REASONING UNDER INCOMPLETE INFORMATION IN ARTIFICIAL INTELLIGENCE

A Comparison of Formalisms Using a Single Example

Léa Sombé

JOHN WILEY & SONS, INC.
New York / Chichester / Brisbane / Toronto / Singapore

Raisonnements sur des informations incomplètes
Authorized english language translation.
All rights reserved. Published simultaneously in Canada.

The *International Journal of Intelligent Systems* (ISSN: 0884-8173) is published quarterly, one volume per year, by John Wiley & Sons, Inc., 605 Third Avenue, New York, NY 10158.

Copyright © 1990 by John Wiley & Sons, Inc. All rights reserved. Reproduction or translation of any part of this work beyond that permitted by Sections 107 and 108 of the U.S. Copyright Law without the permission of the copyright owner is unlawful. Application to mail at second-class rates is pending at New York, NY, and at additional mailing offices.

The code and copyright notice appearing at the bottom of the first page of an article in the journal indicate the copyright holder's consent that copies may be made for personal or internal use, or for the personal or internal use of specific clients, on the condition that the copier pay for copying beyond that permitted by Sections 107 and 108 of the United States Copyright Law. The per-copy fee for each item is $4.00 and is to be paid through the Copyright Clearance Center, Inc., 21 Congress St., Salem, MA 01970. This consent does not extend to other kinds of copying, such as copying for general distribution, for advertising or promotional purposes, for creating new collective works, or for resale. Such permission requests and other permission inquiries should be addressed to Permissions Dept.

Subscription price (1990): $185.00 per volume. Outside U.S.A.: $228.00 (air service and handling included). Please allow four weeks for processing a change of address. For subscription inquiries, please call customer service at (212) 692-6035 or write to the above address.

Claims for undelivered copies will be accepted only after the following issue has been received. Please enclose a copy of the mailing label or cite your subscriber reference number in order to expedite handling. Missing copies will be supplied when losses have been sustained in transit and where reserve stock permits. If claims are not resolved satisfactorily, please write to Timothy B. King, Vice President and Director of Publishing Operations, Scientific & Technical Division, John Wiley & Sons, Inc., 605 Third Avenue, New York, NY 10158.

Postmaster: Send address changes to *International Journal of Intelligent Systems,* Susan Malawski, Fulfillment Manager, Subscription Department, John Wiley & Sons, Inc., 605 Third Avenue, New York, NY 10158.

Advertising/Reprints: Inquiries concerning advertising and reprints should be forwarded to Ms. Tasi Manicas, Advertising/Reprints Sales, John Wiley & Sons, Inc., 605 Third Avenue, New York, NY 10158, (212) 850-6000. Advertising Sales, European Contact: Michael Levermore, Advertising Sales Manager, John Wiley & Sons, Ltd., Baffins Lane, Chichester, Sussex PO19 1UD, England.

Other Correspondence: Address all other correspondence to: Margaret Irwin, Publisher, Scientific & Technical Division, John Wiley & Sons, Inc., 605 Third Avenue, New York, NY 10158.

The contents of this journal are indexed in the following: *Automatic Subject Citation Alert®, Compumath Citation Index®, Current Contents/Engineering, Technology & Applied Sciences,* **INSPEC,** and *SCISEARCH®.*

Manuscripts should be submitted to the Editor, Dr. Ronald R. Yager, *International Journal of Intelligent Systems,* Machine Intelligence Institute, Iona College, New Rochelle, NY 10801. **Information for contributors** appears in each issue of each volume.

Printed in the United States of America

10 9 8 7 6 5 4 3 2 1

International Journal of Intelligent Systems

Volume 5, Number 4, September 1990

Special Issue
REASONING UNDER INCOMPLETE INFORMATION IN ARTIFICIAL INTELLIGENCE
A Comparison of Formalisms Using a Single Example

Contents

vii	**Foreword**	
324	**Section I.**	**Introduction**
326		A. Work Plan
328		B. The Example under Study and the Comparison Criteria
330	**Section II.**	**Why New Logics are Needed**
331		A. Limitations of Rule-Based Systems
335		B. Limitations of Classical Logic
340		C. Deduction and Nonclassical Logics
342	**Section III.**	**Default Logic**
342		A. Presentation
344		B. Treatment of the Example
346		C. Defaults without Prerequisites
347		D. Priorities among Defaults
348		1. *Ordering the Defaults*
348		2. *Semi-Normal Defaults*
349		3. *Assertion Predicates*
350		E. Conclusion
350	**Section IV.**	**Nonmonotonic Modal Logics**
351		A. A Logic for "Conceivable"
351		1. *Presentation*
353		2. *Discussion*
356		B. Autoepistemic Logic
359		C. A Logic for "All I Know"
361		D. Logics of Likelihood
362	**Section V.**	**Closed World Assumption and Circumscription**
363		A. Circumscription
363		B. Syntactic Definition
364		C. Application 1
365		D. Application 2
366		E. The Complete Example
367		F. Semantics
368		G. Comparison Criteria
369	**Section VI.**	**A Nonmonotonic Logic Based on Suppositions**
370		A. Language and Theory with Supposition
370		1. *Language with Suppositions*

371			2. *Theories with Supposition*
371			3. *Extensions*
372			4. *Consistency*
372			5. *Remarks and Explanations*
373			6. *The Example*
374			7. *Deduction of General Rules*
374			8. *Instanciation and Exceptions*
375		B.	Comparison Criteria
377	Section VII.		**Conditional Logics and "Rough" Implications**
377		A.	Conditional Logics
382		B.	"Rough" Implications
384	Section VIII.		**Logics of Uncertainty**
385		A.	Possibilistic Logic
385			1. *Presentation*
388			2. *Discussion*
392		B.	Probabilities and Belief Functions
394	Section IX.		**Fuzzy Logic**
394		A.	The Sorites Paradox
395		B.	Automated Reasoning in Fuzzy Logic
396		C.	Variants of Fuzzy Conditional Statements
398		D.	Fuzzy Logic and Possibilistic Logic
399		E.	Approximate Reasoning and Default Reasoning
401		F.	Conclusion
401	Section X.		**Numerical Quantifiers and Conditional Probabilities**
401		A.	Presentation
404		B.	Discussion
411	Section XI.		**Causal Models**
412		A.	Bayesian Approach
412			1. *Presentation*
414			2. *Discussion about Knowledge Representation*
416			3. *Other Points of Discussion*
416		B.	Relational Approaches
418	Section XII.		**Reasoning by Analogy**
424	Section XIII.		**Truth-Maintenance Systems**
424		A.	TMS
424			1. *Presentation*
431			2. *Comparison Criteria*
434		B.	ATMS
434			1. *Presentation*
435			2. *Treatment of the Example*
436			3. *Comparison Criteria*
438	Section XIV.		**Theories of Action and the Frame Problem**
440		A.	A Temporal Logic of Change
440			1. *The Modelling of Actions and the Frame Problem*
443			2. *The Deduction of the Resulting States by Means of a Tableau Prover*
445			3. *Multiple Extensions*
447			4. *The Comparison Criteria*
447		B.	A Theory of Action Based on Circumscription
449	Section XV.		**Revision Theory**
452	Section XVI.		**A Tentative Conclusion**
457	**References**		
471	**Index**		

Members of the Group Léa Sombé

Philippe Besnard

I.R.I.S.A., Campus de Beaulieu, Avenue du Général Leclerc, 35042 Rennes Cedex, France

Marie-Odile Cordier

I.R.I.S.A., Rennes

Didier Dubois

I.R.I.T, Université Paul Sabatier, 118 route de Narbonne, 31062 Toulouse Cedex, France

Luis Fariñas del Cerro

I.R.I.T., Toulouse

Christine Froidevaux

L.R.I., Université de Paris Sud, Bâtiment 490, 91405 Orsay Cedex, France

Yves Moinard

I.R.I.S.A., Rennes

Henri Prade

I.R.I.T., Toulouse

Camilla Schwind

G.I.A., Faculté des Sciences de Luminy, 70 route Léon Lachamp, Case 901, 13288 Marseille Cedex, France

Pierre Siegel

E.I.R.P., Université de Provence, Case H, 3 place Victor Hugo, 13331 Marseille Cedex 3, France

> "Logic, n. The art of thinking and reasoning in strict accordance with limitations and incapacities of the human misunderstanding."
> **Ambrose Bierce**
> (The Devil's Dictionary)

> "A false error is not necessarily a genuine truth."
> "If in pure reality it is always right not to be wrong, in altered reality it is often wrong to be right."
> **Pierre Dac**
> (Pensées, Le Cherche-Midi Editeur, Paris)

FOREWORD

The formalisms proposed nowadays in Artificial Intelligence to account for so-called "commonsense" reasoning, capable of compensating for incomplete available information, are plentiful. The potential user faces a confusing profusion of methods, the description of which is scattered in an abundant literature, and few elements of comparison exist between the approaches often defended by different schools of thought.

That is what a group of French researchers became fully aware of, at the time of the first meeting, held at Prélenfrey (Isère), on March 3 and 4, 1986, of the "Inference and Control" project of a research program (PRC-GRECO Artificial Intelligence) formed shortly before under the sponsorship of the French Ministry of Research and Technology and of the French National Centre for Scientific Research (CNRS). During these two days it appeared, indeed, that the same examples were used to illustrate and support the interest of often radically different approaches, some purely symbolic, others based on numerical theories of uncertainty. Some time later, a working group including nine people (Philippe Besnard, Marie-Odile Cordier, Didier Dubois, Luis Fariñas del Cerro, Christine Froidevaux, Yves Moinard, Henri Prade, Camilla Schwind and Pierre Siegel) took the name of Léa Sombé (from "les A sont B," which means "the A's are B's" in French) and decided to make a comparative study based on an illustrative example.

Subsequent meetings held at Carry-le-Rouet (October 1987) and at Luminy (January 1988) near Marseilles led to the first version of this work, presented at the Second National Meeting of the PRC-GRECO in Artificial Intelligence held at Toulouse, on March 14 and 15 1988, and published in the proceedings of this meeting (available from Teknea, Toulouse). Léa Sombé proposes today a revised, updated and substantially augmented version of that study, the fruit of further meetings of the group, notably at Gif-sur-Yvette near Paris in July 1988.

Léa Sombé
February 1989
(Translation of the Foreword to the French edition, Teknea, 1989)

The present text is a slightly revised and updated translation of the French edition.

Léa Sombé
June 1990

Reasoning under Incomplete Information in Artificial Intelligence: A Comparison of Formalisms Using a Single Example

Léa Sombé
P.R.C.-G.R.E.C.O., Artificial Intelligence

Translated by Sandra A. Sandri, I.R.I.T., University Paul Sabatier, Toulouse, France & I.N.P.E., São José dos Campos, Brazil

Man is capable of reasoning when the available information is incomplete. The conclusions obtained are based on knowledge considered as "generally true." These conclusions are temporary as they are liable to be challenged by the arrival of new pieces of information which will refine the information previously available (without necessarily contradicting it). Numerous studies have independently dealt with the formalization of this kind of revisable reasoning over the last ten years. The approaches used have been very diverse: some are purely symbolic, others make use of numbers to quantify the uncertainty; some are close to formal logic, and others are much less formalized; some only deal with exceptions, a smaller number which are somewhat more ambitious tackle the problem of knowledge base revision. This work presents the above approaches and compares them on a single example in order to better evaluate their similarities, their differences, their abilities to formalize certain aspects of so-called "commonsense" reasoning, and also in order to try to lay bare the fundamental principles that underlie the different approaches. The logics considered in this work are default logic, nonmonotonic modal logics, including autoepistemic logic, circumscription, circumscription-like approaches, supposition-based logic, conditional logics, logics of uncertainty, i.e., probabilistic, and possibilistic logics as well as belief functions, numerical quantifier logic, and fuzzy logics. We also consider formalisms oriented towards causal reasoning and analogical reasoning. Lastly, we study the contribution of works on truth maintenance, action logic, as well as recent attempts to formalize the process of revision of a set of formulae closed by deduction. The systematic use of a single example and of the same evaluation criteria for each formalism, will enable the reader to better perceive the rationale behind the various approaches as well as to appreciate their interest.

I. INTRODUCTION

In a recent, perhaps intentionally provocative article, Drew McDermott[1] expresses his discouragement with the logic-based methodology to Artificial Intelligence to which he previously subscribed and explicitly declares that this approach cannot succeed. Such an uncompromising stand has given rise to numerous strong reactions which were collected together by Levesque in an issue of the Canadian journal *Computational Intelligence*.[2] In 1988, the same journal published another issue[3] in which Cheeseman,[4] adding to McDermott's remarks, proposes Bayesian induction as a formalization of plausible reasoning, giving rise again to lively reactions from the "logicists," the supporters of the logical approach, as well as the supporters of other numerical formalisms. Actually, every study of nonclassical reasoning in Artificial Intelligence raises the question of the relevance of the opinions of McDermott's as well as those of his partisans and disparagers. At the beginning of his article, McDermott describes what he calls the "logicist" work plan. Its basic postulate is that Artificial Intelligence programs should rely on a large amount of knowledge, particularly "commonsense" knowledge characterizing "what everybody knows" and allowing the extraction of conclusions "obvious to everybody," and it is necessary to represent this knowledge inside programs. At this stage, the logicist's point of view, according to McDermott, is that the representation of such knowledge should be independent of the nature of the programs themselves and in fact, that this knowledge should be represented before any of these programs are written. From then on, still according to McDermott, the logicist considers that logic is the most preferable approach if not the only possible one. McDermott takes a stand against this procedure, affirming that it rests on the implicit but essential hypothesis which reads: "An important part of the reasoning process is deductive." He also rejects the idea that the methodology proposed by logic is of a viable generality for knowledge representation.

In fact, wanting to clear the table of logic, McDermott proposes "programming" as the only alternative, as the general procedure of research in Artificial Intelligence. He declares that the idea of representing knowledge without knowing how it is going to be used, notably in nondeductive reasonings, is completely wrong, (hence his rejection of representing knowledge by means of a logical language). From his point of view, every representation should include a minimal amount of information indicating how the knowledge represented is going to be used in order to contribute to non-deductive reasoning. We note that a debate foreshadowing this one, logic against programming, at the time termed the declarative/procedural controversy, had already taken place during the 1970s (Minsky,[5] Winograd,[6] Hayes[7]).

Among the answers to McDermott there emerges the idea that logic furnishes an incomparable methodological basis for reasoning formalization. The arguments put forward to that effect include the following[2]:

> ...only formal theories, which deal with well-defined entities and relationships, and are expressed in a language with a clear denotational semantics, are precise enough to be understood by others besides the original author.
>
> (Allen & Kautz)

There is no convincing sense of "works" without an independent account of what the program should be doing. At some point prior to making a claim for a program's success, we need to understand in precise terms what to expect from it.

(Brachman)

Logic used in the right way can provide just the appropriate sort of independent means of justification – a true correctness measure – for knowledge-based programs.

(Brachman)

Ultimately what distinguishes a logical representation formalism from non-logical ones is that it is *systematically interpretable;* and the reason for wanting systematic interpretability is to ensure that the knowledge represented in the formalism is understandable, verifiable, and expandable, and the inference methods used (whether deductive, inductive, abductive, or something else) are *justifiable*.

(Schubert)

The lesson drawn from these reactions is that logic permits a real objective evaluation of the undertaking of reasoning formalization[2]:

We admit...that logical deduction may be inappropriate for modeling many reasoning tasks. It is very significant, however, that McDermott can sit down and write a paper exposing these failures, and inspire the rest of us to try to overcome them. This means that the paradigm is alive and has great potential. We challenge McDermott to write a similar paper pointing out specific problems with a "program" based approach to AI.

(Allen & Kautz)

Among McDermott's objections to the logical approach to Artificial Intelligence is the claim that it cannot provide a solution to the problem of the formalization of nondeductive reasoning. Rather than trying to synthesize here the opposite arguments, formulated by researchers such as John McCarthy and Vladimir Lifschitz, it is easier to use the following (characteristic) quotation[2]:

Similarly, if a special inference rule is used to encode an inductive generalization step, it won't necessarily be a sound rule – but committing oneself to a logical approach does not oblige one to use sound rules of inference.

(Nilsson)

The feeling expressed by most of the logicists who answered McDermott in the special issue of *Computational Intelligence*[2] is that an approach to Artificial Intelligence which is driven solely in terms of program development lacks all kinds of points of reference permitting one to draw comparisons, to isolate specific difficulties, and to make progress. With this feeling is linked the conviction that the logic-based approach to Artificial Intelligence is the only scientifically rigorous one. Nevertheless, this presupposes that no dogma qualifying "commonsense" reasoning as deductive will limit the contribution of logic to constructing a system of reasoning[2]:

> Logics worthy of consideration by logicists (small "l") should not necessarily have standard notations or rules of inference. In fact, while notation is just notation, the right notation can lead to insights about the domain or a reasoning problem in the domain. This seems to have been the case with certain network-style forms of representation.
>
> (Brachman)

We summarize and express the opinion of Léa Sombé by saying that the modeling of commonsense reasoning should be based on a formal procedure of the logical type, but without limiting itself to the tools of classical logic and deduction, the limited expressive power of which should be acknowledged.

The problem of incomplete information has brought to light the insufficiencies of first order logic, (as well as those of the empirical approaches employed in expert systems), as a means of knowledge representation and commonsense modeling, and has given rise to numerous works on nonclassical logics. Each of these logics has dedicated itself to deal with a particular aspect of human reasoning, and consequently offers only a partial solution to the problems discussed by McDermott and Cheeseman. It thus becomes interesting to measure the expressive power of each of these logics, already partially surveyed by Turner,[8] Smets et al.,[9] Brown,[10] by comparing them on a test-example.

Here we are particularly interested in the logics developed in order to treat statements of the type "the A's are B's", as for instance, "young people are single." This type of statement is often tempered by expressions such as "in most cases," "up to exceptions," "typically," "supposing that," "generally," etc, or may be rewritten in the form of statements of a gradual character such as "the younger, the more likely one is single."

A. Work Plan

In the first part of Section II, the insufficiencies of the expert system approach, where a certainty degree is attached to a production rule in order to introduce uncertainty into the statement "the A's are B's," are discussed. Besides, it is clear that the translation of "the A's are B's" into "all the A's are B's" in first order logic rules out the possibility of exceptions. One might imagine getting around the difficulty by writing "all the A's except the C's are B's," the expression of which in first order logic assumes all the C's to be known. But it is not realistic to wish to be able always to express all the exceptions. Besides, the knowledge of new exceptions entails a complete reconsideration of the knowledge base, which raises enormous modularity problems as will be seen in the second part of Section II. Moreover, in order to infer B it is then necessary not only to establish A but also to verify that we are not in any of the exceptional cases (which presupposes that the necessary information is available).

In nonclassical approaches that are studied here, the sentence "the A's a does not express a universal property for the A's, of the form "*all* the A's are B a weakened form of the type "*generally* the A's are B's." Each formalism de "generally" in its own manner. We are now faced with the problem of redefinin we understand by "inference," and of specifying its expected properties. This tackled in a very general framework in the last part of Section II, prelimina systematic analysis of the existing formalisms. In the formalisms examined study, the sentence "the A's are B's" will be translated into

- "an A is a B, up to exceptions" in Reiter's *default logic* (Section III)
- "if B is conceivable and if A, then B" in Doyle and McDei *nonmonotonic modal logic*, and into "if a given A was not B, we woulc it" in Moore's *autoepistemic logic* (Section IV)
- "every A that is not abnormal is B" in McCarthy's *circumscription* (Secti
- "every A for which we assume B is B" in Besnard and Siegel's *suppo based logic* (Section VI)
- "typically the A's are B's" in Delgrande's *conditional logic*; this appro close to the logic of "counterfactual" conditionals of the type "if it were then it would be a B" developed by Stalnaker (Section VII)
- "an A is almost certainly a B" in *logics of uncertainty* and notably in Dubois and Prade's *possibilistic logic* (Section VIII)
- "the more one is A, the more certainly one is B" or "the more one is A, the more one is B" depending on the case, in Zadeh's *fuzzy logic* (which authorizes gradual or vague predicates) (Section IX)
- "most of the A's are B's" or "being an A without being a B is rare", depending on whether we are dealing with relative or absolute quantifiers in the (possibly vague) *numerical quantifiers logic* (Section X).

Although they may seem to resemble one another, these various formulations will lead to logical systems whose behavior and results are sometimes highly differentiated.

Moreover, the example will also be treated with respect to two other approaches:

- causal models (A causes B), Bayesian, or relational ones (in the sense of Reggia, or Sanchez), which are adapted to diagnostic problems (Section XI),
- reasoning by analogy which exploits the similarities between particular examples ("the examples of A that we know are mostly B") (Section XII).

In the three sections preceding the conclusion an attempt is made to link the issues of commonsense nonmonotonic reasoning with the formalisms oriented towards truth-maintenance (Section XIII), the modeling of the idea of action and the resulting changes of states (Section XIV), or the general problem of knowledge base revision (Section XV). We can also treat the example with the systems TMS of Doyle and ATMS of De Kleer, even though these systems do not, strictly speaking, perform inference but are designed with the aim of maintaining the consistency of a set of deductions. Besides, we go beyond the example framework to investigate the logics of action and revision theories.

B. The Example under Study and the Comparison Criteria

A test-example, capable of being modelled at least partly, if not completely, by most of the approaches is used as the common point of reference to compare the various formalisms. Moreover, a certain number of questions relating to the meaningful properties of these formalisms have arisen, and have led to the definition of comparison criteria. With these criteria the specific problems tackled by these formalisms as well as their expressive power can be better characterized, in order to establish a classification in the future; however the latter point goes beyond the ambitions of this work and is only outlined in the conclusion.

The knowledge base of the test-example which will be treated by each of the considered formalisms is the following:

$e1$. Students are young
$e2$. Young people are single
$e3$. Single people are young
$e4$. Some young people are students
$e5$. Students who have children are married or cohabitants
$e6$. Cohabitants are young
$e7$. Single, married, and cohabitant are mutually exclusive.

Only $e7$ will always be interpreted in the sense of classical logic; the other statements will be interpreted in various ways. Figure 1 sketches the links between the predicates involved in the example. Apart from the statements $e1$ to $e7$, this figure contains various inferences which are valid in classical logic.

In this work, the notations should be understood as follows:

- The expressions Sdnt(x), Yng(x), Sng(x), Pnt(x), Mrd(x), Chbt(x) mean: x is respectively "student," "young," "single," "parent (having one or more children)," "married," and "cohabitant."
- The usual notations of the predicate calculus ($\neg$, $\wedge$, $\vee$, $\exists$, $\forall$, $\vdash$, $\models$...) are used; the classical logic material implication is denoted by $\rightarrow$, while the particular implication of a considered formalism is denoted by $\Rightarrow$.

We will try to situate each formalism in relation to the following criteria, considered as the most meaningful.

Point 0. Representation – Is there only one possible translation of the example? Several interpretations of the proposed assertions may exist in one formalism; the choice of the representation may be guided by the intuition we have of the meaning of the assertions, as well as by the answers that we intend to give to questions.

REASONING UNDER INCOMPLETE INFORMATION

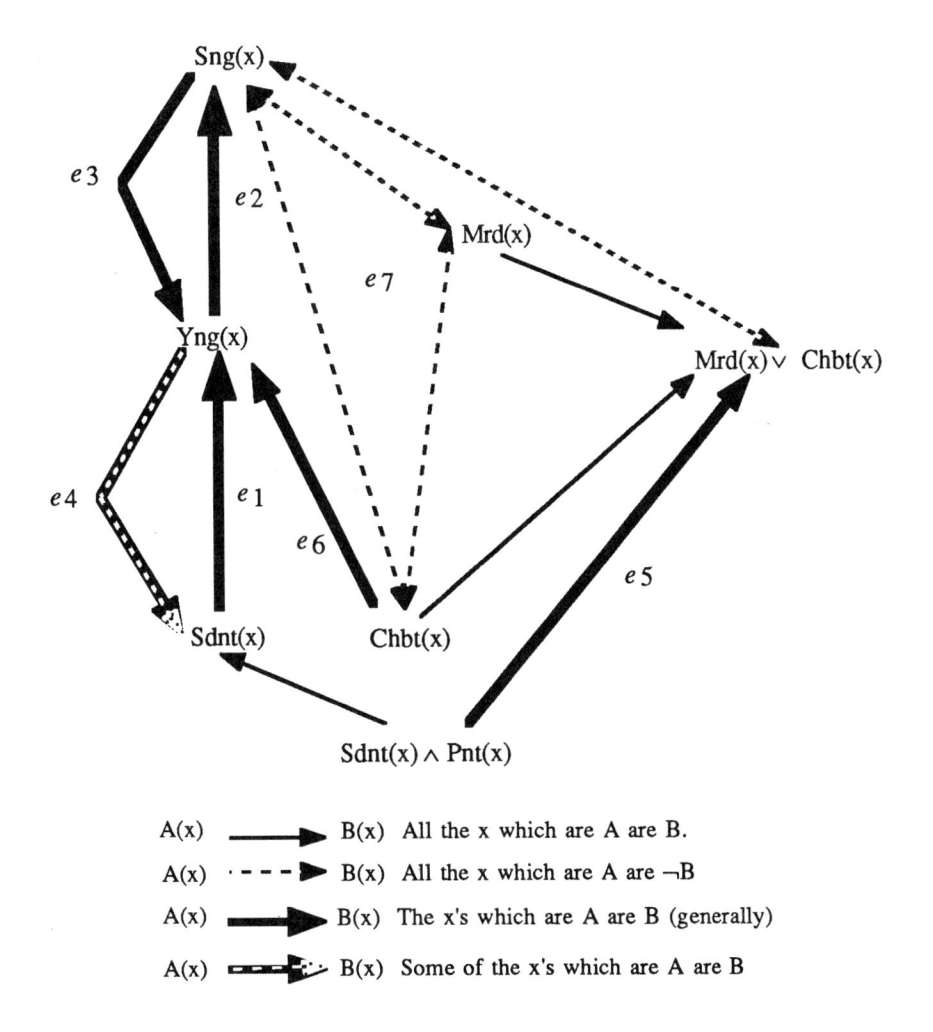

Figure 1. The example under study.

A(x) ⟶ B(x)   All the x which are A are B.
A(x) ⋯⋯▶ B(x)   All the x which are A are ¬B
A(x) ⟹ B(x)   The x's which are A are B (generally)
A(x) ⟹ B(x)   Some of the x's which are A are B

Point 1. General scope / instantiated character of the conclusions – Is it possible to answer questions of a general nature such as "are students single?" or only questions referring to individuals such as "is the student Léa single?" Do we distinguish between default answers and sure answers (obtained using only non-default information held for certain)?

Point 2. Transitivity – For example, is it possible to conclude from "students are young" and "young people are single" that "students are single"?

Point 3. Contraposition – For example, can we use e2 ("young people are single") to answer the question "are married people not young?"

Point 4. Monotonicity – If knowing *A* we conclude *B*, can we still do it knowing *A and C*?

Point 5. Tackling disjunctive information – Knowing that "x is an A or a B" and knowing that the A's are C's, that the B's are C's, can we conclude x is a C?

Point 6. Quantifiers – Is it possible to represent quantifiers expressing "a few," "some," "most," "many," ...?

Point 7. Conflicting conclusions – Is it possible to obtain several distinct and partially conflicting sets of conclusions? If it is so, we have a choice problem. Do we accept all the sets of conclusions? If not, which one(s) do we finally retain? What are the preference criteria used?

Point 8. Representation modularity – Is it possible to take new information into account without modifying the existing representation?

Point 9. Knowledge revision – Does the formalism provide a possibility of questioning a piece of information initially taken to be true? Do there exist any mechanisms for handling the suppression or the addition of information, thereby maintaining a certain form of coherence?

Point 10. Complexity and calculability of the treatment of a question.

In the study of criteria 2, 3, 4, 5, it may be convenient to treat the considered question in terms of an implication (when it exists) specific to the considered approach, and also in terms of the inference rule.

In the following we briefly present, for each formalism, the fundamental definitions and properties necessary for treating the example. The numbering of a formula or an expression refers to the section in which it appears. In the remaining discussion, we refer to criterion $n°i$ by sometimes indicating "(Point i)."

II. WHY NEW LOGICS ARE NEEDED

Classical logic is a formal system composed of:

(i) a language,
(ii) a set of axioms,
(iii) inference rules, and a description of the manner in which these axioms and rules are to be used in order to yield theorems.

Moreover a semantics is associated with the formal system, and is generally defined by means of a function which assigns a truth value to every formula.

For a quick (and dense) introduction to classical logic, the reader should refer to Lyndon.[11] Predicate calculus is well-adapted to mathematics, but does not easily take into account certain aspects of human reasoning (common sense, uncertainty, temporality...). This observation led to the development of a large number of "nonclassical" or "nonstandard" logics, which were designed to describe various forms of inference. These logics have been created by modifying the three components considered above. Several manners of enlarging the classical logic framework may be envisaged and combined:

- *The language is extended* by introducing particular predicates (supposition-based logic) or operators (for example "possible" and "necessary" in modal logic, "I believe" in autoepistemic logic, operators indicating the past or the future in temporal logic,...). It is equally possible to use an implication different from the material one (conditional logic), to introduce quantifiers other than "For all..." and "There exists...," or lastly to take into account the vague character of predicates (fuzzy logic) or of quantifiers. Finally, uncertainty degrees can be assigned to the propositions (possibilistic logic for instance).

- *New axiom schemata are added* (especially in the circumscription approach).

- *New notions of inference are defined,* which permit the formulation of answers of the type "P is true in a certain vision of the world..." (in default logic, we speak of extensions). A new notion of semantics may correspond to it (maximal (minimal) model in the nonmonotonic logics, universe of possible worlds in modal logic for example). We no longer impose certain properties of classical deductive systems, such as inference monotonicity in particular (nonmonotonic logics). We do not limit ourselves to the classical rule of modus ponens; we authorize new inference rules (necessitation rule in modal logic for example).

Before studying a number of non-classical logics in the light of our example, we are going to explain how certain reasoning problems in an uncertain environment have been dealt with in the area of expert systems, and the difficulties that the empirical approaches using "certainty factors" have encountered. We will then show why classical logic itself is insufficient to handle commonsense reasoning. Lastly, some general considerations on the notion of deduction (in the nonclassical logics) seem to be relevant to achieving a better understanding of the problems that have to be faced whenever we step outside the framework of first order logic.

A. Limitations of Rule-Based Systems

The development of non-classical logics to treat the exceptions to general rules and uncertain or imprecise pieces of information, is partially linked to the advent of so-called "expert" systems and to the difficulties which they face. These systems are programs for solving diagnostic, classification, or decision problems in a limited knowledge domain. Their novelty lies in the presence of modular operational pieces of knowledge (rules) which are kept apart from the algorithms capable of exploiting such knowledge, which endows them with explanation capabilities. Just as in logic, a separation occurs between language and inferential mechanism. Nevertheless, the active pieces of knowledge are represented most of the time by means of production rules triggered by pattern matching from a factual base that contains a description of the situation to be studied. A production rule has the form "if A_1 and A_2 and... A_n

then B" where A_i is an elementary condition and B an action to be executed. The triggering of this rule takes place as soon as the conditions $A_1 \ldots A_n$ are satisfied by the factual base (the most elementary case being the one where $A_1 \ldots A_n$ appear explicitly therein). The resulting action B may be the addition of a new fact to the base, the withdrawal of a fact or the execution of a procedure. This corresponds to the so-called "forward-chaining" strategy. In backward-chaining, it is the conclusion part of the rule that is used to trigger the rule, by producing new facts to be demonstrated. The theoretical status of these production rules is rather obscure since they are similar to (Horn) clauses as well as to inference rules with specific contents. Consequently, the theoretical status of the "expert system" approach, as compared to a rigorous approach of the "classical logic" type, has not yet been completely elucidated.

In this poorly formalized framework the need to represent production rules pervaded with uncertainty, imprecision, or exceptions appeared very early in order to better represent human expertise. Systems such as MYCIN (Buchanan and Shortliffe[1,2]) model knowledge of the type "the presence of A *strongly* suggests (or confirms) the hypothesis B" in the form of production rules "if A then B" to which a "certainty factor" is added to express in numerical terms the "strongly" that appears in the expression of the rule in the current language. Certainty factors are also attached to the available facts, which are matched against the condition part of these rules. Uncertainty is thus handled by propagation of the certainty factors from the condition part of the rules, towards their conclusions, through the network which represents the knowledge. We will note that the uncertainty in a rule suggests the existence of exceptions; but there is no explicit treatment of exceptions in systems such as MYCIN. We calculate the certainty factors, deduced with the help of intuitive but empirical composition laws are not completely well-grounded, theoretically speaking.

Example. Here is how we could express the test-example in MYCIN's style:

r_1 :   if Sdnt   then   (.9) Yng
r_2 :   if Yng   then   (.8) Sng
r_3 :   if Sng   then   (.7) Yng
r_4 :   if Yng   then   (.3) Sdnt
r_5 :   if Sdnt and Pnt   then   (.95) Mrd-or-chbt
r_6 :   if Chbt   then   (.8) Yng
r_7 :   if Sng   then   (-1) Chbt, etc...
       (six rules for three pairs of mutually exclusive predicates)
r_8 :   if Mrd   then   (+1) Mrd-or-chbt
       if Chbt   then   (+1) Mrd-or-chbt
       if Mrd-or-chbt   then   (-1) Sng

Note that in many rule-based systems neither disjunction nor logical negation exists. Hence the symbol Mrd-or-chbt is used with the addition of rules r_8 to rule r_5 for translating the statement $e5$ in the test-example. The number in parentheses is the certainty factor (CF) of the rule, with a value of +1 when the conclusion is certainly true, provided that the conditions are also true, and -1 when the conclusion is certainly false. This last value permits us to translate statements of the mutual exclusive type into the form "if A then (-1) B" and "if B then (-1) A," both rules being necessary because of the absence of contraposition of the production rules. In particular the calculation of certainty factors is such that $CF(\neg A) = - CF(A)$. The numerical value of the likelihood coefficients reflects information that is not explicitly contained in a statement of the type "the A's are B's." The use of numbers permits us to weight the strength of the rules, in a completely empirical way.

This approach encounters many difficulties, especially because the production rules weighted with a certainty factor have no rigorous semantics; they may have several meanings, which do not correspond to a single treatment of the coefficients. Moreover, the assignment of a precise value to a certainty factor proves to be even harder, since these numbers have neither a clear practical interpretation, nor a rigorous axiomatics. A particularly delicate problem is that of conflict resolution among several rules that lead to conflicting conclusions about a fact or about its denial. The systematic use of a combination operation in order to resolve these conflicts cannot be fully justified, and is sometimes even dangerous (since the separate processing of the rules which leads to partial conclusions which thus have to be combined, cannot take into account all the dependencies jointly expressed by the rules). Moreover, the reasoning mode may be of the inductive type as in the Bayesian approach, or of the deductive type as in systems such as MYCIN (production rules worked by modus ponens), depending on whether or not the rules are written in a more "causal" form: if B then A (interpreted as B causes A, for example, "if fire then smoke"), or rather in the "evidential" form: if A then B (interpreted as A suggests B, for example "if smoke then fire"); in both cases, knowing A ("smoke" in the example) we (more or less) certainly infer B ("fire" in the example): see Pearl[13] for a discussion on the distinction between "causal" and "evidential" rules. It is in fact difficult to understand what we are doing exactly, when we make use of rules with coefficients to represent knowledge, since the status of these coefficients is not clear (as in MYCIN where the certainty factors propagated deductively are originally defined in terms of a relative difference between an *a posteriori* probability and an *a priori* probability).

Example (continued): Let us suppose that sure facts (i.e., held for certain), Sdnt and Pnt, concerning Léa are available. A system such as MYCIN works by backward-chaining, i.e., it tries to answer a question by going back to the initial facts from a fact corresponding to the question. For example, if we want to know if Léa is young, we construct the deduction tree of Figure 2 with the help of an inference engine:

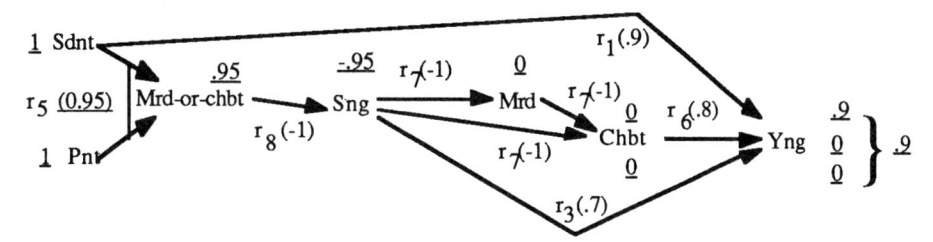

Figure 2. Evaluation of a conclusion in a rule-based system manner.

The presence of indirect recursion (due in particular to the rules r_7) in the knowledge base of our example requires certain stopping procedures in order to avoid loop phenomena. In the above graph we have ruled out the repetition of a fact in any path from the root to a leaf. Thereafter the uncertainty coefficients are propagated from the initial facts, along each path, and combined on each "and" node and on each "or" node of the graph. MYCIN proposes the following formulae:

- propagation along the rule $A \xrightarrow{CF} B$: $CF(B) = \max(0, CF(A)) \cdot CF$, i.e., we propagate only facts which are fairly sure.
- "or" node (case of two rules concluding on A):

$$CF(A) = CF_1(A) + CF_2(A) - CF_1(A)CF_2(A) \quad \text{if } CF_1(A) > 0 \quad CF_2(A) > 0$$

$$= CF_1(A) + CF_2(A) + CF_1(A)CF_2(A) \quad \text{if } CF_1(A) < 0 \quad CF_2(A) < 0$$

$$= \frac{CF_1(A) + CF_2(A)}{1 - \min(|CF_1(A)|, |CF_2(A)|)} \quad \text{otherwise;}$$

this combination mode is associative.
- "and" node (conjunction of elementary conditions A_1 and A_2 in a rule)

$$CF(A_1 \wedge A_2) = \min(CF(A_1), CF(A_2))$$

In the case of the above example the terminal combination of 0, 0, and .9 gives .9. This result, which is paradoxical since we do not use the information Pnt, is due to the absence of modus tollens which would permit the propagation of the negative facts. Let us note that the absence of modus tollens for the uncertain rules is sometimes natural; for instance we will hardly be able to contrapose rule r_3 since from the fact that most of the singles are young, we cannot deduce without risk that most of the nonyoung are married or cohabitants. On the other hand contraposition is more natural for r_2. But in MYCIN it would be necessary to write this contraposition explicitly in order to be able to use the fact Pnt. We indeed obtain the conclusion $\neg$ Sng with a high certainty factor (.95), which would permit us, should modus tollens be applied to r_2, to conclude $\neg$ Yng with a certainty factor that could be estimated as .8 x .95 = .76 (using the product, by analogy with the propagation rule). Nevertheless, the combination of $CF_2(\text{Yng}) = -.76$ with $CF_1(\text{Yng}) = .9$ would then be performed and would give a debatable result (.9 - .76) / 1 - .76 = .14 / .24 $\simeq$ 0.58. In fact the partial solutions obtained come from the two justification sets {Yng} and {Yng, Pnt} which are far from being independent. The system, in general, does not provide any means of detecting these dependencies, and carries out the combination in a systematic way.

Yet MYCIN (and in the Bayesian setting PROSPECTOR[14]) has strongly influenced research on the treatment of uncertainty in reasoning systems: there have been attempts to formalize the likelihood coefficients, and the development of computer systems using weighted production rules. Let us mention Friedman[15] who tried to generalize the certainty factors to the four reasoning modes considered by Polya[16] (direct deduction or modus ponens, modus tollens, and the two "plausible" modes: confirmation and denial). Heckerman[17] tried to find the combination laws of the certainty factors in accordance with their original probabilistic interpretation. Hajek[18] discussed the mathematical properties of the combination and propagation laws in MYCIN. Rich[19] and Ginsberg[20] sought to treat the particular phenomena linked to the presence of exceptions with a numerical approach. Many systems which are variants of MYCIN and attempt with variable degrees of success to improve the expression of knowledge, or to achieve a greater flexibility in the combination or propagation laws, have been built; let us mention, among the most recent systems, PROTIS,[21] SLOP,[22] RUM,[23] TAIGER,[24] MILORD,[25] etc.

These systems, however efficient or useful they might be, are unsatisfactory at the theoretical level, and they still suffer from the same drawbacks as MYCIN on the matter of the semantics of the weighted production rules, particularly on conflict resolution (cf. Dubois and Prade[26] for a systematic analysis of these problems).

Besides what one might call the "numerical school" of expert systems, another trend has been developed that attempts to solve, at a practical level, the conflict resolution problems posed by the certainty factor approach. This trend deeply distrusts numbers, as Cohen and Grinberg[27] state: "The number is presumably a summary of the reasons for believing or disbelieving the inference; but once summarized, these reasons are inaccessible." This tendency, illustrated by works of Cohen ("Endorsement theory") and Fox,[28] focus on the notion of "endorsement," and intends to reason *about* uncertainty rather than *under* uncertainty. In France, studies by Gascuel in the LEZARD system,[29] and by Ganascia[30] follow the same line. Although this approach does not propose, strictly speaking, any theory, it has the merit of raising important problems and asking good questions, even if the answers it provides are often *ad hoc*. We are close to the ideas formalized by nonmonotonic logics (principle of preference for the more specific rules, in LEZARD) and by the truth maintenance systems (propagating the endorsements along the inferences as proposed by Cohen). Nevertheless, we observe the persistence of the idea of certainty factors even in the framework of these approaches. There is no opposition between reasoning with uncertain information and reasoning about uncertainty. Moreover, the certainty factors permit us to detect the potential presence of exceptions that we do not know how to record, and which remain even when we have explicitly treated the known exceptions. The expert system MUM[31] is a good example of a piece of software in which reasonings *about* uncertainty and *under* uncertainty coexist.

We thus see that non-classical logics for the treatment of uncertainty and exceptions belong to, but with a greater concern for rigour, the line of research dealing with the development and the critique of expert systems methodology.

B. Limitations of Classical Logic

"Students are young" is meant to express "Generally, students are young." From a very elementary point of view this might mean that, knowing that Léa is a student, we want to deduce that Léa is young as long as it has not been said, either explicitly or implicitly, that Léa was not young.

One way of expressing this type of information, which seems natural at first sight, is of course to use a first order logic formalism. "Students are young" will thus be translated into "*All* students are young":

$$e1. \quad \forall x \; \text{Sdnt}(x) \rightarrow \text{Yng}(x)$$

Such a formulation is sound if the only known information is "Léa is a student", but it rules out the possibility of an exception. In fact, if it is moreover known that "Léa is not-so-young," the global knowledge base is contradictory. In order to restore consistency, while still keeping the interesting deductions, we have to express "All students, except Léa, are young." Predicate calculus with equality seems to allow for this kind of formulation. We will then write "Every student, who is not Léa, is young":

$$e1'. \quad \forall x \; (\text{Sdnt}(x) \wedge \neg (x = \text{Léa})) \rightarrow \text{Yng}(x)$$

which is rewritten denoting $\neg (x = \text{Léa})$ as $(x \neq \text{Léa})$:

$$e1'. \quad \forall x \; (\text{Sdnt}(x) \wedge (x \neq \text{Léa})) \rightarrow \text{Yng}(x)$$

Such an approach poses several problems and leads to logical systems (or to techniques) that, although sophisticated, do not yield any really satisfactory solutions. We will point out some of these problems.

• *Expressing all the exceptions is unrealistic*, since it is difficult, to say the least, to handle general rules containing a large number of explicit exceptions. On the other hand, if the exceptions are not explicit, but inferred, it would be necessary to calculate them somehow. Lastly, and this is fundamentally the most important thing in the construction of a real logical system, suppose all we know is that there exists an old student:

$$\exists x \; \text{Sdnt}(x) \wedge \neg \text{Yng}(x)$$

without being able to give him/her a name. We need a complete revision of the rules in order to be able to deduce that all students, except for this old one, are young.

In practice, by stepping outside the classical logic framework, we may try to solve the problem using the notion of negation as failure, as will be seen further on.

• *"Different"($\neq$) is not provable*: indeed formula e1' in predicate calculus does not permit us, knowing that "Paul is a student," to deduce that "Paul is young." Nothing permits us to assert that $\neg$ (Paul = Léa) and thus to infer our result. It is possible of course, to add to the knowledge all the formulae expressing that two different names correspond to different individuals ($\neg$ (Paul = Léa), $\neg$ (Jean = Léa),...). This method, often implicitly used in programming languages, in data bases ("unique names assumption"), and in applications, leads to essentially propositional formal systems.

This difficulty is just the most straightforward form of the problem of nonexceptions: for every case which is not *a priori* exceptional, in order to deduce the desired conclusions, it is first necessary to prove that indeed it is not an exceptional case, and this is not necessarily feasible. For example, no individual that is a student in an adult educational program (Aep) is young. Instead of e1', we have thus to consider

$e1''$. $\forall x\ (\text{Sdnt}(x) \land x \neq \text{Léa} \land \neg\,\text{Aep}(x)) \rightarrow \text{Yng}(x)$

Simply knowing that Paul is a student, it is impossible to deduce from $e1''$ that Paul is young since it is then absolutely required to demonstrate not only Paul ≠ Léa but also $\neg\,\text{Aep}(\text{Paul})$.

• *The representation is not modular* since the addition of any exception requires a complete revision of the knowledge base. It raises enormous problems if this knowledge is not trivial. As an example, let us consider a possible formulation of our knowledge base by means of universal quantifiers:

$e1.\quad \forall x\ \text{Sdnt}(x) \rightarrow \text{Yng}(x)$
$e2.\quad \forall x\ \text{Yng}(x) \rightarrow \text{Sng}(x)$
$e3.\quad \forall x\ \text{Sng}(x) \rightarrow \text{Yng}(x)$
$e4.\quad \exists x\ \text{Yng}(x) \rightarrow \exists y\ (\text{Yng}(y) \land \text{Sdnt}(y))$
$e5.\quad \forall x\ (\text{Sdnt}(x) \land \text{Pnt}(x)) \rightarrow (\text{Mrd}(x) \lor \text{Chbt}(x))$
$e6.\quad \forall x\ \text{Chbt}(x) \rightarrow \text{Yng}(x)$
$e7.\quad \forall x\ \neg\,\text{Sng}(x) \lor \neg\,\text{Mrd}(x)$
$\forall x\ \neg\,\text{Sng}(x) \lor \neg\,\text{Chbt}(x)$
$\forall x\ \neg\,\text{Chbt}(x) \lor \neg\,\text{Mrd}(x)$

If we know that
  "Léa is a student who cohabits with someone,"
since Léa is a student we obtain that:
  "Léa is young" (from $e1$ and also, in another way, from $e6$)
and thus that:
  "Léa is single" ($e2$).
But since we know that Léa cohabits with someone, we know that:
  "Léa is not single" ($e7$).
which is inconsistent with the previous deduction.

In order to restore consistency we may, after study, transform the knowledge base into:

$e1.\quad \forall x\ \text{Sdnt}(x) \land (x \neq \textbf{Léa}) \rightarrow \text{Yng}(x)$
$e2.\quad \forall x\ \text{Yng}(x) \rightarrow \text{Sng}(x)$
$e3.\quad \forall x\ \text{Sng}(x) \rightarrow \text{Yng}(x)$
$e4.\quad \exists x\ \text{Yng}(x) \rightarrow \exists y\ (\text{Yng}(y) \land \text{Sdnt}(y))$
$e5.\quad \forall x\ (\text{Sdnt}(x) \land \text{Pnt}(x)) \rightarrow (\text{Mrd}(x) \lor \text{Chbt}(x))$
$e6.\quad \forall x\ (\text{Chbt}(x) \land (x \neq \textbf{Léa})) \rightarrow \text{Yng}(x)$
$e7.\quad \forall x\ \neg\,\text{Sng}(x) \lor \neg\,\text{Mrd}(x)$
$\forall x\ \neg\,\text{Sng}(x) \lor \neg\,\text{Chbt}(x)$
$\forall x\ \neg\,\text{Chbt}(x) \lor \neg\,\text{Mrd}(x)$

In this way, we obtain a sound representation at the expense of transforming our knowledge base. After some additions of exceptions of different types, the representation may fail to be understandable. On the other hand, we are faced with the problem of automating this transformation. There exists at least another way of restoring the consistency of the base:

$e1.\quad \forall x\ \text{Sdnt}(x)\ \rightarrow\ \text{Yng}(x)$
$e2.\quad \forall x\ \text{Yng}(x) \land (x \neq \textbf{Léa})\ \rightarrow\ \text{Sng}(x)$
$e3.\quad \forall x\ \text{Sng}(x)\ \rightarrow\ \text{Yng}(x)$
$e4.\quad \exists x\ \text{Yng}(x)\ \rightarrow\ \exists y\ (\text{Yng}(y) \land \text{Sdnt}(y))$
$e5.\quad \forall x\ (\text{Sdnt}(x) \land \text{Pnt}(x))\ \rightarrow\ (\text{Mrd}(x) \lor \text{Chbt}(x))$
$e6.\quad \forall x\ \text{Chbt}(x)\ \rightarrow\ \text{Yng}(x)$
$e7.\quad \forall x\ \neg \text{Sng}(x) \lor \neg \text{Mrd}(x)$
$\quad \forall x\ \neg \text{Sng}(x) \lor \neg \text{Chbt}(x)$
$\quad \forall x\ \neg \text{Chbt}(x) \lor \neg \text{Mrd}(x)$

The question of *choosing the "good" transformation* then arises. We also face this problem again when, with certain formalisms, it is necessary to choose the appropriate "view" of the world we want to describe ("extension" in default logic; truth-maintenance algorithms of the TMS type).

• *The symbols $\land$ and $\exists$ alone are not capable of representing the information according to which some young people are students.* Indeed, the formula:

$e4.\quad \exists x\ \text{Yng}(x)\ \rightarrow\ \exists y\ (\text{Yng}(y) \land \text{Sdnt}(y))$

which says that "if there exists a young person, there exists a young student" is a very poor formulation. The reason is the extreme imprecision of the term "some" which seems risky to interpret as anything but "there exists at least one." But there exists at least one young person that is a student as soon as there exists at least one student, and that the first piece of information expressing that all students are young is true in at least one of the cases to which it applies.

We have seen that we could restore the consistency of the knowledge base, given the information "Léa is a student who cohabits with someone" in two different ways, neither of which was completely satisfying. The first way of proceeding was to say that all students, except Léa, are young. Such an approach suppressed the contradiction resulting from the opposed conclusions Sng(Léa) and Chbt(Léa) but it no longer permitted us to infer that Léa is young, information which is quite compatible with the facts Sdnt(Léa) and Chbt(Léa). In order to avoid this drawback, we could envisage a third approach where the exception would concern not only Léa but all the cohabitants. We would then obtain the following formulae:

$e1:\quad \forall x\ \text{Sdnt}(x)\ \rightarrow\ \text{Yng}(x)$
$e2:\quad \forall x\ (\text{Yng}(x) \land \neg\ \textbf{Chbt(x)})\ \rightarrow\ \text{Sng}(x)$
$e3:\quad \forall x\ \text{Sng}(x)\ \rightarrow\ \text{Yng}(x)$
$e4:\quad \exists x\ \text{Yng}(x)\ \rightarrow\ \exists y\ (\text{Yng}(y) \land \text{Sdnt}(y))$
$e5:\quad \forall x\ (\text{Sdnt}(x) \land \text{Pnt}(x))\ \rightarrow\ (\text{Mrd}(x) \lor \text{Chbt}(x))$
$e6:\quad \forall x\ \text{Chbt}(x)\ \rightarrow\ \text{Yng}(x);$

$e7$: $\forall x \ \neg \text{Sng}(x) \lor \neg \text{Mrd}(x);$
$\forall x \ \neg \text{Sng}(x) \lor \neg \text{Chbt}(x);$
$\forall x \ \neg \text{Chbt}(x) \lor \neg \text{Mrd}(x);$

The knowledge base thus formed is consistent and, from Sdnt(Léa) ∧ Chbt(Léa), we can deduce Yng(Léa). Unfortunately, from Yng(Léa) (without any other information), we are no longer able to conclude Sng(Léa). In fact, the formula $e2$ is equivalent to:

$$\forall x \ \text{Yng}(x) \rightarrow (\text{Sng}(x) \lor \text{Chbt}(x))$$

This formulation does not correspond to what we wanted to say since, due to the symmetrical character of disjunction, we do not translate the fact that the property "single" is attached to a young person in a privileged way in relation to the property "cohabitant." What we need here, is a mechanism that would permit us to distinguish $C \lor B$ from $\neg C \rightarrow B$, where the meaning of the last formula would be: B except for C.

The introduction of *negation as failure* by Clark[32] for logical data bases, solves this case. A logical data base consists of clauses of the form:

$$(A_1 \land A_2 \land ... \land A_n \land \neg C_1 \land \neg C_2 \land ... \land \neg C_p) \rightarrow B, \quad (1)$$
$(n \geq 0, p \geq 0)$, where $A_1,..., A_n, B, C_1,..., C_p$ are positive literals.

Clark proposes a query evaluation algorithm based essentially on ordered linear resolution for Horn clauses (SLD) augmented by the negation as failure inference rule: "$\neg C$ may be inferred if every possible proof of C fails" (SLDNF). This algorithm is the one employed in PROLOG for the interpretation of the negation operator **not**. The links between negation as failure, completed data bases,[32] and the closed world assumption[33] have been studied in a very precise way. A complete survey of these studies can be found in (Lloyd[34]). The drawback of the SLDNF approach is that there exist simple data bases that cannot be interrogated: although the expected answer to certain queries is clear, the evaluation algorithm does not supply it (loop problems).

Another way of breaking the symmetry of clauses is to associate with a logical data base (or logical program) a canonical model that gives a new semantics to negation. While the first notion was a procedural one borrowed from classical logic, this second notion is a logical one that steps outside the classical framework. Several declarative semantics have been proposed: iterated fixed point,[35] perfect model,[36,37] default model,[38,39] stable model,[40]... which coincide at least in the case where the logical program is *stratified* (any recursion through a negative literal is forbidden). In fact, Bidoit and Froidevaux[39,41,42] have shown that stable models defined by Gelfond and Lifschitz are totally equivalent to the previously introduced default models. All these various declarative semantics are constructions that go beyond the classical logic framework. Besides, some of these approaches are directly inspired by the nonclassical logics that we are dealing with here: Reiter's default logic gave rise to the default model semantics and Moore's autoepistemic logic gave rise to the stable model semantics.

We do not propose here to treat statements according to one or another of these points of view, since some pieces of information in the knowledge base cannot be translated into clauses of the form (1).

C. Deduction and Nonclassical Logics

Given a language, i.e., a set of well-formed expressions E, we can define a logic L as a set of pairs (A,B) where A and B are sets of expressions in E. The meaning associated with the pair (A,B) is: given all the elements of A, at least one element of B follows; this is denoted by $A \vdash B$ (which means, from A we can infer, or if we prefer, deduce B). Generally, the set of pairs is defined from a particular set of pairs called axioms of the form $(\emptyset, a)$ *, and from a set of rules which permits new pairs to be generated. An example of a rule is: if $(\emptyset, a)$ and $(\emptyset, a \to b)$ belong to L then $(\emptyset, b)$ also belongs to L (where $\to$ denotes material implication). Generally (or rather classically) speaking, we suppose that the logic L, or the set of corresponding pairs, has the three following properties:

Reflexivity: $(A, A) \in L$ for every set A of expressions
Transitivity: if $(A, B \cup b)$ and $(C \cup b, D) \in L$ then $(A \cup C, B \cup D) \in L$ for all the sets A, B, and C of expressions
Monotonicity: if $(A, B) \in L$ then $(A \cup A', B \cup B') \in L$ for all the sets A, A', B, and B' of expressions.

Recently the monotonicity property aroused strong criticism, or more specifically its restriction: if $(A, B) \in L$ then $(A \cup A', B) \in L$. This is at the heart of the so-called nonmonotonic logics in which the monotonicity property has been suppressed. Gabbay[43] proposes other properties that he takes to be natural for nonmonotonic inference:

Reflexivity: $(A, A) \in L$ for every set A of expressions.
Restricted monotonicity: if $(A, b) \in L$ and $(A, c) \in L$ then $(A \cup b, c) \in L$ for all the set of expressions A and expressions b and c.
Weak transitivity: if $(A, b) \in L$ and if $(A \cup b, c) \in L$ then $(A, c) \in L$ for all the set of expressions A and expressions b and c.

In general we will write $A \mathrel{\mid\!\sim} B$ if the pair (A, B) belongs to L and if L is a nonmonotonic logic. This means that B can be inferred (or deduced) from A in a nonmonotonic manner.

A logic is thus characterized by structural properties on the set formed by the pairs (A, B).

A set A of expressions is consistent in a logic L if and only if $(A, \emptyset)$ does not belong to L. We assume that the language contains the Boolean connectives $\vee$, $\wedge$,

---

* We use lower case letters for denoting well-formed expressions and { } are ommitted around singletons.

$\rightarrow$, $\neg$, plus possibly an implication connective $\Rightarrow$ which will be called the "weak implication." In what follows it will permit us to represent the statements in our example.

We are now in a position to state the following problem: given a knowledge base $\mathcal{B}$, i.e., a set of expressions, and an expression q called the question, we would like to know whether $\mathcal{B}$ allows an answer to q. Various meanings of the word "answer" can be envisaged. We give here some examples. We may say that we can positively answer q from $\mathcal{B}$ if:

(1) We can deduce q from $\mathcal{B}$ (using the rules of the logic), thus ($\mathcal{B},q$) belongs to the logic
(2) We can deduce $\mathcal{B} \Rightarrow q$ in the logic, (where "$\equiv$>" is a certain implication operator; in our case "$\equiv$>" can be either material implication, or the weak implication) therefore the pair ($\emptyset$, $\mathcal{B} \equiv$> q) must belong to the logic
(3) There exists a set A of consistent expressions containing $\mathcal{B}$ and q
(4) Each set of consistent expressions that contains $\mathcal{B}$ is contained in a consistent set containing q.

It should be noted that, generally speaking, these definitions are not necessarily equivalent. In particular, we see that in the second definition the notion of an answer is formalized by making use of the implication operator "$\equiv$>" of the language, as opposed to the first definition which formalizes the notion of an answer either with $\vdash$ or with $\vdash\!\sim$, and hence in the metalanguage.

On the other hand, in classical logic, definitions (1), (2), and (4) are equivalent if "$\equiv$>" is material implication. This demonstrates the tight link that may exist between the metalanguage inference symbol $\vdash$ (or $\vdash\!\sim$) and the language implication operator "$\equiv$>." In this way, it is possible for the operator "$\equiv$>" to satisfy the three classical properties of the symbol $\vdash$ even though their expressions are different:

Reflexivity: ($\emptyset, b \equiv$> b) $\in L$ for every expressions b.
Transitivity: If ($\emptyset, b \equiv$> c) $\in L$ and ($\emptyset, c \equiv$> d) $\in L$ then ($\emptyset, b \equiv$> d) $\in L$ for every expressions b, c and d.
Monotonicity: If ($\emptyset, b \equiv$> c) $\in L$ then ($\emptyset, (b \wedge b') \equiv$> $(c \vee c')$) $\in L$ for every expressions b, b', c and c'.

As for the material implication, these three properties are satisfied, but as we will see below, if we consider the weak implication "$\Rightarrow$," properties such as transitivity or monotonicity are not necessarily true.

Thus, in nonclassical logics we are led to distinguish between the monotonicity and the transitivity of the inference, and those of the weak implication. Moreover we can easily imagine definitions of the transitivity property, other than the ones given above:

Transitivity of the inference: ($D \cup \{a \equiv$> b, $b \equiv$> $c\}$, $a \equiv$> c) $\in L$ for every set D of expressions.
Transitivity of the implication: (D, ($a \equiv$> $b \wedge b \equiv$> c) $\rightarrow$ ($a \equiv$> c)) $\in L$ for every set D of expressions.

In the following the treatment of the comparison criterion $n° 2$ (transitivity) will refer to one of these definitions, the one which is the most "natural" in the particular formalism. The last two definitions, however, seem to be the best adapted to the problems considered throughout the test-example, i.e., the representation and use of pieces of information of the type "the A's are B's."

We may also be interested in another property verified by the material implication, but not necessarily by the weak implication:

Contraposition: if $(\emptyset, a \equiv> b) \in L$ then $(\emptyset, \neg b \equiv> \neg a) \in L$ for all expressions a and b.

The multiplicity of possible definitions clearly shows how difficult it is to characterize in a single way the comparison criteria established in the definition. The study of the links between these definitions goes beyond the scope of this work, and requires further consideration.

III. DEFAULT LOGIC

A. Presentation

Default logic is a nonmonotonic logic introduced by Reiter[44] in order to formalize default reasoning. A default theory $\Delta = (D,W)$ consists of a set of facts W which are closed first order formulae, and of a set of defaults D which are specific inference rules. An open *default* is any expression of the form: $\dfrac{u(x) : v(x)}{w(x)}$ where $u(x)$, $v(x)$ and $w(x)$ are first order well-formed formulae (wff) containing the free variable x *. $u(x)$ is the *prerequisite*, $v(x)$ the *justification*, and $w(x)$ the *consequent* of the default. The meaning of such a formula is the following: if $u(x)$ is known and if $v(x)$ is consistent with what is known, then infer $w(x)$. A default is called *normal* if $v(x) = w(x)$. The default $\dfrac{A(x) : B(x)}{B(x)}$, where A and B are unary predicates, may be read as: A is B with exceptions. A normal default may be used to express assertions of the form "Normally or typically, the A's are B's (possibly with exceptions)."

The use of defaults augments the first order knowledge contained in W: we obtain *extensions* which are sets of nonmonotonic theorems. Let $\Delta = (D,W)$ be a default theory whose defaults are closed, (i.e., whose free variables were instantiated with the grounded terms of the language, in our example, the individual Léa; each open default produces therefore a family of closed defaults, here a single one). An extension for Δ is a set E of formulae, closed under deduction, containing W and satisfying the

---

* We consider here that defaults have a unique free variable. The case of defaults having many free variables is treated by a reduction to closed defaults, by instantianting them with grounded terms.

following property: if d is a default of D whose prerequisite is in E and whose negation of its justification is not in E, then its consequent is in E.

Formally the extensions are characterized by the following property:

E is an extension for Δ if and only if $E = \bigcup_{i=0...\infty} E_i$, with

$E_0 = W$ and for $i \geq 0$,

$$E_{i+1} = \text{Th}(E_i) \cup \{C \,/\, (\frac{A:B}{C}) \in D, A \in E_i \text{ and } \neg B \notin E\},$$

where $\text{Th}(E_i)$ denotes the set of theorems obtained from E_i in a monotonic way:

$$\text{Th}(E_i) = \{w \,/\, E_i \vdash w\}.$$

It is important to note the occurrence of E in the definition of E_{i+1}. The sequence does not allow us to build E, as E should already be known to obtain the E_i's. E is a fixed point of a nonmonotonic operator. This definition is not constructive in general, but it may be adapted to a constructive one in the case of normal default theories.[45]

Default theories may have many extensions or none. The existence of at least one extension is assured in the case in which all the defaults are normal. An example of a theory with no extension is $\Delta = (D,W)$, with $D = \{\frac{:\neg A}{A}\}$ and $W = \{B\}$. In this case, the absence of an extension, due to the presence of an intrinsically contradictory default, excludes all information, even that contained in W (which is now inaccessible). We will see in Section VI that supposition logic behaves differently. Let us also point out that Lukaszewicz[46] proposes a variant of default logic, such that every default theory admits at least one m-extension (modified-extension).

We will propose several translations of the example; each one of them treats some aspect of the knowledge contained therein, but none is completely satisfactory. We will begin with some general considerations.

- The extensions are calculated from the instantiated defaults and contain only first order formulae of the type $\forall x\, P(x) \to Q(x)$, or $\exists x\, P(x) \to Q(x)$. We cannot get as a theorem a formula expressing a generality; the extensions do not contain formulae such that $\frac{A(x):B(x)}{B(x)}$ (Point 1).

- We have no modus tollens: from the default $\frac{A(x):B(x)}{B(x)}$, we cannot deduce that generally the non-B's are non-A's; we have to add explicitly the default:

$\frac{\neg B(x):\neg A(x)}{\neg A(x)}$ in order to obtain it (Point 3).

- Default logic gives account for only three quantification degrees:

(1) there exists x such that... (2) all the x are... (3) with exceptions, the x are...

Consequently, default logic is more powerful than classical logic insofar as it permits us to take normality assertions into account, but it is rather poor when representing quantifiers such as "a (big, small) part of" (Point 6).
- About truth maintenance, let us point out that Reiter showed that if W is consistent, and if the default theory (D,W) has an extension, then this extension is consistent. As for the problem of belief revision, no mechanism is provided (Point 9).

B. Treatment of the Example

We propose a first translation into normal defaults.

$$e1 : d1 \quad = \quad \frac{Sdnt(x) : Yng(x)}{Yng(x)} ;$$

$$e2 : d2 \quad = \quad \frac{Yng(x) : Sng(x)}{Sng(x)} ;$$

$$e3 : d3 \quad = \quad \frac{Sng(x) : Yng(x)}{Yng(x)} ;$$

$$e5 : d5 \quad = \quad \frac{Sdnt(x) \wedge Pnt(x) : Mrd(x) \vee Chbt(x)}{Mrd(x) \vee Chbt(x)} ;$$

$$e6 : d6 \quad = \quad \frac{Chbt(x) : Yng(x)}{Yng(x)} ;$$

Statement $e7$ is represented by the three following formulae:

$$e7 : \quad \begin{aligned} w1 &= \forall x \; \neg Sng(x) \vee \neg Mrd(x) ; \\ w2 &= \forall x \; \neg Sng(x) \vee \neg Chbt(x); \\ w3 &= \forall x \; \neg Chbt(x) \vee \neg Mrd(x). \end{aligned}$$

We will propose a representation for statement $e4$ later. We have already pointed out that default logic can handle statements like $e4$ only imperfectly. In the following, we denote $D = \{d1, d2, d3, d5, d6\}$ and $W = \{w1, w2, w3\}$.

We now show some examples of queries. A formula f is an answer to a question to the knowledge base represented by (D,W), if there exists at least one extension E for (D,W) such that $f \in E$.

$q1$: *Léa is a student. What is her marital status?* We add: $w4 = Sdnt(Léa)$; $S1 = (D, W \cup \{w4\})$ has an extension, $E1$. $E1$ contains, among others: $Sdnt(Léa)$,

Yng(Léa), Sng(Léa), ¬ Mrd(Léa), ¬ Chbt(Léa). Léa is a student, young, and single. The transitivity of the instantiated defaults is effective: for a given individual, we conclude from $e1$ and $e2$ that if he is a student, then he is single. However from $d1$ and $d2$, we cannot construct a default such as $\dfrac{\mathrm{Sdnt}(x) : \mathrm{Sng}(x)}{\mathrm{Sng}(x)}$ (Point 2).

$q2$: *Léa is a student and married. What is her status?* We add: $w4$ and $w5$ = Mrd(Léa); $S2 = (D, W \cup \{w4, w5\})$ has an extension $E2$. $E2$ contains, among others: Sdnt(Léa), Yng(Léa), Mrd(Léa), ¬ Chbt(Léa), ¬ Sng(Léa).

Default theories are *nonmonotonic*: the addition of $w5$ to $S1$ yields $S2$ which admits only one extension $E2$ in which we no longer have the theorem Sng(Léa). The set of theorems does not increase while the set of axioms does (Point 4).

However, if we limit ourselves to normal defaults, this nonmonotonicity can only arise when W is modified, and not by the simple addition of a new default. This property (semimonotonicity of normal defaults) limits the need to revise the old proofs when some new piece of information is added, and it allows us to define a "proof theory" for normal defaults.[44]

$q3$: *Léa is young. What is her status?* We add: $w6$ = Yng(Léa); let $E3$ be the extension for $S3 = (D, W \cup \{w6\})$. $E3$ contains among others: Yng(Léa), Sng(Léa), ¬ Mrd(Léa), ¬ Chbt(Léa) but contains neither Sdnt(Léa) nor ¬ Sdnt(Léa). We do not know whether Léa is a student or not.

$q4$: *Léa is a student and maybe has children. What is her status?* We add $w4$ and the two defaults: $d7 = \dfrac{: \mathrm{Pnt}(\mathrm{Léa})}{\mathrm{Pnt}(\mathrm{Léa})}$ and $d8 = \dfrac{: \neg \mathrm{Pnt}(\mathrm{Léa})}{\neg \mathrm{Pnt}(\mathrm{Léa})}$. The "maybe" is translated by the existence of two types of extensions: those where Léa has children, and those where she does not. $S4 = (D \cup \{d7, d8\}, W \cup \{w4\})$ admits three extensions $E4$, $E4'$, and $E4''$.

In each of them we have: Sdnt (Léa), Yng(Léa).
In $E4$ we have moreover: Pnt(Léa), Mrd(Léa) ∨ Chbt(Léa), ¬ Sng(Léa);
in $E4'$ we have: Pnt(Léa), Sng(Léa), ¬ Mrd(Léa), ¬ Chbt(Léa);
in $E4''$ we have: ¬ Pnt(Léa), Sng(Léa), ¬ Mrd(Léa), ¬ Chbt(Léa).

We do not know whether Léa is single or not but we know that it is possible; namely, there exists an extension with ¬ Sng(Léa) and two extensions with Sng(Léa). Let us note that this situation is different from the preceding one where we had a unique extension in which neither Sdnt(Léa) nor ¬ Sdnt(Léa) were present: the knowledge was incomplete. Here, we could introduce modalities at the level of the answers and say that the fact Sng(Léa) is *possible* because there exists an extension that contains it, whereas the facts Sdnt(Léa) and Yng(Léa) are *necessary* because they belong to all extensions. The introduction of the two defaults $d7$ and $d8$ is not completely satisfactory, since these two defaults play the same role, (each of them can be applied in order to generate an extension), while the English statement suggests a preference for default $d7$.

Remark: This process could also be used to translate $e4$: we will introduce the two following defaults

$$\frac{\text{Yng}(x) : \text{Sdnt}(x)}{\text{Sdnt}(x)} \text{ and } \frac{\text{Yng}(x) : \neg \text{Sdnt}(x)}{\neg \text{Sdnt}(x)}$$

This translation presents the same drawback that was just pointed out; it might as well be used for the statement "a part of the young people are not students."

C. Defaults without Prerequisites

A second possibility of translation consists of using normal defaults without prerequisites as suggested by Besnard[47]. We would keep w1-3, and would modify the defaults in the following way:

$$e1 : d1' = \frac{: \text{Sdnt}(x) \to \text{Yng}(x)}{\text{Sdnt}(x) \to \text{Yng}(x)}; \quad e2 : d2' = \frac{: \text{Yng}(x) \to \text{Sng}(x)}{\text{Yng}(x) \to \text{Sng}(x)};$$

$$e3 : d3' = \frac{: \text{Sng}(x) \to \text{Yng}(x)}{\text{Sng}(x) \to \text{Yng}(x)}; \quad e6 : d6' = \frac{: \text{Chbt}(x) \to \text{Yng}(x)}{\text{Chbt}(x) \to \text{Yng}(x)};$$

$$e5 : d5' = \frac{: (\text{Sdnt}(x) \land \text{Pnt}(x)) \to (\text{Mrd}(x) \lor \text{Chbt}(x))}{(\text{Sdnt}(x) \land \text{Pnt}(x)) \to (\text{Mrd}(x) \lor \text{Chbt}(x))};$$

$D' = \{d1', d2', d3', d5', d6'\}$.

Defaults $d1$ and $d1'$ do not have exactly the same meaning: $d1$ expresses circumstantial knowledge, and $d1'$, a permanent one. With $d1$, it is only when we hear about a student that we think that he is a priori young. With $d1'$, we know from the beginning that every individual, if he is a student, is a priori young.[47]

The answers to the preceding questions are slightly different now, but here are the questions exhibiting the two main differences: contraposition (Point 3) and disjunction (Point 5).

q5: Léa is not young. What is her status? We add $w7 = \neg$ Yng(Léa) to W. With the first translation $(D, W \cup \{w7\})$ nothing much may be deduced, as the extension we get contains nothing more than the theorems obtained from W. All we know is that Léa is not young. With the second translation, the extension $E5$ for the theory $S5 = (D', W \cup \{w7\})$ contains $\neg$ Yng(Léa) and Sdnt(Léa) $\to$ Yng(Léa) and thus also $\neg$ Sdnt(Léa); it contains likewise $\neg$ Sng(Léa), $\neg$ Chbt(Léa). Léa is neither a student, nor single, nor cohabitant.

q6: I cannot remember very well whether Léa told me she was a student, or single. We add $w8 =$ Sdnt(Léa) $\lor$ Sng(Léa) to W. The first translation $(D, W \cup \{w8\})$ gives nothing else concerning Léa, while the second one permits us to conclude that Léa is young: the extension $E6$ for the theory $S6 = (D', W \cup \{w8\})$ contains Sdnt(Léa) $\to$ Yng(Léa), Sng(Léa) $\to$ Yng(Léa) and Sdnt(Léa) $\lor$ Sng(Léa) and thus also Yng(Léa). We conclude that Léa is young (Point 5).

In situation $q5$ (contraposition, Point 3), it may be argued against the choice made here. Not everybody agrees with the idea of systematically "contraposing" the rules with exceptions. One argument runs as follows: suppose we write a field-guide about "birds and bats." We describe a world in which: (1) birds fly, (2) bats fly, and (3) non-flying individuals are birds. These three rules may have exceptions. Now we do not want to have the contraposition: contraposing the first rule would give an unwanted rule, contradicting the third rule.

In situation $q6$ (disjunction, Point 5), the expected answer is clearly the answer given by the defaults without prerequisite. So, the choice between these two translations using normal defaults (with prerequisite versus without prerequisite) is mainly dictated by the expected behavior in these two situations.

In Section IV-B, we will see a third translation, introduced by Konolige[48]:

$$e1 \quad \text{is translated by} \quad \frac{: \text{Yng}(x)}{\text{Sdnt}(x) \rightarrow \text{Yng}(x)}, \text{ and so on for } e2\text{--}6.$$

This default without prerequisite is not normal (although it is semi-normal, see below). The answer in situation $q5$ is the answer given by normal defaults with prerequisite; we do not get the contraposition, contrary to Konolige's claim: the justification of the default prevents the full contraposition here. (However, some kind of "shadow contraposition" remains. From $\neg \text{Yng}(\text{Léa}) \lor \neg \text{Sdnt}(\text{Léa})$ we get $\neg \text{Sdnt}(\text{Léa})$).

In situation $q6$, we get the answer given by *normal* defaults without prerequisite, as we get a conclusion from a disjunctive information. This behavior is sometimes considered as the ideal one with respect to these two points. However, the problem of the *shadow contraposition* is a significant drawback.

D. Priorities among Defaults

q7: Léa is a student and has children. What is her status? We add: $w4$ and $w9 = \text{Pnt}(\text{Léa})$. We are interested only in the first translation process. With the second one there would be more extensions to consider, as is often the case, but the problem treated here would remain the same.

$$S7 = (D, W \cup \{w4, w9\}) \text{ admits two extensions: } E7 \text{ and } E7'.$$

In each of the extensions, we have: Sdnt(Léa), Yng(Léa), Pnt(Léa) (we use $e1$ in either case). In $E7$, we have moreover: Mrd(Léa) $\lor$ Chbt(Léa), $\neg$ Sng(Léa) (obtained with $e5$); while in $E7'$, we have: Sng(Léa), $\neg$ Mrd(Léa), $\neg$ Chbt(Léa) (obtained with $e2$).

We get two extensions that give different information depending on whether Léa is single or not. Contrary to what happened with $q4$, this ambiguity is rather undesirable. It seems better to choose $E7$, since the information contained in $e5$ is more specific than that obtained from $e1$ and $e2$ (Point 7). The ambiguity actually results from the fact that general rules ($e1$ and $e2$) and more specific ones ($e5$) are translated into contradictory defaults which are alternatively activated. In commonsense discourse $e5$, which concerns a more particular case, behaves as an exception to the more general rules $e1$ and $e2$. It is thus normal to give it some applicability priority: we define an order among the defaults. Another way of solving this ambiguity consists of modifying the defaults representing general rules in order to render them ineffective in presence of exceptions, by the use of semi-normal defaults.

1. Ordering the Defaults

Touretzky[49] and Poole[50] have proposed to complete default logic in order to take this notion of specificity into account (see also Moinard[51]). Their solutions (or rather the derived solutions) would keep here only extension $E7$, as there exists an *inference chaining* from the prerequisite of default $d5$, Sdnt(Léa) $\wedge$ Pnt(Léa), to the prerequisite of default $d2$, Yng(Léa), constructed with the help of Sdnt(x) $\wedge$ Pnt(x) $\rightarrow$ Sdnt(x) and $d1$, whereas there exists no such chaining from the prerequisite of $d2$ to the prerequisite of $d5$. That is why $d5$ prevails over its concurrent $d2$, $d5$ being considered more specific.

A drawback to these definitions is that, even if the theoretical formulation is reasonably easy to handle, at least for the simple theories able to represent our example, the effective deduction of these preferences requires a substantial number of comparisons.

Furthermore, Etherington[52] objects that the role of logic is not to tell which extension should be chosen, by providing an explicit ordering, for example, but only to tell which are the extensions. It is up to the user (an external agent) to establish the preference criteria with the help of extralogical properties.

Another approach consists of making explicitly precise the priorities that we might eventually give to one rule over another. We could content ourselves with ordering only certain defaults. We would add to D and W for example: "$d5$ should be applied before $d2$". The advantage of this solution is that it permits the restriction to normal defaults, the main drawback being that it would then be necessary to define a new default logic, which would incorporate this notion of priority order but would lose, in particular, the semi-monotonicity of normal defaults.

In the following we present two other solutions, using other default types to give preference to certain defaults over some others.

2. Semi-Normal Defaults

The first method makes use of semi-normal defaults and has been proposed and discussed by Reiter and Criscuolo,[53] and resumed later by Etherington and Reiter.[54]

A *semi-normal default*, is any default of the form: $\dfrac{u : v \wedge w}{w}$ (that is, the justification implies the consequent).

$$\text{Let } d2'' = \frac{\text{Yng}(x) : \neg \text{Pnt}(x) \wedge \text{Sng}(x)}{\text{Sng}(x)} \ ;$$

$d2''$ means that being a parent is an exception to the fact that a young person should *a priori* be single. Let $D'' = D \setminus \{d2\} \cup \{d2''\}$. $S7' = (D'', W \cup \{w4, w9\})$ has then a unique extension, $E7$, which corresponds to our intuition. Let us note that $(D'', W \cup \{w4\})$ admits the same extension $E1$ as $S1$.

Such semi-normal defaults lead to the same answers as the normal defaults when there is no ambiguity, and choose the expected extension, otherwise. Thus it seems better to use semi-normal defaults rather than the normal ones. Unfortunately, the existence of extensions for the semi-normal default theories is not, in general, assured.

Etherington[55] has however demonstrated that the *ordered* finite semi-normal default theories (i.e., which correspond to hierarchical knowledge with no cycles in the inferences) admit at least an extension.

This solution presents however a major drawback: the writing of the rules is not modular. In fact, the addition of new exceptions may require the addition of new formulae to the justifications of the semi-normal defaults and consequently the modification of the already existing rules (Point 8). But, if we allow the modification of previous rules, classical logic permits us to represent all the situations described in this section (except "maybe" and "a part of"). Nonmonotonic logics have been introduced, in large part, exactly in order to avoid modifying the previous rules. The solution we propose below also uses semi-normal defaults, but preserves modularity.

3. Assertion Predicates

To each default di''', we associate an assertion predicate Ri such that Ri (x) means that default di''' may be applied to x; there are as many assertion predicates as defaults. These predicates permit us to reason by default over inferences and to block certain inferences, not valid in the presence of exceptions (see Froidevaux and Kayser[56]).

The default theory corresponding to our case is then the following one:

$$e1 : d1''' = \frac{Sdnt(x) : Yng(x) \wedge R1(x)}{Yng(x)} \; ; \; e2 : d2''' = \frac{Yng(x) : Sng(x) \wedge R2(x)}{Sng(x)} \; ;$$

$$e3 : d3''' = \frac{Sng(x) : Yng(x) \wedge R3(x)}{Yng(x)} \; ; \; e6 : d6''' = \frac{Chbt(x) : Yng(x) \wedge R6(x)}{Yng(x)} \; ;$$

$$e5 : d5''' = \frac{Sdnt(x) \wedge Pnt(x) : (Mrd(x) \vee Chbt(x)) \wedge R5(x)}{Mrd(x) \vee Chbt(x)} \; ;$$

In order to give preference to $d5'''$ over $d2'''$, we introduce a default $d7'''$ which blocks default $d2'''$. Default $d7'''$ expresses the fact that being a student and a parent is a situation in which the fact of being young no longer permits us to infer that one is single.

$$d7''' = \frac{\text{Sdnt}(x) \wedge \text{Pnt}(x) : \neg R2(x) \wedge R7(x)}{\neg R2(x)}$$

We denote $D''' = \{d1''', d2''', d3''', d5''', d6''', d7'''\}$.

The acquisition of a new exception such as $e5$ is translated into two more defaults $d5'''$ and $d7'''$: $d5'''$ corresponds to an assertion itself, and $d7'''$ plays a control role, indicating that $e5$ is an exceptional situation for $e2$. The addition of an exception thus leaves unchanged the already existing defaults $d1'''$ and $d2'''$. It is in this sense that the proposed translation is considered modular.

$S7''' = (D''', W \cup \{w4, w9\})$ has then a single extension $E7'''$ which contains Sdnt(Léa), Yng(Léa), Pnt(Léa), Mrd(Léa) $\vee$ Chbt(Léa), $\neg$ Sng(Léa), $\neg$ R2(Léa). We obtain the desired conclusion: if Léa is a student and has children, then she is young and non-single.

The obtained default theory is still an ordered semi-normal one, and thus admits at least an extension. Moreover, with this translation we obtain a modular representation. Let us note that if we eliminate in the justification of these defaults the part that is equal to the consequent, and if the represented knowledge is acyclic, (which is not the case in the example), we obtain a theory whose defaults are neither normal, nor semi-normal, but which admits at least one extension.[57]

E. Conclusion

Default logic is well-adapted to the treatment and representation of rules with exceptions; its vocabulary and its ideas have become standards in the subject. The definition is "syntactic-semantical," and the effective calculability is not simple, even when we limit ourselves to normal defaults (Point 10). However there do exist some theorem-provers that are able to work with fragments of default logic (for example, for the normal theories without prerequisites: Besnard, Quiniou, and Quinton,[58] for normal theories: Schwind[59]). This theory does not produce any new general rule of the type "students are young," but it permits us to give the properties of a particular individual. As well, it is not quite satisfactory for the problem of disjunction. Moreover, the answers to questions may vary according to the chosen representation and there exists no systematic procedure that permits us to find the appropriate representation for the statements. It is a non-numerical formalism that treats rules with exceptions as describing "the normal course of things," but does not necessarily express "the most frequent" situation.

IV. NONMONOTONIC MODAL LOGICS

Starting with the notion of information, statements may be classified in three categories. Indeed, pieces of information are nothing but statements to which the truth value *true* is ascribed. Conversely, statements contradicting a given statement of this first category are the ones to which the truth value *false* is ascribed. Lastly, we may find still other statements that do not fit in a true-false classification of this kind. For an information system, all this means is a distinction between what is *provable*, what is *refutable,* and what is *conceivable*. In relation to logic, this illustrates the interest of being able to form from a formula p not only the formula ¬*p* but also the formula ◊*p* which is then read as "p is conceivable." The truth of *p*, ¬*p* or ◊*p* thus corresponds respectively to the fact that *p* is provable, refutable, or conceivable. Intuitively, the truth of ◊*p* represents the complement of the truth of ¬*p* (*p* is conceivable whenever *p* is not refutable).

This gives us some insight about the question of taking into account and exploiting knowledge of the kind given in our test-example (that is, the knowledge relative to students, young people, singles,...). It is thus natural to express the fact that students are typically young by means of something like "if someone is a student and if it is conceivable that this person is young, then he/she is young." Using the notation described above this yields the formula $\forall x$ Sdnt(x) ∧ ◊Yng(x) → Yng(x) from which the formula Sdnt(Léa) should permits us to infer the conclusion Yng(Léa) (through the truth of ◊Yng(Léa), i.e. provided that nothing permits us to deduce the contradiction ¬ Yng(Léa)).

The ideas presented above motivate two nonmonotonic modal logics which are the subject of Sections A and B of this chapter.

A. A Logic for "Conceivable"

1. Presentation

The logic defined by McDermott and Doyle[60] relies on the language briefly described above, in which the operator ◊ has the status of a modal operator, i.e., it may prefix (in other words apply to) every formula. The set of all the formulae constructable in the modal language L_M will be denoted by F_M.

This logic aims at interpreting the notion of "conceivable" as a notion dual (vis à vis the negation connective ¬) to the notion of "provable": a proposition p is conceivable if its contradictory proposition ¬ *p* is not provable. This objective is achieved by McDermott and Doyle by considering all the situations induced by the truth of what is conceivable: for each proposition ¬ *p* which is not provable, the proposition ◊*p* is added; several possibilities may result as shown in the following example.

For purposes of illustration, we adopt the following convention: the proposition *m* means "I am married," the proposition *p* means "I am a young, single student," and the proposition *r* means "I am responsible." Let us now consider (maybe like the automobile insurance companies) the following:

◊*m* → *r*   "if it is conceivable that I am married then I am responsible"
◊*p* → ¬*r*   "if it is conceivable that I am a young single student then I am irresponsible"

Consider the principle that whatever is not conceivable is not true (a principle expressed by the schema ¬ ◊*q* → ¬ *q* being valid for all formulae *q*). Of course, I cannot be responsible and irresponsible at the same time, so that two possibilities follow:

either $\lozenge m$ is true and thus also r (and $\neg \lozenge p$ and thus $\neg p$)
or $\lozenge p$ is true and thus also $\neg r$ (and $\neg \lozenge m$ and thus $\neg m$)

In a certain manner, there are two possible solutions, corresponding to what are called extension in the preceding section. The definition of importance here is the following.[61]

Definition. Given a theory T, every enumeration $p_1, p_2,...$ of all the formulae without variables of F_M, produces a sequence $T_0, T_1,...$ built as follows:

$$T_0 = T$$
$$T_{i+1} = \begin{cases} F_M & \text{if there exists a } q \text{ such that } \lozenge q \in T_i \text{ and } T_i \vdash \neg q \\ T_i \cup \{\lozenge p_i\} & \text{if } T_i \nvdash \neg p_i \\ T_i & \text{otherwise} \end{cases}$$

The *fixed point* associated with the given enumeration $p_1, p_2,...$ is the collection T_∞ of all the T_i's.
Similar to the above example another case of a theory having two fixed points is given next.

Example. Let $T = \{\lozenge p \to \neg q, \lozenge q \to \neg p\}$ be a theory.

With an enumeration $p_1, p_2,...$, taking p for p_i and q for p_j it turns out that

if $i < j$ then $T_{j+1} \vdash \lozenge p \wedge \neg q$ which determines the first fixed point
if $i > j$ then $T_{j+1} \vdash \lozenge q \wedge \neg p$ which determines the second fixed point.

The name "fixed point" (of a theory T) comes from the fact that, essentially, we are interested in the solutions to the equation $S = \text{Th}(T \cup \{\lozenge p \mid \neg p \notin S\})$. For all degenerate cases, especially the absence of a solution to the equation, F_M is, by convention, the only fixed point of T, as illustrated in the example below.

Example. In the theory $T = \{\lozenge p \to \neg p\}$, the equation has no solution. Evidently, $T_0 \nvdash \neg p$ which entails $\lozenge p \in T_1$ and thus $T_2 = F_M$.

Given a theory, McDermott and Doyle do not consider the notion of inference based on the presence or absence of a formula in a fixed point of the theory. Rather, they are interested in the notion of inference linked to the presence or absence of a formula in all the fixed points of the theory:

$T \mathrel{\vdash\mkern-5mu\sim} p$ if and only if $T_\infty \vdash p$ for every enumeration $p_1, p_2,...$

In light of the equivalence between the fixed points of a theory T and the solutions to the equation $S = \text{Th}(T \cup \{\lozenge p \mid \neg p \notin S\})$, in order to get the notion of inference described above, McDermott and Doyle consider the intersection of all the fixed points of T:

$T \hspace{2pt}\vdash\hspace{-6pt}\sim\hspace{2pt} p$ if and only if $p \in \cap \{S \mid S = \text{Th}(T \cup \{\Diamond p \mid \neg p \notin S\})\}$.

The logic of McDermott and Doyle falls into category (1) of the classification established in Section II-C: to answer a question q on a knowledge base $\mathcal{B}$, amounts to verifying if q is in the intersection of all the fixed points of $\mathcal{B}$.

2. Discussion

We now examine the logic of McDermott and Doyle according to the eleven points listed in the general introduction. For these eleven points, it is understood that wherever it is written "from formula..." one should read "in the considered theory and from formula...," where the considered theory consists of the five formulae below, that give a representation of the test-example in the logic of McDermott and Doyle:

$\forall x$ $\text{Sdnt}(x) \wedge \Diamond \text{Yng}(x) \rightarrow \text{Yng}(x)$ "students are young"
$\forall x$ $\text{Chbt}(x) \wedge \Diamond \text{Yng}(x) \rightarrow \text{Yng}(x)$ "cohabitants are young"
$\forall x$ $\text{Sng}(x) \wedge \Diamond \text{Yng}(x) \rightarrow \text{Yng}(x)$ "singles are young"
$\forall x$ $\text{Yng}(x) \wedge \Diamond \text{Sng}(x) \rightarrow \text{Sng}(x)$ "young people are single"
$\forall x$ $\text{Sdnt}(x) \wedge \text{Pnt}(x) \wedge \Diamond(\text{Mrd}(x) \vee \text{Chbt}(x)) \rightarrow \text{Mrd}(x) \vee \text{Chbt}(x)$
         "students who have children are married or cohabitants"

The specificity of the statements above is reflected in the structure of the formulae that represent them: $\forall x\ A(x) \wedge \Diamond B(x) \rightarrow B(x)$. The language L_M permits us to express statements having a different form, for instance $\forall x\ A(x) \wedge \Diamond B(x) \rightarrow C(x)$, $\forall x\ A(x) \wedge \Diamond B(x) \wedge \Diamond C(x) \rightarrow D(x)$,....

Information describing which part of the young people consists of students, is not taken into account in the case of the logic of McDermott and Doyle (no more than in the case of all the purely symbolic logics presented in this work, for the reasons indicated in the general introduction). It is possible to think of representing a rule of the type "students are young" not by $\forall x\ \text{Sdnt}(x) \wedge \Diamond \text{Yng}(x) \rightarrow \text{Yng}(x)$ but by $\forall x\ \Diamond(\text{Sdnt}(x) \rightarrow \text{Yng}(x)) \rightarrow (\text{Sdnt}(x) \rightarrow \text{Yng}(x))$ (the formula corresponding to the default without prerequisites) which would permit us to obtain the contraposition property. As a result of the existence of various alternatives at the rule representation level in the framework of the logic of McDermott and Doyle, it is meaningless to consider the weak implication $A \Rightarrow B$ for a rule "the A's are B's." Indeed, it would be possible to define $A \Rightarrow B$ as $A \wedge \Diamond B \rightarrow B$ as well as $A \wedge \Diamond C \rightarrow B$, which lead to two radically different notions of weak implication.

Point 1: Generality/Individuality – Even if the formula $\exists x\ \text{Sdnt}(x) \wedge \neg \text{Yng}(x)$ is not deducible from the considered theory, it is impossible to obtain the conclusion $\forall x\ \text{Sdnt}(x) \rightarrow \text{Yng}(x)$. This is because the theory has only one fixed point (containing both $\Diamond(\exists x\ \text{Sdnt}(x) \wedge \neg \text{Yng}(x))$ and $\Diamond(\forall x\ \text{Sdnt}(x) \rightarrow \text{Yng}(x))$, but not containing $\forall x\ \text{Sdnt}(x) \rightarrow \text{Yng}(x)$). It is thus impossible to answer general questions (or even to conclude $\forall x\ \text{Yng}(x)$ if $\forall x\ \text{Sdnt}(x)$), but possible only to answer questions regarding individuals: for example, from the formula Sdnt(Léa) it is possible to obtain the conclusion Yng(Léa).

Point 2: Transitivity – There is a partial transitivity for the developed notion of inference but, according to what has just been said, that cannot be expressed by general statements, only by statements concerning individuals. It is not possible to obtain the formula $\forall x\ \text{Sdnt}(x) \to \text{Sng}(x)$ as a conclusion, and not even $\forall x\ \text{Sdnt}(x) \land \Diamond \text{Sng}(x) \to \text{Sng}(x)$. However, from the formula Sdnt(Léa), there is no problem in inferring the formula Sng(Léa), since there exists an attenuated transitivity here in the form of $\forall x\ \text{Sdnt}(x) \land \Diamond \text{Yng}(x) \land \Diamond \text{Sng}(x) \to \text{Sng}(x)$.

Point 3: Contraposition – Contraposing $\forall x\ \text{Sdnt}(x) \land \Diamond \text{Yng}(x) \to \text{Yng}(x)$ yields $\forall x\ \neg \text{Yng}(x) \land \Diamond \text{Yng}(x) \to \neg \text{Sdnt}(x)$, which yields nothing interesting: neither $\forall x\ \neg \text{Yng}(x) \to \neg \text{Sdnt}(x)$ nor $\forall x\ \neg \text{Yng}(x) \land \Diamond \neg \text{Sdnt}(x) \to \neg \text{Sdnt}(x)$ are admitted as a conclusion, whereas $\neg \text{Sdnt}(\text{Léa})$ does follow from $\neg \text{Yng}(\text{Léa})$. But the translation corresponding to the default without prerequisites (i.e., $\forall x\ \Diamond(\text{Sdnt}(x) \to \text{Yng}(x)) \to (\text{Sdnt}(x) \to \text{Yng}(x))$ permits the contraposition property to be recovered.

Point 4: Monotonicity – The property of monotonicity is not respected. Indeed, although the theory permits us to conclude Yng(Léa) from Sdnt(Léa), the same theory does not of course permit us to conclude Yng(Léa) from Sdnt(Léa) and $\neg$ Yng(Léa).

Point 5: Disjunction – From the formula $\text{Sdnt}(\text{Léa}) \lor \text{Sng}(\text{Léa})$ representing the hypothesis $q6$, it is possible to infer Yng(Léa). To reason by cases, on the one hand from Sdnt(Léa) and on the other hand from Sng(Léa), is equivalent to reason from the single formula $\text{Sdnt}(\text{Léa}) \lor \text{Sng}(\text{Léa})$. This comes from the fact that, as opposed to what happens with default logic, the formula $\forall x\ (\text{Sdnt}(x) \lor \text{Sng}(x)) \land \Diamond \text{Yng}(x) \to \text{Yng}(x)$ is equivalent to the conjunction of the formulae translating $e1$ and $e3$. In short, the notion of inference developed allows for reasoning by cases.

Point 6: Generalized quantifiers – The modal language L_M does not have, strictly speaking, any new quantifiers. But it provides some means of representing the statements involving such quantifiers. For example, it seems reasonable (but not completely satisfactory) to translate "many young people are single" by $\forall x\ \text{Yng}(x) \land \Diamond \text{Sng}(x) \to \text{Sng}(x)$ as well as to translate "few of the young people are married" by the formula $\forall x\ \text{Yng}(x) \land \Diamond \neg \text{Mrd}(x) \to \neg \text{Mrd}(x)$. On the other hand, a quantifier such as "a part of" would not be meaningful in the logic presented here (this point was already mentioned).

Point 7: Multiple extensions – The fixed points in the logic of McDermott and Doyle correspond to extensions in default logic, except for a few special theories.[44] In this sense, the logic of McDermott and Doyle admits multiple extensions, although the authors are only interested in the intersection of the extensions. What is most important is that there exists no notion of preference in this logic, for that we should borrow the corresponding principles developed for default logic.

Point 8: Modularity – Fundamentally, monotonicity is sacrificed for modularity in such a way that finding out an exception (should it be the first or the

nth) to a rule of the type "the A's are B's" is taken care of by a simple addition (of a formula representing this exception). There is otherwise absolutely no need to modify the knowledge base. The formula Sdnt(Léa) $\wedge \neg$ Yng(Léa) for example is simply added to the considered theory without anything else to be done. In particular, the formula $\forall x$ Sdnt(x) $\wedge$ ◊Yng(x) → Yng(x) is left unaltered even though it allowed us to obtain the formula Sdnt(Léa) → Yng(Léa) as a conclusion. Modularity is not extended to the case of a rule of the type "the A's are B's" which is presented as an exception to a rule of this type. As an illustration, consider the rule (represented by formula $\forall x$ Sdnt(x) $\wedge$ Pnt(x) $\wedge$ ◊$\neg$ Yng(x) → $\neg$ Yng(x)) according to which the students who have children are not young, which is presented as an exception to the rule (represented by the formula $\forall x$ Sdnt(x) $\wedge$ ◊Yng(x) → Yng(x)) according to which students are young. To take fully into account the former rule, the formula $\forall x$ Sdnt(x) $\wedge$ ◊Yng(x) → Yng(x) should be transformed into $\forall x$ Sdnt(x) $\wedge \neg$ Pnt(x) $\wedge$ ◊Yng(x) → Yng(x). Otherwise, neither of the two rules would overrule the other, as testified by the existence of two fixed points. In other words, modularity is limited by the absence of a solution to the problem of preference between fixed points.

Point 9: Revision – Essentially, the logic of McDermott and Doyle does not lend itself to information updating with data withdrawal.

Point 10: Complexity and decidability – The limits on the decidability of the logic of McDermott and Doyle correspond to those of classical logic in the following sense: a fragment of the modal logic L_M is decidable, when the part of the language where no modal operator intervenes is involved, form a decidable fragment in classical logic. Moreover, McDermott and Doyle[60] furnish a decision procedure for the propositional fragment of their logic. As to complexity, no result is known at present.

There exist several versions[62] of the logic of McDermott and Doyle according to whether the modal operator ◊ follows simply the rules of classical logic, or the rules of the modal logics M or $S4$. On the other hand it is out of the question to appeal to $S5$: two axiom schemata of $S5$, one, ◊$\neg$ ◊p → $\neg$ ◊p, characteristic of $S5$, and the other, p → ◊p characteristic of M, impose the monotonicity property by reducing the intersection of the fixed points of a theory T, to T itself. This is very unfortunate since $S5$ seems to be the one that comes closest to the notion of consistency required by the logic of McDermott and Doyle: a long tradition of studies in modal logics tends to consider $S5$ as the logic that best captures the notion of consistency in the logical language using the modal operator ◊.

Gabbay[63] has proposed a version of the logic of McDermott and Doyle in which the basic logic is neither classical logic nor a modal logic but intuitionistic logic. Another type of nonmonotonic intuitionistic logic is given by Clarke and Gabbay,[64] and Clarke.[65]

B. Autoepistemic Logic

Moore[66,67] adapts the approach of McDermott and Doyle by referring to the dual notion of "conceivable" which is, according to him, the same as "believe" (for as much as believing something amounts to considering as false that its contrary is conceivable: usually, this reduces to the equivalence between $\neg \Diamond \neg p$ and $\Box p$ which is read as "believe p").

Moore proposes to look in a different way at the reasoning by which, from the fact that students are typically young, we conclude that if Léa is a student then she is young. Moore qualifies this type of reasoning as autoepistemic since we reason on what we know or believe. The idea is that if Léa, although a student, were not young we would know it. But to know is, all the more so, to believe. We do not believe that Léa is a student who is not young, hence the conclusion. In fact, we start with the hypothesis according to which if a student were not young then we would know it (that he is not young). This is represented symbolically by $\forall x\ Sdnt(x) \wedge \neg Yng(x) \rightarrow \Box \neg Yng(x)$. The equivalence between $\neg \Diamond \neg p$ and $\Box p$ (and thus between $\Diamond \neg p$ and $\neg \Box p$, as well as between $\neg \Diamond p$ and $\Box \neg p$) shows that this is another way of writing the formula $\forall x\ Sdnt(x) \wedge \Diamond Yng(x) \rightarrow Yng(x)$. The notion of inference defined by Moore concerns ideal autoepistemic reasoning, since it reflects the principle according to what is provable is believed; this is where lies the difference between the fixed points equation of a theory and the definition below.

Definition. In a given theory T, an *expansion* of T is a solution to the equation

$$S = Th(T \cup \{\neg \Box p\ /\ p \notin S\} \cup \{\Box p\ /\ p \in S\})$$

It is the second brace that differentiates Moore's equation from that of McDermott and Doyle. Applied to the two examples presented above, this definition yields the following results.

Example. The theory $T = \{p \rightarrow \Box \neg q, q \rightarrow \Box \neg p\}$ (that is $\{\Diamond p \rightarrow \neg q, \Diamond q \rightarrow \neg p\}$) has two expansions, one containing $\neg q$ and $\neg \Box \neg p$, and the other containing $\neg p$ and $\neg \Box \neg q$.

Example. The theory $T = \{p \rightarrow \Box \neg p\}$ (that is $\{\Diamond p \rightarrow \neg p\}$) has no expansion.

In autoepistemic logic, the modal operator $\Box$ follows the rules of the modal logic $K45$ (see Chellas[68]) which is nothing but the modal logic $S5$ deprived of the axiom schema $\Box p \rightarrow p$ (which is equivalent to $p \rightarrow \Diamond p$). In view of the intended interpretation of the modal operator $\Box$, it seems natural to discard $\Box p \rightarrow p$ ("believe" p implies p). The logic of McDermott and Doyle, in the version where the modal operator $\Diamond$ follows the rules of the modal logic $S4$, brings interesting elements to the comparison since $S5$ is nothing but $S4$ enlarged with the axiom schema $\Diamond p \rightarrow \Box \Diamond p$. The difference between Moore's logic and that of McDermott and Doyle comes from this difference between $K45$ and $S4$, which is apparent at the level of negation of the modal operators. In fact, following $K45$, only the implications $\neg\Box\neg\Box p \to \Box p$ and $\Diamond p \to \neg\Diamond\neg\Diamond p$ are satisfied, while following $S4$, only the converse implications $\Box p \to \neg\Box\neg\Box p$ and $\neg\Diamond\neg\Diamond p \to \Diamond p$ are satisfied.

The first of the two situations differentiating autoepistemic logic from that of McDermott and Doyle may be paraphrased as follows. In autoepistemic logic it is not possible to believe something without any kind of justification whatsoever. As regards the logic of McDermott and Doyle, nothing prevents us to state without any justification that a certain proposition is inconceivable. In order to justify this analysis, we now give an example, in which to illustrate the problem, we will say that the proposition p means "I am married." The formula of interest is $\Box(\Diamond\neg p \to \neg p)$ which is also written in the form of $\Box(p \to \Box p)$, and in the form of $\neg\Diamond(p \land \Diamond\neg p)$. Following Moore, the formula $\Box(p \to \Box p)$ is then read as "I believe that if I were married I would know it". Following McDermott and Doyle the formula $\neg\Diamond(p \land \Diamond\neg p)$ is then read as "I cannot conceive that being married I would conceive that I am not married." In these two cases, the formula represents a meaningful statement. However, the theory $\{\Box(p \to \Box p)\}$ has no expansion. On the other hand, the theory $\{\neg\Diamond(p \land \Diamond\neg p)\}$ has a fixed point (that contains the formula $\neg p$, i.e., I am not married, a conclusion that seems opportune: indeed, should it be conceivable or not that I am married, nothing in the theory avoids my still conceiving that I am not married; but then I am not married otherwise I would be able to conceive that being married I conceive that I am not married, contradicting what the theory expresses; symbolically, from $\neg\Diamond(p \land \Diamond\neg p)$ by the modal logic $S4$, it follows that $\Diamond\neg p \to \neg p$ and thus $\neg p$).

The formula $\Box(\text{Sdnt}(\text{Léa}) \land \neg \text{Yng}(\text{Léa}) \to \Box\neg \text{Yng}(\text{Léa}))$ illustrates this first situation: it has no expansion in autoepistemic logic, in other words, to believe that if Léa were a student without being young then we would believe that Léa is not young, leads to a deadlock (autoepistemic logic generating here what is comparable to reasoning in a vicious circle).

Concerning the second situation, it is the case that in autoepistemic logic we might not believe that we do not believe a certain proposition. In contrast, in the logic of McDermott and Doyle, it is out of question to state that it is conceivable that a proposition is inconceivable. Here it is an example where, as above, we will say that the formula p means "I am married." The formula of interest is the conjunction, on the one hand of $\Diamond\Box p$, which is also written as $\neg\Box\neg\Box p$ ("I do not believe that I do not believe that I am married"), or $\Diamond\neg\Diamond\neg p$ ("I conceive that I do not conceive that I am not married") and on the other hand of $\Box p \to p$ ("I believe that I am married only if I am married") which is also written as $\neg p \to \Diamond\neg p$ ("if I am not married then I conceive that I a not married"). Although each formula represents a meaningful statement, the theory $\{\Diamond\neg\Diamond\neg p, \neg p \to \Diamond\neg p\}$ has no fixed point, whereas the theory $\{\neg\Box\neg\Box p, \Box p \to p\}$ has an expansion (containing the formula p, i.e., that I am married, a very rational conclusion: if I was not married, I would not believe to be married and thus I would believe not to believe that I am married, contradicting what the theory expresses; symbolically, from $\neg\Box\neg\Box p$, in modal logic $K45$ it follows $\Box p$ and thus p due to $\Box p \to p$).

The test-example is represented in autoepistemic logic with the same theory as in the logic of McDermott and Doyle, as can be seen from the equivalences between $\neg\Diamond\neg p$ and $\Box p$, between $\Diamond\neg p$ and $\neg\Box p$ as well as between $\neg\Diamond p$ and $\Box\neg p$.

The comments relative to the eleven points should also be applied to autoepistemic logic (for which a decision procedure for the propositional fragment is due to Niemelä[69]). However, as opposed to McDermott and Doyle, Moore does not consider the intersection of the expansions. Autoepistemic logic also falls into the category (1) of the classification established in Section II-C: to answer a question q to a knowledge base $\mathcal{B}$, is to verify if there exists an expansion of $\mathcal{B}$ containing q.

In spite of the impression that the preceding discussion might give, autoepistemic logic turns out to be more satisfactory than the logic of McDermott and Doyle. The modal logic $K45$ indeed constitutes a very satisfactory logic of belief on which the development of autoepistemic logic was founded. On the contrary, for all versions of the logic of McDermott and Doyle, the underlying logic only partially accounts for the required concept of consistency insofar as even the modal logic S4, though richer than classical logic and modal logic M, still lacks the principle $\Diamond\Box p \to \Box p$ (expressing that if it is conceivable that a proposition is inconceivable then this proposition is inconceivable).

Besides, Konolige[48] has established that autoepistemic logic corresponds, in a strong sense, to default logic, but with a richer language (in which the general ordering rules, which can only be postulated in default logic, are represented by real formulae). The correspondence defined by Konolige associates with the default

$$\frac{U(x) : V(x)}{W(x)}$$

the formula

$$\forall x \ (\Box U(x) \wedge \Diamond V(x)) \to W(x)$$

of autoepistemic logic. Consequently, a default theory may be translated into a theory of autoepistemic logic with the result that every extension for the default theory is contained in an expansion of the theory (of autoepistemic logic) associated with that default theory. For the exact result involving notions of strong expansions and weak extensions, see Marek and Truszczynski.[70] The correspondence established by Konolige also permits us to find the same differences existing between the defaults with and without prerequisites. For example, the formula $\forall x \ Sdnt(x) \wedge \neg Yng(x) \to \Box \neg Yng(x)$, in autoepistemic logic, corresponds to the semi-normal default without prerequisite

$$\frac{: Yng(x)}{Sdnt(x) \to Yng(x)}$$

for the statement "students are typically young." The formula corresponding to the normal default with prerequisites is written as $\forall x \ \Box Sdnt(x) \wedge \neg Yng(x) \to \Box \neg Yng(x)$ ("if a person whom I believe to be a student were not young, then I would believe it"). This permits us to find, in default logic and in autoepistemic logic, which variants satisfy or falsify the contraposition (Point 3) and the disjunction properties (Point 5).

The logic of minimal knowledge by Halpern and Moses[71] resembles autoepistemic logic with the difference that, where one refers to what is believed, the other refers to what is known. According to the definition given by Halpern and Moses, for a given theory T, we are interested in finding the solution to the equation $S = \text{Th}(T_0 \cup \{\neg \Box p \:/\: p \notin S\} \cup \{\Box p \:/\: p \in S\})$, such that $T \subseteq S \subset F_M$, where T_0 is the set of formulae without a modal operator which follows from T in the modal logic S5. Halpern and Moses restrict their study to the theories T such that, if $T \vdash \Box F_1 \vee \ldots \vee \Box F_n$, where the F_i are formulae without modal operators then $T \vdash \Box F_i$ for a certain $i \in [1,n]$, and the symbol $\vdash$ refers to the modal logic S5. Such theories, are said to be "honest" by Halpern and Moses, since they describe without ambiguity a state of knowledge (to the image of $\Box(p \vee q)$ which expresses that $p \vee q$ is known, as opposed to $\Box p \vee \Box q$ which expresses that either p is known or q is known). For honest theories, it turns out that every expansion (in the sense of autoepistemic logic) of T is a solution to the equation. That the opposite should be true comes up against the difference between K45 and S5, that is $\Box p \rightarrow p$, which explains why, for the theory $T = \{\Box p\}$, the equation above admits a solution (containing p, $\Box p$, $\neg \Box \neg p$,...) while there exists no expansion in the sense of autoepistemic logic.

C. A Logic for "All I Know"

According to Levesque,[72] the exploitation of rules with exceptions is carried out in relation to what is believed: if I believe that the student Léa is young it is because I have no reason to believe that she is not young, and the reason for which I do not believe that a student is young is that, effectively, this student is not young. The way Levesque found to model this kind of reasoning goes through the definition of a modal operator o meaning "all that is known is that." Rather than working directly with this modal operator, Levesque prefers to consider the modal operator $\Box$ meaning "what is known to be true is at least that" (Levesque thus assigns to the modal operator $\Box$ the same meaning as Moore), conjunctively with the modal operator Δ meaning "what is known to be false is at most that." The passive expression "is known" may refer to any agent: for example, $\Box\text{Sdnt}(\text{Léa})$ may be read as "I believe, at least, that Léa is a student" and $\Delta\text{Mrd}(\text{Léa})$ may be read as "I believe, at most, that it is false that Léa is married." Now Levesque identifies the idiomatic expression "all I know" with "what at least I believe to be true of which I believe that at most the contrary is false." With the symbols introduced above, this yields the equivalence $op \leftrightarrow (\Box p \wedge \Delta \neg p)$. The axiom schemata are those of the first order logic together with

☆p if p is a valid formula without a modal operator
☆$(p \rightarrow q) \rightarrow (\text{☆}p \rightarrow \text{☆}q)$
$(\forall x\ \text{☆}p) \rightarrow (\text{☆}\forall x\ p)$
$p \rightarrow \text{☆}p$ if every occurrence of a predicate in p is in the scope of a modal operator

where ☆ may be either $\Box$ or Δ.
Lastly,

$\Delta p \to \neg \Box p$ if $\neg p$ is a satisfiable formula containing no modal operator.

The inference rules are those of first order logic.

Levesque suggests that the application of his logic to the modelling of the reasoning on rules with exceptions be completed by a definition of a notion of nonmonotonic inference:

c is a conclusion of p if and only if $op \to \Box c$ is a theorem in the logic of "all I know"

Levesque's logic falls into the category (2) of the classification established in Section II-C: to answer a question q to the knowledge base $\mathcal{B}$, is to determine whether $o\mathcal{B} \to \Box q$ is a theorem.

The test-example is represented in Levesque's logic by taking the same formulae

$\forall x \quad \text{Sdnt}(x) \land \Diamond \text{Yng}(x) \to \text{Yng}(x)$
$\forall x \quad \text{Chbt}(x) \land \Diamond \text{Yng}(x) \to \text{Yng}(x)$
$\forall x \quad \text{Sng}(x) \land \Diamond \text{Yng}(x) \to \text{Yng}(x)$
$\forall x \quad \text{Yng}(x) \land \Diamond \text{Sng}(x) \to \text{Sng}(x)$
$\forall x \quad \text{Sdnt}(x) \land \text{Pnt}(x) \land \Diamond(\text{Mrd}(x) \lor \text{Chbt}(x)) \to \text{Mrd}(x) \lor \text{Chbt}(x)$

as in the case of the logic of McDermott and Doyle but with the addition of the conjunction F of the formulae governed by the modal operator o in order to obtain the single formula oF.

The logic defined by Levesque is purely monotonic (Point 4), even if it is extremely natural and easy to derive a notion of nonmonotonicity following the procedure indicated before. At the modularity level (Point 8), the logic of Levesque cuts a poor figure even though the operation of changing premises is perfectly codified, representing a radical improvement in comparison to first order logic. The process of changing the premises corresponds to a revision of the knowledge base (Point 9), though excessively limited as it is only concerned with the formulae representing individual counter-examples of the rules with exceptions.

The absence of an extension for a set of premises p is translated in the logic of Levesque by the simple fact that op is false, i.e., that $\neg o(\neg \Box p \to \neg p)$ is a theorem in the logic of Levesque. The existence of multiple extensions (Point 7) is translated into an explicit alternative concerning "all that is known": $o(\neg \Box p \to \neg q \land \neg \Box q \to \neg p) \to (o(\neg \Box p \land \neg q) \lor o(\neg \Box q \land \neg p))$ is a theorem in the logic of Levesque.

The satisfiability condition attached to the axiom schema $\Delta p \to \neg \Box p$ entails not only the undecidability of the logic of Levesque but also the impossibility of furnishing a recursively enumerable axiomatization. However, in view of what has been said about the logics of McDermott and Doyle, and that of Moore, the logic of Levesque is decidable for that part of the language which is purely propositional apart from the modal operators (see Bieber,[73] Bieber and Fariñas del Cerro[74] for a tableau method). The reason is the essential similarity of the modal languages defined by Levesque, Moore, McDermott and Doyle. This is also why, for the generalized quantifiers (Point 6), nothing changes similar to the logic of McDermott and Doyle: there is no quantifier apart from $\forall$ and $\exists$. So we have to be content with the interpretation of the formulae to arrive at some approximation to quantifiers such as "few of" for example.

Brown[75] adopts an approach, somewhat similar but neither as general nor as elegant as the one taken by Levesque, in which the modal operator □ means "it is logically true that" and the modal operator ◊ means "it is logically possible that." The approach employs a proposition symbol, say K to refer to the knowledge base, it represents ordinary propositions, for instance "if p and q then r," by formulae ($p \wedge q \to r$ for the given example), it represents assertions of the type "if p then q in the absence of a proof to the contrary" with $p \wedge \Diamond(K \wedge q) \to q$, and lastly it postulates that it is logically true that the knowledge base is equivalent to its contents, which for the example used so far, yields the formula $\Box(K \leftrightarrow ((p \wedge q \to r) \wedge (p \wedge \Diamond(K \wedge q) \to q)))$. It must also be postulated that all the combinations of literals are logically possible, which for our example yields $\Diamond(p \wedge q \wedge r)$, $\Diamond(p \wedge q \wedge \neg r)$, $\Diamond(p \wedge \neg q \wedge r)$, $\Diamond(p \wedge \neg q \wedge \neg r)$,.... Brown's logic generally permits us to deduce an equivalence $K \leftrightarrow F$ where F is a formula that contains no occurrence of the symbol K, so that the conclusions to be taken from the knowledge base are formulae that follow from F. Although it is based on a first order modal language, concerning inferencing Brown's logic is purely propositional: even $\Box(K \leftrightarrow (\forall x \Diamond(K \wedge p(x)) \to p(x)))$ does not yield the conclusion $K \leftrightarrow \forall x\, p(x)$.

D. Logics of Likelihood

The original motivation for the LL logic of Halpern and Rabin[76] was that decision making involves a qualitative perception of likelihood. The language of this logic contains a modal operator ⌑ intuitively meaning "it is likely that" in addition to the modal operator □ meaning "it is necessary that." This logic, which actually extends the modal logic $S5$, of which the modal operator □ follows the rules, presents a notion of classical inference that does not need a fixed point equation definition. In addition to the axiom schemata and inference rules of the modal logic $S5$, it has the following axiom schemata:

$p \to ⌑p$
$\Box p \to \neg ⌑ \neg p$
$\Box(p \to q) \to (⌑p \to ⌑q)$
$⌑(p \vee q) \leftrightarrow (⌑p \vee ⌑q)$

The various modalities (sequences of the modal operator ⌑) determine different likelihood degrees, which are, from the strongest to the weakest, $\neg ⌑...⌑\neg p,..., \neg ⌑\neg p, \neg ⌑\neg p, p, ⌑p, ⌑⌑p,..., ⌑...⌑p$. This is why the logic LL, which is monotonic, can be used to reason with rules with exceptions. For example, "students are young" would be represented as $\forall x\, \text{Sdnt}(x) \to ⌑\text{Yng}(x)$. It follows that, for every student who is not considered *a priori* as an exception to the rule, he is likely to be young: from $\forall x\, \text{Sdnt}(x) \to ⌑\text{Yng}(x)$ and $\text{Sdnt}(\text{Léo})$ it follows that $⌑\text{Yng}(\text{Léo})$. Similarly, for an exception to the rule, $\text{Sdnt}(\text{Léa}) \wedge \neg \text{Yng}(\text{Léa})$, the two formulae $\neg \text{Yng}(\text{Léa})$ and $⌑\text{Yng}(\text{Léa})$ would be inferrable; the first one dominates the second for the following reason: if $⌑\text{Yng}(\text{Léa})$ and $⌑\neg \text{Yng}(\text{Léa})$ are considered as formulae of the same likelihood, that from the fact that $\Box\neg$ Yng(Léa) is weaker than $\neg$ Yng(Léa), it seems natural to consider that $\neg$ Yng(Léa) prevails over $\Box$Yng(Léa). It is important to point out that the logic of Halpern and Rabin reproduces the degradation of the likelihood attached to the chaining of different steps in likelihood reasoning: from $p \to \Box q$ and $q \to \Box r$ it follows that $p \to \Box\Box r$ (only as an inference since $(p \to \Box q) \wedge (q \to \Box r) \to (p \to \Box\Box r)$ is not a valid formula in the logic of Halpern and Rabin) but not $p \to \Box r$.

The axiom schema $\Box(p \vee q) \leftrightarrow (\Box p \vee \Box q)$ underlines the fact that $\Box$ (as opposed to $\Box\Box$ which does not exhibit an equivalence between $\Box\Box(p \vee q)$ and $(\Box\Box p \vee \Box\Box q)$) is not compatible with the mathematical idea of probability, but rather with the one of possibility. In addition, both of the axiom schemata $p \to \Box p$ and $\Box(p \vee q) \leftrightarrow (\Box p \vee \Box q)$ are found in the possibility based axiomatization of the modal logic M (in the form of two axiom schemata due to von Wright, $p \to \Diamond p$ and $\Diamond(p \vee q) \leftrightarrow (\Diamond p \vee \Diamond q)$[77]). Moreover, every numerical possibility measure Π (cf. Section VIII-A) indeed satisfies, for every p and q, $\Pi(p \vee q) = \max(\Pi(p), \Pi(q))$. A counterpart in terms of modal logic to the all-or-nothing possibility measures was proposed by Dubois, Prade, and Testemale[78] in which the extension to the case of the possibility measure taking values in [0,1] leads to a notion of gradual accessibility (among incomplete knowledge states). An analogous procedure, for the translation of modal logic into probabilistic logic (but not the other way around), was proposed by Frisch and Haddawy.[79] Additionally, Fagin and Halpern[80] have presented a modal logic whose formulae permits us to express that "according to the agent i, the formula p is true with a probability of at least α." This work lies within a framework similar to the type of procedure undertaken by Ruspini[81] to endow the theory of belief functions of Shafer (cf. Section VIII-B) with logical foundations. Lastly, the logic of Bacchus[82] which admits conditional probabilities in a first order language, is close to these other approaches.

V. CLOSED WORLD ASSUMPTION AND CIRCUMSCRIPTION

Logic is faced with the problem of incomplete information because, in practice, it is often difficult to store all the facts that describe a world to be modelled. Indeed, everything that is not true constitutes such a mass of information that the problem of its description is pendent. One solution consists in considering this knowledge as being implicit, due to the closed world assumption,[83] written in its most elementary form as:

If A is not deducible, then infer $\neg A$ (A is a variable free atomic formula)

For example, if all we know is that Léa is a person, we will deduce that she is not a student. The closed world assumption leads to nonmonotonic reasoning since the addition of new pieces of information (Léa is a student) may invalidate the preceding conclusions (Léa is not a student) without producing any incoherencies. This permits us to satisfy Point 8 in a natural manner (modularity of representation) since any addition or suppression of information will require no modification of the global representation.

The closed world assumption is enough for simple problems (data bases), but leads to contradictions when the represented knowledge goes beyond the framework of Horn clauses or production rules (disjunctions lead to incoherences). On the other hand, this assumption is essentially propositional. McCarthy's circumscription[84,85] extends the closed world assumption to first order logic, by the introduction of an axiom schema.

A. Circumscription

In order to express that "Students are young"" we will say that "Every non-abnormal student is young." We thus introduce the new predicate *abnormal* (the abnormality refers here to the property of being young) and our sentence will be translated in first order logic:

$$\forall x \; Sdnt(x) \wedge \neg abnormal(x) \rightarrow Yng(x) \quad (1)$$

Intuitively, the *circumscription* of a set of predicates pi means that we only take into account, in order to define inference, world representations (models) for which the sets of individuals that make each of its predicates true are the smallest possible. We can also *vary* other predicates qi in order to enable pi to have an influence on the value of the qi. On the other predicates of the language which are neither circumscribed, nor varying, the circumscription will have no influence. In our example, we wish that the property of being abnormal be circumscribed, that is cirscumscription should affect the property of being young but it should have no influence on the property of being a student.

B. Syntactic Definition

Formally, circumscription is composed of an axiom schema, named circumscription schema, which extends the demonstration theory for the first order logic. In a finite set T of closed formulae of the first order calculus, *the circumscription schema that carries out the circumscription of the predicates $p1,...,pn$ by varying the predicates $q1,...,qm$ is of the form:*

$$\wedge \quad \begin{array}{l} (T[\Phi_{p1},..., \Phi_{pn}; \varphi_{q1},..., \varphi_{qm}] \\ [\forall X1 \; \Phi_{p1}(X1) \rightarrow p1(X1)] \wedge ... \wedge [\forall Xn \; \Phi_{pn}(Xn) \rightarrow pn(Xn)]) \end{array}$$
$$\rightarrow \quad ([\forall X1 \; p1(X1) \rightarrow \Phi_{p1}(X1)] \wedge ... \wedge [\forall Xn \; pn(Xn) \rightarrow \Phi_{pn}(Xn)])$$

- Each of the Φ_{pi} and each of the φ_{qi} may be any formula, even an open one.
- $T[\Phi_{p1},..., \Phi_{pn}; \varphi_{q1},..., \varphi_{qm}]$ is the set T inside which for all pi (respectively qj) every occurrence of pi (qj) is replaced by an occurrence of Φ_{p_i} (φ_{q_j}).
- The set of all the instances of this schema is denoted $Circums_T[p1,..., pn; q1,..., qm]$.

A formula f is *derivable by circumscription* if:

$$T \cup \text{Circums}_T[p1,...,pn\,;\,q1,...,qm] \vdash f$$

C. Application 1

If the set of formulae T is composed of a single formula:

$$\forall x \;\; \text{Sdnt}(x) \wedge \neg\,\text{abnormal}(x) \to \text{Yng}(x) \quad (1)$$

The circumscription in T of the predicate *abnormal* by varying Yng may permit us to conclude:

$$\forall x \;\; \text{Sdnt}(x) \to \text{Yng}(x) \quad (2)$$
"All students are young."

We obtain indeed $T[\Phi_{abnormal}\,;\,\varphi_{Yng}]$ by replacing in T, *abnormal* by $\Phi_{abnormal}$, and Yng by φ_{Yng}:

$$T[\text{abnormal}\,;\,\text{Yng}] = \forall x \;\; \text{Sdnt}(x) \wedge \neg\,\Phi_{abnormal}(x) \to \varphi_{Yng}(x)$$

The Circumscription schema $Circums_T[abnormal\,;\,Yng]$ is then written as:

$$([\forall x \;\; \text{Sdnt}(x) \wedge \neg\,\Phi_{abnormal}(x) \to \varphi_{Yng}(x)]$$
$$\wedge \quad [\forall x \;\; \Phi_{abnormal}(x) \to \text{abnormal}(x)])$$
$$\to \quad [\forall x \;\; \text{abnormal}(x) \to \Phi_{abnormal}(x)]$$

It should be noted that this is an *axiom schema*, that is a notation which expresses *all* the formulae of the language obtained by replacing, in the schema, $\Phi_{abnormal}$ and φ_{Yng} by *no matter which* formula.

We will now show that (2) is derivable by circumscription, that is that:

$$T \cup \text{Circums}_T[\text{abnormal}\,;\,\text{Yng}] \vdash \forall x \;\; \text{Sdnt}(x) \to \text{Yng}(x)$$

All the instances of the circumscription schema belong to the theory and can thus be used to establish the desired result (2). It is evident that most of the instances are useless in our case. In order to prove (2) we make use of the instance that corresponds to the trivial choices of formula $\mathbb{0}$ (always false) in place of $\Phi_{abnormal(x)}$ and formula $\mathbb{1}$ (always true) in place of $\varphi_{Yng}(x)$:

$$\Phi_{abnormal}(x) \Leftrightarrow \mathbb{0} \;\;;\;\; \varphi_{Yng}(x) \Leftrightarrow \mathbb{1} \;\;;$$

These choices correspond to "Everybody is young" and "Nobody is abnormal" and yield the instance of the circumscription schema:

$$([\forall x \;(\text{Sdnt}(x) \wedge \neg\,\mathbb{0}) \to \mathbb{1}] \wedge [\forall x \;\; \mathbb{0} \to \text{abnormal}(x)]) \to [\forall x \;\; \text{abnormal}(x) \to \mathbb{0}]$$

The formulae $[(\forall x \;\text{Sdnt}(x) \wedge \neg\,\mathbb{0}) \to \mathbb{1}]$ and $[\forall x \;\; \mathbb{0} \to abnormal(x)]$ are deducible from T (they are tautologies). Modus ponens permits us to derive the conclusion:

$$\forall x \text{ abnormal}(x) \to \mathbb{O}$$

i.e., $\forall x \neg \text{abnormal}(x)$. The latter formula yields, with (1), the desired formula (2).

D. Application 2

We complicate a little by adding to the previous set T the pieces of information "Léa is a student" and "Paul is not young." The set T' is then:

$$\text{Sdnt(Léa)} \wedge \neg \text{Yng(Paul)} \wedge (\forall x \text{ Sdnt}(x) \wedge \neg \text{abnormal}(x) \to \text{Yng}(x)) \quad (3)$$

The circumscription in T' of the literal *abnormal* by varying Yng no longer allows us to conclude, as before, that "All students are young." We have therefore a nonmonotonic reasoning since the addition of pieces of information to T invalidates a conclusion of T.

We will show that we may nevertheless conclude:

$$\forall x \text{ Sdnt}(x) \wedge (x \neq \text{Paul}) \to \text{Yng}(x) \quad (4)$$

The circumscription schema $circums_{T'}[abnormal\,;\,Yng]$ is indeed:

$$([\text{Sdnt(Léa)} \wedge \neg \varphi_{Yng}(\text{Paul}) \wedge (\forall x \text{ Sdnt}(x) \wedge \neg \Phi_{abnormal}(x) \to \varphi_{Yng}(x))]$$
$$\wedge \quad [\forall x \, \Phi_{abnormal}(x) \to \text{abnormal}(x)])$$
$$\to \quad [\forall x \text{ abnormal}(x) \to \Phi_{abnormal}(x)]$$

In order to deduce (4), we use the instance of this schema that correponds to the choice:

$$\Phi_{abnormal}(x) \Leftrightarrow \text{Sdnt}(x) \wedge (x = \text{Paul})$$
$$\varphi_{Yng}(x) \Leftrightarrow (x \neq \text{Paul})$$

This instance is:

$$([\text{Sdnt(Léa)} \wedge \neg(\text{Paul} \neq \text{Paul}) \wedge (\forall x \text{ Sdnt}(x) \wedge \neg(\text{Sdnt}(x) \wedge (x=\text{Paul})) \to (x \neq \text{Paul}))]$$
$$\wedge \, [\forall x \, (\text{Sdnt}(x) \wedge (x=\text{Paul})) \to \text{abnormal}(x)])$$
$$\to [\forall x \text{ abnormal}(x) \to (\text{Sdnt}(x) \wedge (x=\text{Paul}))]$$

We show that the premises of the instance are deducible from T', and thus the conclusion:

$$\forall x \text{ abnormal}(x) \to (\text{Sdnt}(x) \wedge (x=\text{Paul}))$$

is validated. With T' this conclusion yields the desired result (4). Let us notice that if "Léa is a student," it cannot be inferred that Léa is young, but only

$$(\text{Léa} \neq \text{Paul}) \rightarrow \text{Yng}(\text{Léa})$$
"If Léa and Paul do not represent the same person, then Léa is young."

Indeed we cannot, in circumscription, infer the equalities or inequalities which are not deducible from the initial set of formulae T. This is expressed by stating that equality dominates circumscription.[86]

The two applications show the difficulties that arise in order to implement circumscription on a computer. Actually, to derive a result by circumscription, we have to find, within the large number of instances of the circumscription schema, those that will permit us to prove the result. But the automation of this search for good instances is difficult.

E. The Complete Example

The complete example may be described by a set T of 8 first order formulae of which the last three ones represent mutual exclusion (the rule $e4$ is not translated):

$\forall x \quad \text{Sdnt}(x) \land \neg \text{abnormal1}(x) \rightarrow \text{Yng}(x)$
$\forall x \quad \text{Yng}(x) \land \neg \text{abnormal2}(x) \rightarrow \text{Sng}(x)$
$\forall x \quad \text{Sng}(x) \land \neg \text{abnormal3}(x) \rightarrow \text{Yng}(x)$
$\forall x \quad \text{Sdnt}(x) \land \text{Pnt}(x) \land \neg \text{abnormal4}(x) \rightarrow (\text{Mrd}(x) \lor \text{Chbt}(x))$
$\forall x \quad \text{Chbt}(x) \land \neg \text{abnormal5}(x) \rightarrow \text{Yng}(x)$
$\forall x \quad \neg \text{Sng}(x) \lor \neg \text{Mrd}(x)$
$\forall x \quad \neg \text{Sng}(x) \lor \neg \text{Chbt}(x)$
$\forall x \quad \neg \text{Chbt}(x) \lor \neg \text{Mrd}(x)$

We now have to define what are the predicates to circumscribe and what are the ones to vary. If it is natural to circumscribe all the variables referring to abnormality, thus exceptions, the choice of the varying predicates is more subtle. In effect, to vary all the predicates other than the abnormal ones would prevent any inference. To obtain interesting results, we can only vary Yng, Sng, Mrd, and Chbt. We then obtain the formulae:

$\forall x \quad \text{Sdnt}(x) \land \neg \text{Pnt}(x) \rightarrow \text{Yng}(x)$
$\forall x \quad \text{Yng}(x) \land \neg (\text{Sdnt}(x) \lor \text{Pnt}(x)) \rightarrow \text{Sng}(x)$
$\forall x \quad \text{Sng}(x) \rightarrow \text{Yng}(x)$
$\forall x \quad \text{Chbt}(x) \rightarrow \text{Yng}(x)$

The problem of choosing the right predicates to circumscribe and the right ones to vary is not simple. Moinard[87] presents a complete study of this problem.

F. Semantics

To give an approximate semantical definition we may employ the approach of the "preferential models".[88,89] In order to define the *circumscription* of the predicates *p1,..., pn while varying the predicates q1,...,qm*, we establish a partial order relation between the interpretations:

An interpretation *I* is *dominated by* an interpretation *J* if:

(1) *I* and *J* have the same domain
(2) *I* and *J* interpret the variables and the functional symbols *f* in the same way (the terms will thus be interpreted in the same way).
(3) For each circumscribed predicate *pi*, the extension of *pi* in *I* is included in the extension of *pi* in *J* (if *pi* is of rank n, the extension for *pi* in *I* is the set of the *n*-tuples of the domain *D* for which *pi* is true). We then say that *pi* is *minimized*.
(4) For each variable predicate *qi*, the extensions of *qi* in *I* and *J* are unconstrained.
(5) All other predicates have the same extension in *I* and *J*.

A *minimal model* of a theory *T* is a model of *T* that is minimal for this ordering relation, in the set of models of *T*. And we have the following result

if $T \cup \text{Circums}_T[p1,...,pn \; ; \; q1,...,qm] \vdash f$
then every minimal model of *T* satisfies *f*.

This semantical definition permits us to emphasise one of the major problems of circumscription, i.e., the addition of the circumscription schema to the theory may yield an inconsistent theory $T \cup \text{circums}_T[p1,...,pn \; ; \; q1,...qm]$. At the semantical level, this is translated by the fact that *T* may have no minimal model. The main general result on the existence of minimal models is that every set of clauses has a minimal model.[90,91,86] The converse of the property which links circumscription and minimal values is not true in general, but several partial solutions to this converse problem exist.[92,93]

Besnard and Siegel[88] use the definition in terms of preferential models to compare circumscription to the closed world assumption and to subimplication.[90,91]

In the closed world hypothesis, all the predicates are minimized, and we add to the theory all the variable-free atomic formulae which are true in at least one minimal extension. The problem is that if we step out of the Horn clauses framework we obtain inconsistent theories. Indeed, if "Léa is married or single," we will infer that "Léa is not married" *and* that "Léa is not single" which contradicts the initial information.

The subimplication is the first purely semantical approach:

– All the predicates are minimized.
– We restrict to discriminant interpretations that interpret two different terms in a distinct way (unique name assumption).

- A formula f is deducible from T if f is true for all the interpretations of a closed lower bound E of the set of discriminant models of T (E is a closed lower bound if every model of T dominates an element of E, and if every interpretation that is dominated by an element of E is in E).
- In the particular case where every model of T dominates a minimal model of T (particularly for every set of clauses), f is deducible from T if every discriminant minimal model of T satisfies f.

The problems caused by disjunctive pieces of information (and equally existential quantifiers) are obviated. The introduction of the closed lower bounds permits us to always have consistent theories (as opposed to circumscription). The restriction to discriminant interpretations permits us to settle the problems related to the fact that circumscription is dominated by the equality (see application 2). This restriction also permits us to devise decidable proof procedures for an interesting class of formulae (groundable clauses and groundable formulas). This proof procedure is based on the production of free variable negative clauses. For production algorithms see Siegel[94] and Jeannicot, Oxusoff and Rauzy.[95] As it is, this formalism is not well-adapted to the example since the minimization of all the literals is here too brutal. It is nevertheless easy, in this framework, to define an ordering relation between interpretations, analogous to the one given by circumscription, which permits a treatment of the example.

G. Comparison Criteria

- Circumscription is a nonmonotonic logic which, in this example, is modular for the treatment of exceptions (Point 8). Inference monotonicity (Point 4) is obviously not assured. The same for inference transitivity.
- There exists no specific implication, but we may consider that a rule such as the ones given in the example are kinds of weak implications ; in this way, in rule (1), the expression "$\wedge \neg$ abnormal(x) $\rightarrow$" could be replaced by a specific weak implication. In this spirit we have the contraposition property and the monotonicity property of this specific implication.
- We have seen that general answers (Point 1) are possible and that these general answers take exceptions into account ("All students, except Paul, are young").
- Circumscription cannot take into account quantifiers other than the basic ones (Point 6), and is not well-adapted to revision (Point 9).
- The implementations of circumscription (Point 10) are, at present, not numerous, partial, and of a great algorithmic complexity. Rather than an effective method, circumscription should be considered as a powerful mechanism capable of describing certain aspects of nonmonotonicity related to the closed world hypothesis. Subimplication is easier to implement for groundable formulas.
- Since circumscription is defined in first order logic, the way the connectives including disjunction, are taken into account is classical. In relation to the contraposition (Point 3) and to the nonclassical implication transitivity (Point 2), the question is not relevant since there does not exist any nonclassical

implication.
- Circumscription does not contain the notion of extension. However, our example raises problems of priority among the predicates. This can be partially solved by making use of a more elaborate form of circumscription, circumscription with priority[85,96] in which the minimization of certain predicates is considered as subordinated to the minimization of predicates of higher priority.

The relationships between default logic and circumscription are more superficial than real. First of all, the correspondence between the circumscription in a theory T, of a predicate P, and the default logic applied to the default theory $(T,\{\delta\})$ where δ is the defaut $\dfrac{:\neg P(x)}{\neg P(x)}$, leads to failure in the general case.

In the second place, the correspondence between default logic applied to a default theory (W,D), where D consists of defaults of the form $\dfrac{H_i(x) : F_i(x)}{F_i(x)}$, and the circumscription of predicates $\text{ABNORMAL}_{H_i;F_i}$ (all predicates in F_i being allowed to vary) in the theory $W \cup \{\forall x\, H_i(x) \wedge \neg \text{ABNORMAL}_{H_i;F_i}(x) \to F_i(x)\}$ is a failure in the general case. This almost complete impossibility of inter-translation may be summed up as follows. In general, each of the two formalisms requires a distinct representation for the same situation in order to carry out the same inferences. On the problem of the relations between default logic and circumscription it is imperative to consult Etherington.[97] Several relationships between circumscription and other formalisms are discussed by Lifschitz,[96] Moinard,[98] Reiter,[99] Gelfond, Przymusinska and Przymusinski,[100] Konolige.[101]

VI. A NONMONOTONIC LOGIC BASED ON SUPPOSITIONS

The main objective of nonmonotonic reasoning is to take into account implicit information that cannot be explicitly stated. In our example, the sentence "Students are young" means that we consider that a student is young as long as that it *does not yield a contradiction*. Most of the existing nonmonotonic logics translate "does not yield a contradiction" into "is consistent" or into "it is possible." Using such a translation, the example can be rewritten as:

"If it is possible (consistent) that a student is young, then this student is young."

This formulation forces, as a first consequence, the reasoning to satisfy a general property of the type:

If p is true, it is not possible (consistent) to have non p

This property, which can be translated by the necessitation rule in modal logic, may be explicit (autoepistemic logic), or a part of the definition of inference (defaults, circumscription). It is very strong and leads to complex logical systems that, in some respects do not really satisfy our objectives. This insatisfaction may for instance stem from the nonexistence, in some cases, of appropriate models (extensions, fixed points, minimal models), or also from the large number of models among which some are not relevant. In some formalisms these problems can be addressed only in the propositional case and the properties of connectives, in particular of the "or" connective, no longer hold. Lastly, the proof procedures are partial and complex even in simple cases.

The supposition-based logic of Besnard and Siegel[102] attempts to adopt a more pragmatic approach, where a nonmonotonic reasoning lies on a supposition about facts (a fact here is a closed formula), and not on possibility which is a much stronger notion. In fact, we do not exclude that what is supposed may be impossible and we may, without any incoherence, have at the same time "p" and "I suppose non p." As a general rule thus, we do not impose anything on the suppositions (a supposition is a simple hypothesis). A specific theory will however put constraints on *certain* suppositions.

For instance, in this formalism, "Students are young" will be translated into

"Every student whom we suppose to be young is young":

– As long as we do not claim that Léa is a student, we may suppose that Léa is young even if we know that Léa is not young. In fact, as long as Léa does not have the property of being a student, our supposition does not lead to contradiction with respect to the *a priori* information (Every student whom we suppose to be young is young).

– On the other hand, if Léa is a student, we can no longer suppose that Léa is young if it is said (or may be deduced) that Léa is not young.

A. Language and Theory with Supposition

1. Language with Suppositions

– Let L be a first order language with equality. To every formula p of L, we associate a new relational symbol, denoted $suppose_p$, whose arity is equal to the number of free variables of p (if p is closed $suppose_p$ is a proposition). These new relational symbols are called *supposition symbols*.

– We denote by LS the first order language obtained from the addition to L of the set RS of these supposition symbols. LS is the *supposition language* associated to L.

– If rs is a supposition symbol of arity n, and $t_1, ..., t_n$ are closed terms of LS then the positive terminal literal $rs(t_1,...,t_n)$ of LS is a *supposition*. The definition and the notation include the case where $n = 0$ (rs is a proposition).

The fact that LS is a first order language allows for the use of theorems and algorithms of predicate calculus.

To the formula $Yng(x)$ we will associate the supposition relational symbol $suppose_{Yng(x)}$. Since $Yng(x)$ has a free variable, this relational symbol is of arity 1, and we can construct the two literals:

$$\text{suppose}_{Yng(x)}(x) \quad (1)$$
$$\text{suppose}_{Yng(x)} (\text{Léa}) \quad (2)$$

Literal (1) is not a supposition since its argument is free whereas (2) is a supposition since its argument is instantiated. It should be noted that in (1), the free variable which appears in the index is not related to variable x which is the argument of the literal. In fact, the writing $suppose_{Yng(x)}$ is only a *notation* which indicates the relational symbol associated to *Jeu(x)*.

A language with suppositions does not attach any specific semantics to the suppositions symbols. This is a desirable feature, since this language should only offer a general and very practical framework in order to define the theories which take the different aspects of supposition into account. In order to define a supposition, two ways are possible: to add either axiom schemata, or general rules to the logical system, or else, to describe the supposition properties inside the theories. The first approach permits us to provide a uniform semantics to supposition, at the expense of a certain rigidity of the logical systems. The second approach is less satisfactory in relation to uniformity, but permits to better take into account certain local aspects of the supposition. The theories with suppositions use this approach in order to the define a class of theories, in which the nature of the occurrences of supposition symbols obeys some constraints. These constraints are not strong and intend to supply the supposition with a skeleton of a minimal semantics.

2. Theories with Supposition

A *supposition theory* of LS is the union $G = F \cup W$, of a set F of closed formulas of L, and of a set W of *supposition.rules*. Each of these rules corresponds:

– to a closed formula of the form:

$$\forall X \, \forall Y \, \text{suppose}_p(X) \wedge q \rightarrow (r \wedge p),$$

where p, q, and r are the formulae of L, X consists of all free variables of p, and Y contains all free variables of the formula $q \rightarrow r \wedge p$ which are not in X.

– and to a closed axiom schema in the form of:

$$\text{suppose}_{\forall X \forall Z} (\alpha \rightarrow p) \rightarrow \forall X \, \forall Z \, (\alpha \rightarrow \text{suppose}_p(X)),$$

where Z consists of all free variables of the formula α (of L) which are not in X.

3. Extensions

If $G = F \cup W$ is a supposition theory and S a set of suppositions such that $E = G \cup S$ is consistent, then E is an *extension* of G. If E is maximal consistent, we will say that E is a *maximal extension* of G.

4. Consistency

In general a tricky problem in nonmonotonic logics is that, in certain cases, consistent maximal extensions (fixed points, minimal models) do not exist. In supposition theory, a maximal extension is defined by the addition to the theory of the largest possible number of suppositions. But since these suppositions are *free variables positive literals*, it is possible to show that every theory with suppositions $F \cup W$ has a maximal extension if F is consistent (in fact we show more generally that every extension of $F \cup W$ is included in a maximal extension of G).

5. Remarks and Explanations

A supposition theory is equivalent to a first order theory of LS (an axiom schema means an infinite number of formulae). The closed formula of a supposition rule intends to express the following pieces of information:

"p being supposed, if q is true then r is true"
and "p being supposed, if q is true then p is true"

The first sentence yields a relationship between q and r ("if q then r") subordinate to the supposition of p. The second sentence simply means that if we make this supposition and if the conditions of application are satisfied ("q is true"), then we are in the situation where the supposition holds ("p is true"). We thus see that if q is not provable, the addition of the supposition of p, in a maximal extension, has no effect and is thus useless (the same as for a "possible") to infer p. On the other hand, if q is provable, then the addition of the supposition of p is linked to the addition of r and *also of p* (which entails that, if $\neg p$ is provable, then adding this supposition is impossible).

The axiom schema of a supposition rule gives a weak semantics to the use of suppositions, which permits the avoidance of uses which would be in too flagrant a contradiction with the intuitive idea associated to the supposition. We will especially be able to go from instancianted sentences to general ones. A particular instance of the schema is indeed:

$$\text{suppose}_{\forall X(\mathbb{1} \to p)} \to \forall X\ (\mathbb{1} \to \text{suppose}_p(X))$$

($\mathbb{1}$ denotes tautology). This instance means that, if we suppose the universal closure of a formula, then we suppose every instance of that formula. Such types of instance permit the inference of general rules in the minimal extensions.

Another instance of the schema is:

$$\text{suppose}_{\forall X(p \to p)} \to \forall X\ (p \to \text{suppose}_p(X))$$

Here $\forall X(p \to p)$ is a tautology, and we may deduce the formula

$$\forall X\ (p \to \text{suppose}_p(X))$$

from the supposition of the tautology. *A priori* nothing forces us to suppose the tautology and this instance is not equivalent, in the general case, to a necessitation.

Since no semantic restriction is imposed, it is always possible to assign to a supposition some semantics, representative of the different manners in which the supposition may be apprehended. We may for instance add a general necessitation rule "If $\vdash p$ then $\vdash$ suppose$_p$," and in this case "suppose" will have the minimal properties of "possible." A rule of the form "If $\vdash$ suppose$_p$ then $\vdash p$," brings the "suppose" close to the "believe" of the autoepistemic logic. It is clear that such additions of inference rules may oblige us to quit the framework of predicate calculus in order to account for the required specific properties.

6. The Example

Representation. The first phrase of the example "Students are young" is translated into the supposition rule composed of a formula $f1$ and a schema $s1$:

$f1.\ \forall x\ \text{Sdnt}(x) \wedge \text{suppose}_{\text{Yng}(x)}(x) \rightarrow \text{Yng}(x) \wedge \text{Yng}(x)$

$s1.\ \text{suppose}_{\forall x\ \forall Z\ (\alpha \rightarrow \text{Yng}(x))} \rightarrow \forall x\ \forall Z\ (\alpha \rightarrow \text{suppose}_{\text{Yng}(x)}(x))$

The relational symbol of LS of rank 1, $\text{suppose}_{\text{Yng}(x)}$, is the supposition symbol associated to $\text{Yng}(x)$, which is an open formula of L.. Likewise, $\text{suppose}_{\forall x \forall Z\ (\alpha \rightarrow \text{Yng}(x))}$ is the supposition symbol (proposition) associated to the closed formula $\forall x\ \forall Z\ (\alpha \rightarrow \text{Yng}(x))$. We recall that $\text{suppose}_{\forall x \forall Z\ (\alpha \rightarrow \text{Yng}(x))}$ is simply the notation of a proposition.

We remark that $f1$ has the general form

$$\forall X\ \forall Y\ (\text{suppose}_p(X) \wedge q \rightarrow (r \wedge p))$$

but in this case, $p=r$. It is often the case that such supposition rules are similar to normal defaults of Reiter. In such a case, the formula $\text{Yng}(x) \wedge \text{Yng}(x)$ reduces to the equivalent formula $\text{Yng}(x)$.

The example will be described by a theory with supposition $G = F \cup W$ in which the set F of formulas of L represents mutual exclusion.

$F = \ \ \forall x\ \ \neg \text{Sng}(x) \vee \neg \text{Mrd}(x)$
$\forall x\ \ \neg \text{Sng}(x) \vee \neg \text{Chbt}(x)$
$\forall x\ \ \neg \text{Chbt}(x) \vee \neg \text{Mrd}(x)$

Each of the six statements in the test-example is represented by a supposition rule (in order to make it lighter we do not write down the axiom schemata associated to the closed formulae).

$f1.\ \ \forall x\ \text{Sdnt}(x) \wedge \text{suppose}_{\text{Yng}(x)}(x) \rightarrow \text{Yng}(x)$
$f2.\ \ \forall x\ \text{Yng}(x) \wedge \text{suppose}_{\text{Sng}(x)}(x) \rightarrow \text{Sng}(x)$
$f3.\ \ \forall x\ \text{Sng}(x) \wedge \text{suppose}_{\text{Yng}(x)}(x) \rightarrow \text{Yng}(x)$

$f4.$ $\exists x$ $Yng(x) \wedge suppose_{\exists y\ (Yng(y) \wedge Sdnt(y))} \to \exists y\ (Yng(y) \wedge Sdnt(y))$
$f5.$ $\forall x$ $Sdnt(x) \wedge Pnt(x) \wedge suppose_{Mrd(x) \vee Chbt(x)}(x) \to Mrd(x) \vee Chbt(x)$
$f6.$ $\forall x$ $Chbt(x) \wedge suppose_{Yng(x)}(x) \to Yng(x)$

We notice that $f4$ is very weak. Just as in the case of circumscription, we have no quantifier to express the implicit exceptions of "Students are young."

7. Deduction of General Rules

We consider, at first, that no supplementary information is given. Then there exists only one maximal extension, obtained by the addition to the theory of *all the suppositions of the language LS* ($suppose_{\forall x\ Yng(x)}$, $suppose_{\neg \forall x\ Yng(x)}$, $suppose Yng_{(x)}(Léa)$, $suppose_{\neg Yng(x)}(Léa),\ldots$, $suppose_{\forall x\ Sdnt(x)}$). In this maximal extension, we can deduce the general formulae:

$g1.$ $\forall x$ $Sdnt(x) \to Yng(x)$
$g2.$ $\forall x$ $Yng(x) \to Sng(x)$
$g3.$ $\forall x$ $Sng(x) \to Yng(x)$
$g4.$ $\exists x$ $Yng(x) \to \exists y\ (Yng(y) \wedge Sdnt(y))$
$g5.$ $\forall x$ $Sdnt(x) \wedge Pnt(x) \to Mrd(x) \vee Chbt(x)$
$g6.$ $\forall x$ $Chbt(x) \to Yng(x)$

In the maximal extension, for example, clause $g1$ is deducible *by making use of the axiom schema associated to $f1$* (if the axiom schema were absent, we would not be able to deduce such a general rule but, as in default logic, only instances of rules). Indeed, the maximal extension contains, in particular, the three formulae:

$f1.$ $\forall x$ $Sdnt(x) \wedge suppose_{Yng(x)}(x) \to Yng(x) \wedge Yng(x)$
$sh1.$ $suppose_{\forall x}\ \mathbb{1} \to Yng(x) \to \forall x\ (\mathbb{1} \to suppose_{Yng(x)}(x))$
$su.$ $suppose_{\forall x}\ \mathbb{1} \to Yng(x)$

Formula $sh1$ is an instance of the axiom schema associated to $f1$, for which α is the tautology; and su is the supposition contained in the maximal extension. From these three formulae we immediately deduce our formula $g1$.

8. Instanciation and Exceptions

We now let $G1 = F1 \cup F \cup W$ where W and F have been previously defined and we have:

$$F1 = \{Sdnt(Léa), Sdnt(Paul), \neg Yng(Paul)\}$$

$G1$ has a single maximal extension obtained by the addition to $G1$ of all the suppositions except $suppose_{Yng(x)}(Paul)$, and $suppose_{\forall x\ \mathbb{1} \to Yng(x)}$ (by using $F1$, $f1$, and $s1$ we prove that the negation of these two suppositions are the theorems of

G1). This extension contains in particular *suppose*$_{Yng(x)}$*(Paul)*, from which we deduce the formula Yng(Léa).

On comparing this formalism with circumscription we remark that in circumscription, equality dominates circumscription, which is not the case here. In circumscription, in fact, we will not deduce Yng(Léa) in this case but only the rule

$$(Léa \neq Paul) \rightarrow Yng(Léa)$$

In supposition logic, as well as in circumscription, we will not, of course, deduce the general rule

$$g1. \quad \forall x \; Sdnt(x) \rightarrow Yng(x)$$

but we may deduce a general rule which takes the exceptions into account:

$$g2. \quad \forall x \; Sdnt(x) \wedge (x \neq Paul) \rightarrow Yng(x)$$

Indeed, the maximal extension contains, among others, the formulae:

- *F*1. Sdnt(Léa), Sdnt(Paul), ¬ Yng(Paul)
- *f*1. $\forall x \; Sdnt(x) \wedge suppose_{Yng(x)}(x) \rightarrow Yng(x) \wedge Yng(x)$
- *sh*2. $suppose_{\forall x \; (x \neq Paul)} \rightarrow Yng(x) \rightarrow \forall x \; (x \neq Paul \rightarrow suppose_{Yng(x)}(x))$
- *s*2. $suppose_{\forall x \; (x \neq Paul)} \rightarrow Yng(x)$

which immediately yield the result.

Other developments. Besnard and Siegel[102] extend the framework by the introduction of a notion of "accepted" facts. This allows in particular to obtain a logic close to default logic. In the same way, Siegel[103] presents a modal framework, which allows to give a formalism equivalent to default logic and a formalism close to circumscription.

B. Comparison Criteria

Since supposition logic is a nonmonotonic logic, the monotonicity of the inference does not hold (Point 4), and the modularity is natural (Point 8). Neither revision, nor addition of quantifiers other than the basic ones (Point 6) are possible. We do not have the transitivity of the inference either. The choice of an extension within several extensions (Point 7) is not included in this formalism. It is always possible to rewrite the supposition rules in order to explicitly establish preferences over the suppositions supporting the application of rules, but this technique is to be avoided, because it has the drawback of destroying modularity for the most part. In the preceding paragraph, we also saw that general and individual responses (Point 1) are possible. We have seen as well that the general answers take the exceptions into account (we deduce $\forall x \; Sdnt(x) \wedge (x \neq Paul) \rightarrow Yng(x)$).

Since the suppositions theories are first order theories, the way of taking connectives and inferences into account is very close to that of predicate calculus:

– The disjunction (Point 5) is taken into account. For example from:
$$a \vee b \qquad a \wedge \text{suppose}_c \to c$$
$$b \wedge \text{suppose}_d \to d$$
we will deduce $c \vee d$ in the single maximal extension.

– There exists no nonclassical implication but, in the same spirit as for circumscription, we may consider that in a supposition rule the expression "$\wedge$ suppose$_{Yng(x)}(x) \to$" is a kind of weak implication. In this spirit the contraposition (Point 3) is partial. Indeed, from the supposition rule:

$$\forall x \; Sdnt(x) \wedge \text{suppose}_{Yng(x)}(x) \to Yng(x)$$

we classically obtain (in first order logic):

$$\forall x \; \neg Yng(x) \wedge \text{suppose}_{Yng(x)}(x) \to \neg Sdnt(x)$$

This formula is not a pure supposition rule.

– As in the case of contraposition, the transitivity of the nonclassical implication (Point 2) is partial, insofar as, from the two rules with suppositions:

$$\forall x \; Sdnt(x) \wedge \text{suppose}_{Yng(x)}(x) \to Yng(x)$$
$$\forall x \; Yng(x) \wedge \text{suppose}_{Sng(x)}(x) \to Sng(x)$$

we cannot deduce the supposition rule

$$\forall x \; Sdnt(x) \wedge \text{suppose}_{Sng(x)}(x) \to Sng(x)$$

but we classically deduce a weaker rule

$$\forall x \; Sdnt(x) \wedge \text{suppose}_{Yng(x)}(x) \wedge \text{suppose}_{Sng(x)}(x) \to Sng(x)$$

which is not a pure supposition rule. It is clear that in this case we obtain, in the single maximal extension,

$$\forall x \; Sdnt(x) \to Sng(x).$$

The problem of the algorithmic complexity of the proof procedures (Point 10) is, first of all, a problem of completeness, as in all nonmonotonic logics. The fact that a maximal extension is obtained by the addition to the theory of the literals without variables (suppositions), permits us to prove that every maximal extension is obtained by the addition of a finite number of suppositions.[102] This compactness property leads to a proof procedure based on the production of negative clauses without variables which only contains suppositions.

VII. CONDITIONAL LOGICS AND "ROUGH" IMPLICATIONS

In modal logic, generally speaking, it is claimed that, in order to represent an expression such as "students are young," it is necessary to find a new implication connective ($\Rightarrow$), capable of formalizing the link between "student" and "young." This expression may be represented by

$$\forall x \, (Sdnt(x) \Rightarrow Yng(x))$$

Which are the modal formalisms capable of representing such statements? To begin with we can say that each modal logic has its own implication symbol. Therefore, if symbol "$\Box$" (necessary) represents the archetype of the modal symbols, its combination with the classical implication "$\rightarrow$" generates a new implication:

$$\Box(p \rightarrow q) =_{\text{definition}} p \Rightarrow q$$

It was this approach that allowed Lewis to define the first modal formalisms.[77]

From this first approximation we find other approaches in modal logic permitting a more explicit formalization of the notion of implication. Some of these are, for instance, presupposition logics, conditional logics, and modal systems which formalize the notion of "rough set."[104,105]

A new question may now be asked, namely: what kind of reasoning do we want to formalize with the help of this implication? Is it a case of formalizing hypothetical reasoning or reasoning with a certain uncertainty degree, or even subjunctive reasoning? Let us return to our example and consider the statement: "students are young." What we want to express is: "normally students are young"; or in other words, that each student, if not otherwise known to be old, should be considered to be young. We shall see in the following how this is formalized in the framework of conditional logics, and in the frameworks based on "rough sets."

A. Conditional Logics

Sentences of the conditional type express a proposition which is a function of two others (the antecedent and the consequent) in the form of "If antecedent then consequent." By "conditional logics representation" it is meant, on the one hand, the fact of giving an adequate definition of the operator which expresses the relation between the two propositions, and on the other hand, the study of its properties.

It is F.P. Ramsey who gives us the first serious elements for the study of the logical problem of conditionals. His suggestions may be expressed in the following terms: the determination of the truth value of a conditional expression may be done by adding the antecedent to the knowledge base (beliefs) and examining afterwards if the consequent is true. It consists thus in transforming the beliefs into truth conditions; this idea is at the origin of new semantic theories, based on the notion of possible world, which have permitted the development of modal logics.

Thence several formal theories have been developed. The first one due to Stalnaker[106] who is interested in the formalization of subjunctive conditionals, of which the statement: if Harry were a woman he would be called Harriet, is an example.

Stalnaker resumes Ramsey's idea and proposes the following intuitive definition of implication:

$A \Rightarrow B$ is true in the actual state if and only if in the state that mostly resembles the actual state and where A is true, B is true.

An important property of the logic of Stalnaker is that its implication is stronger than the classical implication, since $A \Rightarrow B$ only if $A \rightarrow B$, i.e., only if A implies B materially.

These logics have thus been defined in order to formalize conditionals whose premise is false in the state where the statement is made. This kind of logics is not well-adapted to our example, for intuitively, the implicit implication in the sentence "Normally students are young" is weaker than the material implication.

Delgrande[107] has recently defined a new conditional logic, called N, which allows us to take typicality into account. Delgrande proposes the following intuitive definition of implication:

$A \Rightarrow B$ is true in the actual state if and only if B is true in the most typical state where A is true, within the states more typical than the actual state.

Unlike the logic of Stalnaker, the material implication ($\rightarrow$) is stronger than Delgrande's implication, i.e., $A \rightarrow B$ only if $A \Rightarrow B$ and in particular, if $A \rightarrow B$ is a theorem, then $A \Rightarrow B$ is also a theorem.

We will now define the semantics associated to conditional logics. For the sake of being tutorial, we will consider the propositional framework initially. A model M is a triple $<W, f, m>$, where W is a set of states (called "possible worlds" in the specialized literature), f is a function that associates to each state, and to each formula (or more precisely to the set of states where the formula is true), a set of states; m is a meaning function which associates to each propositional variable the set of states in which that variable is true. Let A be a formula, and M a model, $|A|^M$ (or $|A|$ for short) will denote the set of states in M where A is true, also called an extension of A in M. The notion of the satisfiability of a formula A in state w and model M (denoted M, w sat A) is defined by induction over the formula structure. We will therefore have:

M, w sat p if and only if p is true in w (that is $w \in m(p)$)
M, w sat $\neg A$ if and only if M, w non sat A
M, w sat $A \vee B$ if and only if M, w sat A or M, w sat B
M, w sat $A \Rightarrow B$ if and only if $f(w, |A|) \subseteq |B|$

We say that a formula A is satisfiable in a model M if and only if there exists a w in M such that M, w sat A. We say that A is valid if M, w sat A, for each model M and state w in M.

The problem now is to establish a link between the notions of theorem and valid formulae. In other words, given an axiomatics of the implication operator $\Rightarrow$, to find the properties of the function f, so that the syntax-semantics correspondence is exact.

Function f permits the expression of typicality, i.e., $f(w,A)$ represents the set of the most typical states where A is true, within those which are more typical than w.

In the logic of Delgrande, function f has to verify the following properties:

$f(w,|A|) \subseteq |A|$
if $f(w,|A|) \subseteq |B|$ then $f(w,|A|) \subseteq f(w,|A \wedge B|)$
if $f(w,|A|) \not\subseteq |B|$ then $f(w,|A \wedge \neg B|) \subseteq f(w,|A|)$
if $f(w,|A \vee B|) \subseteq |A|$ then $f(w,|A|) \subseteq f(w,|B|)$

It should be noted that the logic developed by Delgrande is a first order logic. In this case the notion of model is extended, in the sense that in each state there will be a first order classical interpretation. Namely, a model is a quadruple $<W,D,f,m>$, where D is a domain of individuals, and, as previously indicated, m furnishes a classical interpretation to each state.

Before studying the behavior of this logic by means of comparison criteria, we define what Delgrande[108] means by answering a question. To do so, some definitions are necessary. For Delgrande, a default theory is a pair $T = <D,C>$, where D is a set of formulae of his conditional logic, called defaults, and C is a set of classical formulas which describe the state of the world.

A formula $\alpha \Rightarrow \beta$ is *supported in* a set of formulas Γ, if there exists a formula γ such that:

(1) $\alpha \rightarrow \gamma$ is a theorem in classical logic
(2) $\gamma \Rightarrow \beta$ is derivable from Γ by the use of Delgrande's logic (denoted $\Gamma \vdash_N \gamma \Rightarrow \beta$)
(3) if there exists a β' such that $\alpha \rightarrow \beta'$ is a classical theorem, and $\Gamma \vdash_N \neg (\beta' \Rightarrow \beta)$, then $\gamma \rightarrow \beta'$ is also a classical theorem.

And finally $E(D)$ is an extension for the default logic $T = <D,C>$, if

$$E(D) = \{\alpha \wedge \gamma \Rightarrow \beta: D \vdash_N \alpha \Rightarrow \beta \text{ and if } \alpha \wedge \gamma \Rightarrow \beta \text{ is supported in } D \cup C\} \cup \{\alpha \wedge \neg \gamma \Rightarrow \beta: D \vdash_N \alpha \Rightarrow \beta \text{ and } \alpha \wedge \gamma \Rightarrow \beta \text{ is not supported in } D \cup C\}.$$

We are now in a position to define how a formula F may be derived from a default theory $T = <D,C>$ (denoted by $T \vdash F$). $T \vdash F$ if and only if $E(D) \vdash_N C \Rightarrow F$. Thus nonmonotonic deduction is reduced to the deduction in N by means of the implication operator. It is in this sense that the notion of deduction will be used from now on.

It should be noted that Delgrande restricts his language to formulae without nested conditional operator "$\Rightarrow$," for instance the formula: $(A \Rightarrow B) \Rightarrow C$ is not allowed.

In the following we study the example with the help of comparison criteria.

In the first place, our example will be translated into the following formulas:

$\forall x\ Sdnt(x) \Rightarrow Yng(x)$ "students are young"
$\forall x\ Chbt(x) \Rightarrow Yng(x)$ "people who cohabit are young"

$\forall x \; \text{Sng}(x) \Rightarrow \text{Yng}(x)$ "singles are young"
$\forall x \; \text{Yng}(x) \Rightarrow \text{Sng}(x)$ "young people are single"
$\forall x \; (\text{Sdnt}(x) \wedge \text{Pnt}(x)) \Rightarrow (\text{Mrd}(x) \vee \text{Chbt}(x))$ "students who have children are married or cohabitants",

where the implication is the one from Delgrande's logic.

Given the restrictions on the above presented language, many properties do not apply to this logic. In this way, it should be proved for the expression $\forall x \; (A(x) \Rightarrow B(x))$, that $E(D) \vdash C \Rightarrow (\forall x \; A(x) \Rightarrow B(x))$, but this expression is not allowed.

As for transitivity (Point 2) the two following properties have to be considered:

(1) The transitivity of the deduction holds. Indeed, if $A \Rightarrow B$ and $B \Rightarrow C$ are the expressions in $E(D)$ we will then have: $E(D) \vdash A \Rightarrow C$, by means of the theorem presented by Delgrande: if A is a classical formula, and $B \Rightarrow C \in D$, then $B \wedge A \Rightarrow C \in E(D)$, or $B \wedge \neg A \Rightarrow C \in E(D)$.

(2) The transitivity of the implication ($\Rightarrow$) does not hold. Since the expression:

$$\forall x \; (\text{Sdnt}(x) \Rightarrow \text{Yng}(x)) \wedge (\text{Yng}(x) \Rightarrow \text{Sng}(x)) \wedge \neg (\text{Sdnt}(x) \Rightarrow \text{Sng}(x)))$$

is a satisfiable formula in the logic of Delgrande, the implication "$\Rightarrow$" is not transitive.

As an example, a model is now defined in which the formula is satisfiable. In order to do so, and for the sake of being tutorial we consider a propositional variant of the formula, namely:

$$(\text{Sdnt}(\text{Léa}) \Rightarrow \text{Yng}(\text{Léa})) \wedge (\text{Yng}(\text{Léa}) \Rightarrow \text{Sng}(\text{Léa})) \wedge \neg (\text{Sdnt}(\text{Léa}) \Rightarrow \text{Sng}(\text{Léa}))$$

Let M be a model where $W = \{w_1, w_2, w_3\}$, $|\text{Sdnt}(\text{Léa})| = \{w_2, w_3\}$, $|\text{Yng}(\text{Léa})| = \{w_2, w_3\}$, $|\text{Sng}(\text{Léa})| = \{w_3\}$, and for state w_1 and the propositional variables, f is defined by: $f(w_1, |\text{Sdnt}(\text{Léa})|) = \{w_2\}$, $f(w_1, |\text{Yng}(\text{Léa})|) = \{w_3\}$, and $f(w_1, |\text{Sng}(\text{Léa})|) = \{w_3\}$. We now have

M, w_1 sat $\text{Sdnt}(\text{Léa}) \Rightarrow \text{Yng}(\text{Léa})$ since $f(w_1, |\text{Sdnt}(\text{Léa})|) \subseteq |\text{Yng}(\text{Léa})|$
M, w_1 sat $\text{Yng}(\text{Léa}) \Rightarrow \text{Sng}(\text{Léa})$ since $f(w_1, |\text{Yng}(\text{Léa})|) \subseteq |\text{Sng}(\text{Léa})|$

But on the other hand, M, w_1 non sat $\text{Sdnt}(\text{Léa}) \Rightarrow \text{Sng}(\text{Léa})$, since $f(w_1, |\text{Sdnt}(\text{Léa})|)$ is not contained in $|\text{Sng}(\text{Léa})|$. As a consequence M, w_1 sat $\neg (\text{Sdnt}(\text{Léa}) \Rightarrow \text{Sng}(\text{Léa}))$, and the formula under consideration will be satisfiable.

In the logic of Delgrande a certain form of transitivity can be recovered. For example, if the formulas $\text{Sdnt}(x) \rightarrow \text{Yng}(x)$ and $\text{Yng}(x) \rightarrow \text{Sng}(x)$ are theorems, formula $\text{Sdnt}(x) \Rightarrow \text{Sng}(x)$ is also a theorem, since $\text{Sdnt}(x) \rightarrow \text{Sng}(x)$ is a theorem. On the other hand the following formula is satisfiable:

$$\forall x \; (\text{Sdnt}(x) \rightarrow \text{Yng}(x)) \wedge (\text{Yng}(x) \Rightarrow \text{Sng}(x)) \wedge \neg (\text{Sdnt}(x) \Rightarrow \text{Sng}(x)))$$

which forbids the composition of the material implication with the weak implication.

Likewise, deduction does not admit the reasoning by contraposition (Point 3), due to language restrictions. Since the expression $\forall x ((Sdnt(x) \Rightarrow Sng(x)) \wedge \neg (\neg Sng(x) \Rightarrow \neg Sdnt(x)))$ is satisfiable, the implication does not permit the contraposition.

And since the expression

$$(Sdnt(Léa) \Rightarrow Yng(Léa) \wedge \neg ((Sdnt(Léa) \wedge Mrd(Léa)) \Rightarrow Yng(Léa))$$

is consistent, the fact of adding new premises may modify the set of conclusions (the implication is nonmonotonic: Point 4). Therefore the symbol $\vdash$ (in $T \vdash F$) is nonmonotonic.

Since the formula

$$((A \Rightarrow C) \wedge (B \Rightarrow C)) \rightarrow ((A \vee B) \Rightarrow C)$$

is one of the axioms in the logic of Delgrande, the disjunction property (Point 5) is true.

As for the generalized quantifiers (Point 6), as in the case of the logics previously studied, conditionals logics only have classical quantifiers. In the logic of Delgrande, for a default theory $T = <D,C>$, there exists only one set $E(D)$, i.e. it has only one extension. No updating of information is done inside the theory.

Nute[109,110] defines a formalism called LDR (Logic for Defeasible Reasoning) based on conditional logics, which permits the treatment of nonmonotonic reasoning. A theory LDR is a pair $<R,K>$, where R is a set of rules and K a set of literals. The rules are expressions constructed by the use of three types of implication $\rightarrow$, $\Rightarrow$, and $?\rightarrow$, and the unary operator E. If L is a finite set of literals, and p is a literal then:

Ep is a formula meaning that p is obvious.
$L \rightarrow p$ is called an absolute rule
$L \Rightarrow p$ is called a defeasible rule
$L \;?\rightarrow p$ is a rule that expresses that if L is achieved, "maybe" p will also be achieved.

Nute distinguishes several types of proof of a literal p from a theory $T = <R,K>$, in the following way:

(a) p has an absolute proof in T (denoted by $T \vdash p$) if there exists a sequence of literals "S", such that the last element of S is p, and for each element s_i in S, we have

(1) $s_i \in K$, or
(2) there exists a rule $L \rightarrow s_i$ in R, such that for each $s_j \in L$, $s_j \in S$ and $j < i$.

(b) p has a defeasible proof in T (denoted by $T \Vdash p$) if there exists a sequence "S" of literals, such that the last element of S is p, and for each element s_j in S, we have:

(1) $T \vdash s_i$, or
(2) if $s_i = Eq$ for a literal q, then $q = s_j$ for a certain $j < i$, or
(3) $L \to q \in R$, non $T \vdash \neg q$, $s_i = Eq$, and there exists $j < i$ such that $Er = s_j$ for each $r \in L$, or
(4) $L \Rightarrow q \in R$, non $T \vdash \neg q$, $s_i = Eq$, and $Er = s_j$, $j < i$ for each $r \in L$, and for each set of literals Q, if $Q \Rightarrow \neg q \in R$, or $Q ?\to \neg q \in R$ then $<R,L> \vdash Q$, and non $<R,Q> \vdash L$.

From this notion of demonstration, Nute introduces the notion of a "defeasible" literal. A literal q is "defeasible" from T if $T \Vdash q$.

This formalism allows to distinguish the literals of which we are sure from the questionable (defeasible) ones. It moreover leads to the definition of a semantics which associates, to each set of formulas T, a single extension. This extension is called conservative in relation to the rules of T.

The formalization of our example will be made in the framework of LDR by means of the use of defeasible rules; we have for example: $\forall x\ (Sdnt(x) \Rightarrow Yng(x))$.

The analysis of the comparison criteria yields results very close to those issued from the logic of Delgrande. However, in the logic of Nute, the disjunction symbol does not exist and, consequently, the criterion on tackling disjunctive information does not apply.

Generally speaking, for all the logics considered in Section VII-A there exists a completeness theorem. The propositional calculus is decidable. The satisfiability in propositional calculus is, in general, a P-SPACE-complete (complete in polynomial space) problem.

B. "Rough" Implications

In this paragraph, we briefly describe the statements of the example by means of the modal logics defined from the notion of "indiscernibility" (see for instance Orlowska and Pawlak[111,112] and Fariñas del Cerro and Orlowska[113]) which permits the definition of rough implications. Independently, Shafer[120] defines a notion of inner and outer reductions which is very close to the notion of approximation induced by an indiscernibility relation. For that, we give a preliminary example in order to illustrate the definitions.

Table I expresses the relation between the attributes "student" and "young," we associate to each attribute a partition defined as follows: two individuals belong to the same class (or are indiscernible), if they have the same value for that attribute. In the example Léa, Léo and Luc are in the same class for "student," since their value for this attribute is "yes."

The class corresponding to an individual O, and to an attribute "a," is denoted by $[a(O)]$. Given a formula F, which expresses a property on the set of objects, we define the notion of extension for F (denoted as before by $|F|$) as the set of objects that satisfy the property associated with F. Let the property of being a student, $Sdnt(x)$, be the extension for "student," $|Sdnt(x)|$ the set {Léa, Léo, Luc}, and $|Yng(x)|$ = {Léo,

Table I. Indiscernibility according to attribute values.

	Student	Young	Single
Léa	yes	no	yes
Léo	yes	yes	no
Luc	yes	yes	yes

Luc}. Thus from the extension of the formulas associated with the attributes (that is with the atomic formulas) we can define an extension of any classical formula, by making use of the definitions

$|\neg F| = -|F|$ (where "-" denotes complementation)
$|F \vee G| = |F| \cup |G|$
$|F \wedge G| = |F| \cap |G|$
$|F \rightarrow G| = -|F| \cup |G|$

We now define two sets which will permit the characterization of new implications. Given a formula F, and an attribute "a", the expressions:

(1) $\bar{a}|F| = \{O : [a(O)] \cap |F| \neq \emptyset\}$
(2) $\underline{a}|F| = \{O : [a(O)] \subseteq |F|\}$

define two approximations of formula F, since $\underline{a}|F| \subset |F| \subseteq \bar{a}|F|$.
   $\bar{a}|F|$ and $\underline{a}|F|$ are pictured on Figure 3.

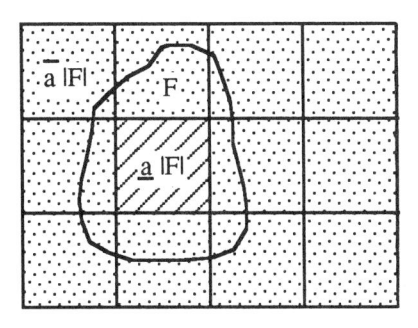

Figure 3. Upper and lower approximations of a set.

where the network represents the partition of the set of objects obtained by attribute "a."

We will say for an attribute "a" that the formula

(1) $Fa \Rightarrow_1 G$ is true if and only if $|F| \subseteq |G|$, and $\bar{a}|F| = \bar{a}|G|$
(2) $Fa \Rightarrow_2 G$ is true if and only if $|F| \subseteq |G|$, and $\underline{a}|F| = \underline{a}|G|$
(3) $Fa \Rightarrow_3 G$ is true if and only if $|F| \subseteq |G|$, and $\underline{a}|F| = \underline{a}|G|$, and $\bar{a}|F| = \bar{a}|G|$

It should be noted that the implications "$a \Rightarrow_1$," and "$a \Rightarrow_2$" are stronger than the material implication, (since $|F| \subseteq |G|$ defines the material implication), in the sense that $Fa \Rightarrow_1 G$ or $Fa \Rightarrow_2 G$ only if $F \rightarrow G$.

Consequently, this type of implication is not very well-adapted to the formalization of an implication which expresses a typicality link. Indeed, as we have seen in the case of the conditional logic of Stalnaker, typicality is less strong than the material implication. This suggests is us the following definitions:

(4) $Fa \Rightarrow_4 G$ is true if and only if $|F| \subseteq |G|$, or $\bar{a}|F| = \bar{a}|G|$
(5) $Fa \Rightarrow_5 G$ is true if and only if $|F| \subseteq |G|$, or $\underline{a}|F| = \underline{a}|G|$
(6) $Fa \Rightarrow_6 G$ is true if and only if $|F| \subseteq |G|$, or $\underline{a}|F| = \underline{a}|G|$, or $\bar{a}|F| = \bar{a}|G|$,

which would permit a more adequate formalization of our example.

These three implications behave in a similar way vis-à-vis the previously studied properties, but they lose interest if the number of classes associated to each attribute (student, young,...) is small. This is the case in our example, since the number of classes is always equal to two.

VIII. LOGICS OF UNCERTAINTY

The idea of associating an uncertainty degree to every formula in classical logic is not new. Indeed, since the beginning of the 60's, Løs[114] and later Fenstad[115] defined and studied a probabilistic logic in which to each formula is assigned a probability degree reflecting the number of interpretations that makes the formula true in a given model, and also a probability distribution on the models. This vision corresponds to the ideas of Carnap[116] and turns out to be seldom employed in Artificial Intelligence, in practice.

A more adapted approach to reasoning with uncertainty considers a set of formulae (seen as axioms) with associated uncertainty degrees, $\{(p_i, \alpha_i) \mid i = 1, n\}$ where $\alpha_i = g(p_i)$. Thus Van Emden[117] and Subrahmanian[118,119] have proposed automatic deduction methods in order to manipulate clauses weighted by numbers, using various operations for combining these numbers without making reference to any precise interpretation of these weights with respect to a theory of uncertainty (for instance, probabilities). The items of knowledge (p_i, α_i) are interpreted in this section as a set of constraints satisfied by an uncertainty measure g thus incompletely characterized (more generally, only bounds on $g(p_i)$ are known). The semantics of (p_i, α_i) is thus a set $\mathcal{P}_i = \{g \mid g(p_i) = \alpha_i\}$ of uncertainty measures g. Reasoning consists in evaluating an interval which contains $g(p)$ for a formula p of which we would like to know the status, such interval being induced by the set $\cap_i \mathcal{P}_i$ associated to the n formulae (p_i, α_i). The answer of a system based on a logic of uncertainty concerning formula p is thus an interval $[\underline{\alpha}, \bar{\alpha}]$ which contains $g(p)$. The interpretation of this interval will depend on the type of uncertainty measure employed (probability, possibility, etc). It should be noted that the numerical logics of uncertainty employ the properties of the corresponding theories of uncertainty in order to define their inference rules in a well-founded manner. For instance, if g is a probability measure, the calculation of the interval bounds containing g(p) will use the additive character of g. Moreover, the degrees employed should have a clear interpretation, stemming from the context where the uncertainty measures are defined. The combination and propagation modes of these degrees are then well-defined. Such is the case in probabilistic and possibilistic logics, and in the one based on Shafer's theory.[120] The advantage of these logics over purely symbolic approaches where the uncertainty marks do not have a clear interpretation (e.g. Duval and Kodratoff[121]) is that even if the use of natural language modalities such as "generally", "typically" instead of the coefficients α_i obviates the numbers estimation problem, it is quite difficult to combine the introduced modalities (apart from using concatenation).

A. Possibilistic Logic

1. Presentation

In possibilistic logic, we employ the formulae of propositional calculus or the closed formulae of first order logic to which a possibility or necessity degree in [0,1] is assigned. Let $\Pi(p)$ be the possibility degree of p and $N(p)$ the necessity degree of p. The following conventions will be adopted:

- $N(p) = 1$ expresses that taking all the available knowledge into account, formula p is certainly true; $\Pi(p) = 0$ expresses that, taking all the available knowledge into account, it is impossible that formula p is true;
- $\forall p$, $\Pi(p) = 1 - N(\neg p)$; in particular, $\Pi(p) = 0 \Rightarrow N(\neg p) = 1$; in other words, saying that p is impossible means also saying that $\neg p$ is certainly true;
- $\forall p$, $\Pi(p) \geq N(p)$: a formula is possibly true before being certainly true;
- $\Pi(p) = \Pi(\neg p) = 1$ expresses that, taking all the available knowledge into account, there is nothing that permits us to either invalidate or confirm p (total ignorance case); this is equivalent to $N(p) = N(\neg p) = 0$;
- $\forall p$, $\forall q$, $\Pi(p \vee q) = \max(\Pi(p), \Pi(q))$ is the fundamental axiom of possibility measures (Zadeh,[122] Dubois and Prade[123]). It supposes that the imprecise or vague information on which the allocation of possibility degrees is based, is described by fuzzy sets, or equivalently by collections of nested subsets of possible worlds. Hence we deduce $N(p \wedge q) = \min(N(p),N(q))$. Moreover, for a classical proposition (that is nonfuzzy) we have $\max(\Pi(p), \Pi(\neg p)) = 1$. This indicates that $N(p) > 0$ implies $\Pi(p) = 1$ (and thus $N(\neg p)= 0$).
- Inconsistency shows up whenever there exists a proposition p for which $N(p) > 0$, and $N(\neg p) > 0$. The closer $\min(N(p), N(\neg p))$ is to 1, the stronger the inconsistency will be. That means effectively saying that p and $\neg p$ are simultaneously surely true.

Possibility measures are the simplest examples of upper and lower probabilities,[123] at the mathematical level. That means saying that the pair (N,Π) of possibility and necessity measures, such that $N(p) = 1 - \Pi(\neg p)$, $\forall p$, can be considered as limiting a set of probability measures $\mathcal{P} = \{\text{Prob} \mid \forall p, N(p) \leq \text{Prob}(p) \leq \Pi(p)\}$, of which N and Π are the upper and lower envelopes, i.e.,

$$N(p) = \inf\{\text{Prob}(p) \mid \text{Prob} \in \mathcal{P}\}, \quad \Pi(p) = \sup\{\text{Prob}(p) \mid \text{Prob} \in \mathcal{P}\}$$

Nevertheless, any set $\mathcal{P}$ of probability measures does not necessarily lead to possibility and necessity measures. However, in order to use the notions of possibility and necessity, such a reference to probabilities is not necessary and possibility and necessity measures can also be introduced and used independently of the idea of probability starting with the fundamental axiom mentioned above.

The calculation of possibility and necessity measures may be carried out by means of a fuzzy pattern matching procedure,[1][24] designed in order to compare the meaning of the formula to be evaluated, with the available information, described by a possibility distribution. The case where $N(p) < 1$ and $N(\neg p) < 1$ indicates a state of incomplete information. For example, let YNG be the extension of predicate Yng, containing all the individuals of age less or equal to a, and Yng(Léa) be the formula to be evaluated. Let A be the set of individuals who are between 20 and 40 years old, and the fact "Léa is between 20 and 40 years old" be the available information. We will have the following cases

– if $a < 20$, YNG $\cap$ $A = \emptyset$, and we have $N(\text{Yng}(\text{Léa})) = \Pi(\text{Yng}(\text{Léa})) = 0$
– if $a \in [20,40]$, YNG $\cap$ $A \neq \emptyset$, and YNG $\cap$ $\bar{A} \neq \emptyset$, where $\bar{A}$ is the complement of A. In this case, we assert $\Pi(\text{Yng}(\text{Léa})) = \Pi(\neg \text{Yng}(\text{Léa})) = 1$
– if $a \geq 40$ (an optimistic conception of the term young !), then $A \subseteq$ YNG, and we state $N(\text{Yng}(\text{Léa})) = 1$.

More generally, the available information may be vague like "Léa is a middle-aged woman" whose meaning might be "is around 35 years old, over 25, but not older than 45." This information will then be represented by a fuzzy set F; each female individual I will satisfy with degree $\mu_F(I)$ the definition of a "middle-aged woman," such a degree will have a value 0 if I is not between 25 and 45 years old, and it will be nearer to 1 the closer the age of I is to 35. In this case we will define

$\Pi(\text{Yng}(\text{Léa})) = \max_{I \in \text{YNG}} \mu_F(I)$ (intersection degree between YNG and F) (1)
$N(\text{Yng}(\text{Léa})) = \min_{I \notin \text{YNG}} 1 - \mu_F(I)$ (inclusion degree of F inside YNG) (2)

These degrees verify the axioms and conventions defined above.

By definition, to assert a statement means assigning to it a necessity degree of which we know a strictly positive lower bound, interpreted as a certainty degree. Therefore

$$N(\forall x \; \text{Sdnt}(x) \to \text{Yng}(x)) \geq \alpha_1$$

where $\alpha_1 > 0$, expresses that "it is relatively certain that all students are young." This statement will be denoted by

$$(\forall x \; \text{Sdnt}(x) \to \text{Yng}(x), \alpha_1).$$

The greater α_1 the surer we are that the statement is true. For instance, e_4 will be expressed by

$$N(\forall x \; \text{Yng}(x) \to \text{Sdnt}(x)) \geq \alpha_4$$

where $0 < \alpha_4 < \alpha_1$, in order to express the shade existing between statements e_1 and e_4. It is clear that in view of the operations which handle possibility and necessity degrees, the ordering among the values is of crucial importance.

To reason with such statements, we use an extended version of the cutting rule and the particularization rule which read[125]

$$\frac{N(\neg p \vee q) \geq \alpha \quad N(p \vee r) \geq \beta}{N(q \vee r) \geq \min(\alpha, \beta)} \qquad \frac{N(\forall x \; P(x)) \geq \alpha}{N(P(a)) \geq \alpha}$$

The resolution principle is thus extended to the case of any first order logic clauses and allows for reasoning by refutation: to prove a fact p we add $(\neg p, 1)$ to the knowledge base. The maximum weight which can be obtained by the empty clause considering the different possible refutations is the best lower bound of the degree $N(p)$ which could be established in the framework of the theory of possibilities/necessities. This way, a *monotonic* logic of uncertainty analogous to Nilsson's[126] proposal is obtained, even though this author makes use of probabilities instead of possibility and necessity measures and does not look after refutation methods. This monotonicity is understood as the fact that the addition of new uncertain clauses to the knowledge base can only contribute to the tightening of the bounds bracketing the uncertainty measure attached to a conclusion, in our case, by increasing the certainty degree. In others words, if a conclusion was established with a certainty degree $(N(p) \geq \alpha)$, it cannot become less certain by the addition of a new piece of information consistent with the pieces of information already in the knowledge base $(N(p) \geq \beta \geq \alpha)$. Let us note that this notion of monotonicity is strongly related to the semantics of the uncertain expressions. From a purely synctatic point of view, however, this logic is not monotonic, since a conclusion (p, α) may be discarded by the addition of a new piece of information, in benefit of another conclusion (p, β), with $\beta \neq \alpha$. Possibilistic logic is not directly adapted to the treatment of default information but to the handling of uncertain conjectures. Nevertheless it can handle revision processes similar to the ones obtained via nonmonotonic reasoning, as well as partial inconsistency, as shown later.

The semantics of this logic is described by means of fuzzy sets of interpretations. If p is a closed formula, and $M(p)$ the set of interpretations I that makes p true (that is, the set of models of p), the models of (p, α) will be defined by a fuzzy set $M(p, \alpha)$ with membership fuction

$$\mu_{M(p,\alpha)}(I) = 1 \text{ if } I \in M(p)$$
$$= 1 - \alpha \text{ if } I \in M(\neg p)$$

In fact, $M(p,\alpha)$ is the largest fuzzy set F of interpretations, such that $N(p) \geq \alpha$ (defined as in (2)), i.e., it corresponds to the least specific information consistent with this inequality.

Under this semantics, a formula such as $(\neg p \vee q, \alpha)$ becomes equivalent (semantically) to $(q, \min(\alpha, \mu_{M(p)}))$. This formal remark, which leads to introduce symbolic weights, allows for several extensions of possibilistic logic.

The consistency degree of a knowledge base $\mathcal{B} = \{e_1,..., e_n\}$, where $e_i = (p_i, \alpha_i)$ is a closed formula followed by its certainty degree, will be defined in the semantic framework by

$$c(\mathcal{B}) = \sup_I \min_{i=1,n} \mu_{M(e_i)}(I)$$

i.e., it measures to what extent the set of models of $\mathcal{B}$ is nonempty. The extended resolution principle was proved complete[127] for the refutation, in the sense that its repeated application over $\mathcal{B}$ allows the computation of the inconsistency degree $1 - c(\mathcal{B})$. This way, we show that this corresponds to maximizing the necessity degree attached to the empty clause. A knowledge base $\mathcal{B}$ such that $1 - c(\mathcal{B}) = \alpha > 0$ is said to be inconsistent to degree α, or α-inconsistent for short. Otherwise it is consistent. It should also be noted that if $S(\mathcal{B})$ denotes the knowledge base obtained by removing the uncertainty degrees, then $\mathcal{B}$ is α-inconsistent if and only if $S(\mathcal{B})$ is inconsistent. Possibility theory mechanisms permit us to reason from a α-inconsistent base, when $\alpha < 1$.

The resolution principle was also extended to the case of two uncertain statements of the form $\Pi(\neg p \vee q) \geq \alpha$, and $N(p \vee r) \geq \beta$. From these two statements, we can deduce $\Pi(q \vee r) \geq \alpha$ if $\alpha + \beta > 1$, and $\Pi(q \vee r) \geq 0$ otherwise (see Dubois and Prade[128]). An inequality of the form $\Pi(p) \geq \alpha$ expresses a very weak statement such as "it is more or less possible (but not at all sure) that p is true." For instance, $\Pi(\text{Pnt}(\text{Léa})) \geq \alpha$ can translate the case evoked in Section III, where Léa might have children (question q_4).

2. Discussion

Point 0. First of all, a statement of the type $N(\forall x\ \text{Sdnt}(x) \to \text{Yng}(x)) \geq \alpha_1$, means that it is relatively sure that all students are young. Thus the idea that most of the students are young (but not all of them) is not well accounted for. Here, universal conjectures are modeled instead of general rules (with exceptions). Let us note that the decomposability property $N(\wedge_{i \in I} p_i) = \min_{i \in I} N(p_i)$ of necessity measures makes $N(\forall x\ P(x)) \geq \alpha$ be equivalent to $\forall x\ N(P(x)) \geq \alpha$. This turns out to be false in the specific case of probability measures. These conjectures will not be used in the example unless instanciated, such as in the case of

$$N(\text{Sdnt}(\text{Léa}) \to \text{Yng}(\text{Léa})) \geq \alpha_1$$

which is logically deduced from the uncertain conjecture (due to the particularization rule) as well as from a general rule; knowing that students are mostly young, and that Léa is a student, we are relatively sure that she is young. Using these conventions the example will be described by

$e_1(\forall x\ \text{Sdnt}(x) \to \text{Yng}(x), \alpha_1)$; $e_2\ (\forall x\ \text{Yng}(x) \to \text{Sng}(x), \alpha_2)$;
$e_3(\forall x\ \text{Sng}(x) \to \text{Yng}(x), \alpha_3)$; $e_4\ (\forall x\ \text{Yng}(x) \to \text{Sdnt}(x), \alpha_4)$ with
$\alpha_4 < \min(\alpha_1, \alpha_2, \alpha_3)$;
$e_5(\forall x\ \text{Sdnt}(x) \wedge \text{Pnt}(x) \to \text{Mrd}(x) \vee \text{Chbt}(x), \alpha_5)$; $e_6\ (\forall x\ \text{Chbt}(x) \to \text{Yng}(x), \alpha_6)$;

with the addition of $(\forall x\ \neg(\text{Sng}(x) \wedge \text{Mrd}(x)), 1)$, $(\forall x\ \neg(\text{Chbt}(x) \wedge \text{Mrd}(x)), 1)$, etc. to express the mutual exclusion among Chbt, Mrd, and Sng.

Point 1. Due to the absence of practical interest in universally quantified uncertain conjectures, we will not use this logic except in order to answer questions relating to particular situations. If we know that Léa is a student, we would deduce, for instance, that $N(\text{Sng (Léa)}) \geq \min(\alpha_1, \alpha_2)$, by applying the modus ponens twice over the assertions e_1 and e_2, i.e. if α_1 expresses "relatively certain" and α_2 "almost certain" ($\alpha_2 > \alpha_1$), then it is relatively certain that Léa is single.

Point 2. The implication obtained is transitive in the sense that

from $\qquad (\forall x\ \text{Sdnt}(x) \to \text{Yng}(x), \alpha_1)$ and from $(\forall x\ \text{Yng}(x) \to \text{Sng}(x), \alpha_2)$,
we deduce $(\forall x\ \text{Sdnt}(x) \to \text{Sng}(x), \min(\alpha_1, \alpha_2))$. The weaker implication thus prevails.

Point 3. The contraposition of the formula $N(\forall x\ \text{Sdnt}(x) \to \text{Yng}(x)) \geq \alpha_1$ is admitted, with the same uncertainty degree. In fact two equivalent formulae have the same uncertainty degree. Therefore e_1 may be employed in order to say that "the non-young are not students," with a necessity degree of at least α_1. This makes sense at least in the instanciated form.

Point 4. Possibilistic logic is monotonic in the sense defined above: if (p, α) is deduced from a consistent knowledge base $\mathcal{B}$, i.e., $\mathcal{B} \vdash (p, \alpha)$, by making use of the resolution principle, the addition of a new piece of information (q, α') to $\mathcal{B}$, which preserves consistency, will only confirm (p, α). We will have $\mathcal{B} \cup \{(q, \alpha')\} \vdash (p, \beta)$, with $\beta \geq \alpha$: p can only become even more certain. This is due to the monotonicity of classical logic, and also to the fact that necessity degrees respect the logic deduction relation: if $p \vdash q$ then $N(q) \geq N(p)$. The monotonicity of the material implication may be stated by $p \to r \vdash p \wedge q \to r$. Hence, $N((p \wedge q) \to r) \geq N(p \to r)$ is inferred, which gives a precise meaning to the monotonicity of the uncertain implication. Nevertheless, that does not prevent from letting $N((p \wedge q) \to r) \geq \alpha$, $N(p \to r) \geq \beta$ with $\beta > \alpha$ (since $N((p \wedge q) \to r) \geq N(p \to r) \geq \beta \Rightarrow \forall\ \alpha < \beta, N((p \wedge q) \to r) \geq \alpha$). It is then possible to show, however, that rule $N(p \wedge q \to r) \geq \alpha$ is redundant and will never be employed in the derivation of a fact! Moreover, the knowledge base containing the certain facts Sdnt(Léa), Pnt(Léa), e_1, e_2, and e_5 will be α-inconsistent. Indeed, from

$$(\text{Sdnt(Léa)} \to \text{Yng(Léa)}, \alpha_1)\ ;\ (\text{Yng(Léa)} \to \text{Sng(Léa)}, \alpha_2) \qquad (\mathcal{B})$$
$$(\text{Sdnt(Léa)} \wedge \text{Pnt(Léa)} \to \neg \text{Sng(Léa)}, \alpha_5)\ ;\ (\text{Pnt(Léa)}, 1)\ ;\ (\text{Sdnt(Léa)}, 1)$$

it can be inferred that $N(\text{Sng}(\text{Léa})) \geq \min(\alpha_1,\alpha_2)$, and $N(\neg\,\text{Sng}(\text{Léa})) \geq \alpha_5$, which leads to $N(\emptyset) \geq \min(\alpha_1, \alpha_2, \alpha_5) > 0$, where $\emptyset$ denotes the empty clause. But unlike classical logic (where all α_i's have value 1), such a base may still be used to make inferences. See Point 8.

Point 5. Disjunctive information is easily dealt with, as in classical logic.

Point 6. As in default logic, the quantifiers are not modeled, since only the instantiated forms are useful. The use of necessity degrees permits us, however, to grade the plausibility of exceptions.

Point 7. Multiple extensions do not exist in possibilistic logic. The presence of uncertainty degrees attached to the conclusions permits us, however, to tolerate inconsistency; the notion of α-inconsistency allows to obtain ambiguous results, in the form of $N(p) \geq \alpha$, $N(\neg\,p) \geq \beta$, with $\min(\alpha,\beta) > 0$. That is the case in the example discussed at Point 4. Base $\mathcal{B}$ furnishes the two opposing conclusions $N(\text{Sng}(\text{Léa})) \geq \min(\alpha_1,\alpha_2)$, and $N(\neg\,\text{Sng}(\text{Léa})) \geq \alpha_5$. They correspond to the two extensions $E7$, and $E7'$ found in case $q7$ of Section III, by default logic. It means that, where default logic leads to many extensions, possibilistic logic leads to a single one, in which partially contradictory pieces of information coexist. The choice may then be guided by the certainty degree (namely, prefer the surest conclusions).

Point 8. Possibilistic logic is monotonic, as long as it deals with a completely consistent knowledge base ($c(\mathcal{B}) = 1$). The addition of some piece of information which does not affect $c(\mathcal{B})$ results therefore in a monotonic behavior. It is no longer the case when some information in contradiction with the base, is added. Indeed, if the necessity degrees assigned to the formulae are well chosen, it is then possible to deduce information from an α-inconsistent base $\mathcal{B}$, with necessity degrees higher than the inconsistency degree of the base, provided that only a sub-base $\mathcal{B}' \subseteq \mathcal{B}$ "more consistent" than the complete base is used, that is $c(\mathcal{B}') > c(\mathcal{B})$. This way, from base $\mathcal{B}$ in Point 4, if $\alpha_5 > \alpha_1$, it is possible to prove by refutation (by adding (Sng(Léa), 1)) that $N(\neg\,\text{Sng}(\text{Léa})) \geq \alpha_5$. Indeed, from $\mathcal{B} \cup \{(\text{Sng}(\text{Léa}), 1)\}$ we infer $N(\emptyset) \geq \alpha_5$ (thus $N(\neg\,\text{Sng}(\text{Léa})) \geq \alpha_5$). To obtain such a result we used exclusively clauses with weight equal to *at least* α_5, (thus not e_1) which constitute sub-base $\mathcal{B}'$. On the other hand, if (Pnt(Léa), 1) is removed from $\mathcal{B}$, we will prove $N(\text{Sng}(\text{Léa})) \geq \min(\alpha_1,\alpha_2)$ with the same strategy, without being any longer able to find a positive lower bound to $N(\neg\,\text{Sng}(\text{Léa}))$. Everything happens as if the addition of a piece of information, making base $\mathcal{B}$ α-inconsistent, would "cancel" the formulae (p,β) with $\beta \leq \alpha$.[127]

This apparently nonmonotonic behavior is due to the refutation strategy, and will appear every time the lower bounds assigned to the rules agree with their specificities: the more specific the rule the surer it should be. It is easy to see that this motto is not always true: we say, for instance, that "most birds fly," but for Antarctic birds it can neither be said that "almost all of the Antarctic birds fly," nor that "almost none of the Antarctic birds fly." It would rather be fifty-fifty considering the number of penguins existing in that region. Here, a more specific rule may also be more uncertain. The presence of uncertainty degrees only partially copes with the absence of the modularity of classical logic.

If certainty decreases as specificity increases ($\alpha_5 < \min(\alpha_1,\alpha_2)$ in $\mathcal{B}$), the conclusions furnished by the knowledge base will no longer be satisfying. Indeed, clause e_5 being disabled, we will deduce $N(\text{Sng}(\text{Léa})) \geq \min(\alpha_1,\alpha_2)$ by e_1 and e_2. In this case we are led to modify e_1 so as to disable it in presence of Pnt(Léa), and write down the rule:

$$(\forall x, \text{Sdnt}(x) \wedge \neg \text{Pnt}(x) \rightarrow \text{Yng}(x), \alpha_1)$$

We are thus faced with the same problems as classical logic encounters in the treatment of exceptions (rule modification strategy, disabling of rules when an exception shows up, etc.). The representation of "default facts" permits, however, the use of rules containing exceptions, when the information is incomplete.

In order to avoid blocking phenomena, we may, in effect, introduce the notion of "default facts." For example, the modification of e_1 must go together with the automatic presence of the default fact $(\neg \text{Pnt}(\text{Léa}), 1 - \varepsilon)$, which will be automatically taken into account, *if needed*, in the absence of information on the fact of whether Léa is a parent or not. We may, of course, condition the presence of $(\neg \text{Pnt}(\text{Léa}), 1 - \varepsilon)$ by the presence of facts such as Sdnt(Léa), and Yng(Léa). With such a mechanism, we deduce $N(\text{Sng}(\text{Léa})) \geq \min(\alpha_1,\alpha_2, 1 - \varepsilon)$ from (Sdnt(Léa),1), and $N(\neg \text{Sng}(\text{Léa})) \geq \alpha_5$ from the two facts (Sdnt(Léa), 1) and (Pnt(Léa), 1). We need a combination mechanism that, in case of conflict, eliminates the uncertain information to the benefit of the more certain one. In such a case, we identify default information and uncertain information, a rule remaining uncertain only if it has unknown exceptions (see Dubois and Prade[129]). This combination mechanism must include criteria such as "specificity," easily borrowed from default theory. For instance, we observe that rule e_5 is more specific than e_1, and we shall not fire rules e_1 and e_2 in sequence unless e_5 cannot be activated. This idea is relatively model-independent.

Point 9. The addition of a piece of information to a possibilistic knowledge base requires a consistency verification. If we deduce the empty clause with a certainty degree at least α, conclusions deduced by refutation from the base with a necessity degree strictly higher than α can still be proved to be correct, contrary to what happens in classical logic. Actually, it turns out that the type of ordering induced by necessity measures on a set of formulas closed under deduction, is very much akin to ordering relations that underlie any revision process of a set of formulas, as studied by Gärdenfors and colleagues (see Section XV).

Point 10. Possibilistic logic in its monotonic form has already been implemented on a computer (see Dubois, Lang and Prade[130]). The adopted strategy is based on the generalized resolution principle and on refutation. It is a linear strategy; moreover it is developed as an A^* algorithm (with a nonadditive heuristic function: + is replaced by min) guided by lower bounds on the uncertainty degrees. When the empty clause is reached, its necessity degree is maximal. Complexity remains of the same order as the one of refutation methods in classical logic (one could not wish more); the use of a heuristic function permits us, in practice, to solve problems dealing with some dozens of clauses in a reasonably short time.

B. Probabilities and Belief Functions

The approach shown in section VIII-A for possibilistic logic is analogous to the one proposed by De Finetti,[131] and rediscovered by Nilsson[126] for the case of probabilistic logic, see also Grosof.[132] We associate a probability degree, or the bounds of a probability degree to each formula (considered as an axiom). For example, from $\text{Prob}(p) = \alpha$, and $\text{Prob}(\neg p \vee q) = \beta$ we deduce that $\text{Prob}(q) \in [\max(0, \alpha + \beta - 1), \beta]$. In fact, this approach has already been discussed, after De Finetti,[131] by Adams and Levine.[133] The resolution principle can also be generalized in this framework.[125] This principle reads, for the lower bounds

$$\frac{\text{Prob}(\neg p \vee q) \geq \alpha \qquad \text{Prob}(p \vee r) \geq \beta}{\text{Prob}(q \vee r) \geq \max(0, \alpha + \beta - 1)}$$

Unfortunately, its repeated use may quickly lead to very weak bounds, whereas the approach proposed by Nilsson,[126] which completely exploits the linear inequalities system constituted by the associated constraints over the uncertain formulae, may yield better bounds. In this sense the resolution principle is not "complete," contrary to its counterpart in terms of necessity measures.

The same approach may be adopted in the framework of the belief functions of Shafer,[120] which mathematically includes as particular cases, possibilities and probabilities at the same time (see Dubois and Prade[123]). A belief function $\text{Bel}(p)$ attached to a formula p implicitly defines a probability allocation m over the set of formulae. That means that there exists a set $\mathcal{F}$ (supposedly finite) of formulae f_i such that $m(f_i) > 0$ and $\Sigma_{f_i \in \mathcal{F}} m(f_i) = 1$. The contradiction does not belong to $\mathcal{F}$, except in case of inconsistency.

The credibility degree $\text{Bel}(p)$ is then defined by

$$\text{Bel}(p) = \Sigma_{f_i \vdash p} m(f_i)$$

A necessity degree is a particular case of a belief function for which the set $\mathcal{F}$ may be completely ordered by the relation $\vdash$ of deduction. $\text{Pl}(p) = 1 - \text{Bel}(\neg p)$ is called plausibility degree; it is such that $\text{Pl}(p) \geq \text{Bel}(p)$. Mathematically, interval $[\text{Bel}(p), \text{Pl}(p)]$ may be viewed as an interval of probabilities. An uncertain knowledge base may be defined by making use of set of valued formulae $\{(p_i, \alpha_i) \mid i = 1, n\}$, where $\alpha_i = \text{Bel}(p_i)$ (it can also be an upper or a lower bound on $\text{Bel}(p_i)$).

To handle the reasoning problems associated to that knowledge base, the two following approaches may be envisaged

– To consider the set of probability allocations $(\mathcal{F}, m)$ such that

$$\forall i = 1, n, \text{Bel}(p_i) = \Sigma_{f_j \vdash p_i} m(f_j)$$

We are now led to choose among functions m according to a minimum specificity principle,[134] which comes down to allocating weights $m(f_j)$ to the formulae having a maximal number of implicants. The solution to the problem is, however, not generally unique.

- To define an allocation of probability combining the credibility degrees associated to each formula p_i by making use of Dempster rule (see Shafer[120]). This is what was attempted by Yager,[135] as well as by Chatalic et al..[136]

In the latter approach, each uncertain formula is then defined by a triple (p_i, α_i, β_i), where $\alpha_i = \text{Bel}(p_i)$, $\beta_i = \text{Pl}(p_i)$ (the pairs (p_i, α_i), $(\neg p_i, 1 - \beta_i)$, where only one credibility degree appears, can be grouped together). The minimum specificity principle is applied to each triple; therefrom an allocation of probability m_i is deduced, defined by

$$m_i(p_i) = \alpha_i$$
$$m_i(\neg p_i) = 1 - \beta_i$$
$$m_i(\mathbb{1}) = \beta_i - \alpha_i$$

where $\mathbb{1}$ denotes tautology. The global allocation of probability is now defined (supposing the m_i to be stochastically independent) by Dempster rule:

$$\forall p, m(p) = \Sigma_{p=f_1 \wedge f_2 \ldots \wedge f_n} \Pi_{i=1,n} m_i(f_i)$$

where Π stands for the product. We will notice that possibly $m(\mathbb{0}) \neq 0$, where $\mathbb{0}$ denotes contradiction. Shafer[120] recommends eliminating this term by dividing m by $1 - m(\mathbb{0})$. This procedure is disputable however (see Zadeh[137] for example), and above all, the probability allocation thus obtained violate the initial constraints defining the knowledge base, i.e., function Bel´ based on $\dfrac{m}{1 - m(\mathbb{0})}$ is not such that $\forall i, \text{Bel}'(p_i) = \alpha_i$, in general. $m(\mathbb{0}) \in (0,1)$ indicates that the uncertain knowledge base is partially contradictory; in possibilistic logic, that corresponds to the case where $c(\mathcal{B}) < 1$, and it was seen that we could still carry out inferences within such a framework.

This approach is adapted to the example to a similar extent as possibilistic logic is. Each knowledge element will be translated by a clause valued by a pair (credibility degree, plausibility degree). We will then have

e_1 $(\forall x \neg \text{Sdnt}(x) \vee \text{Yng}(x), \alpha_1, \beta_1)$
e_2 $(\forall x \neg \text{Yng}(x) \vee \text{Sng}(x), \alpha_2, \beta_2)$
e_3 $(\forall x \neg \text{Yng}(x) \vee \text{Sdnt}(x), \alpha_4, \beta_4)$
e_5 $(\forall x \neg \text{Sdnt}(x) \vee \neg \text{Pnt}(x) \vee \text{Mrd}(x) \vee \text{Chbt}(x), \alpha_5, \beta_5)$

Let us note that $\beta_1 = \text{Pl}(\forall x \neg \text{Sdnt}(x) \vee \text{Yng}(x)) = 1 - \text{Bel}(\exists x \; \text{Sdnt}(x) \wedge \neg \text{Yng}(x))$, therefore $1 - \beta$ reflects the certainty that rule e_1 possesses exceptions. The information is thus richer than with the possibilistic approach, where $\alpha_1 > 0 \Rightarrow \beta_1 = 1$. The behavior of this logic is, with a slight difference (such as the remark above) analogous to possibilistic logic in what concerns the comparison criteria. Some further remarks are yet useful: implication transitivity is accompanied by an attenuation effect; we have for instance

$$\frac{(\neg \text{Sdnt(Léa)} \vee \text{Yng(Léa)}, \alpha_1, \beta_1)}{(\neg \text{Yng(Léa)} \vee \text{Sng(Léa)}, \alpha_2, \beta_2)}$$
$$(\neg \text{Sdnt(Léa)} \vee \text{Sng(Léa)}, \alpha_1\alpha_2, \beta_1 + \beta_2 - \beta_1\beta_2)$$

The attenuation effect comes from the fact that $[\alpha_1\alpha_2, \beta_1 + \beta_2 - \beta_1\beta_2]$ strictly contains $[\alpha_1,\beta_1]$, and $[\alpha_2,\beta_2]$, $[0,1]$ expressing total ignorance. Moreover, this approach allows to take into account of the fact that Léa cannot be an exception to both rules e_1 and e_2 simultaneously (for example being an old student and a young married woman); indeed, when $\beta_1 < 1$ and $\beta_2 < 1$, e_1 and e_2 become slightly contradictory $(m(\mathbb{O}) = (1 - \beta_1)(1 - \beta_2))$.

IX. FUZZY LOGIC

So far, it was supposed that in a formula such as "Young people are single," predicate Yng, which represents the term "young" was a predicate in the usual sense; Yng(Léa) is either true or false according to whether Léa is young or not. Such a semantics of the word "young" is disputable, as the idea of "young" contains shades, gradations, that is from being "young" one does not abruptly become "non-young." Many terms in natural language whose values range within continuous scales (age, size, duration...) are so. In the example, this feature distinguishes only predicate Yng from predicates like Sdnt, Pnt, Sng, Chbt, etc. Consequently, fuzzy logic is not very well-adapted to the test example. The problems due to the vague nature of knowledge are distinct from those relating to exceptions and are here added to the latter.

A. The Sorites Paradox

The fact of not taking into account the gradual nature of vague predicates such as "young" leads to paradoxes, as philosophers have shown a long time ago. This is particularly the case of the "Sorites" paradox, which in our example is stated as follows. Let variable a correspond to Léa's age, and Yng(Léa) admit solely the truth values 0 (false) and 1 (true). Let us suppose that Yng(Léa) is true and that there exists a threshold $\varepsilon > 0$ such that if the age a' of another individual (Léo) older than Léa satisfies

$$0 \leq a' - a \leq \varepsilon$$

then Yng(Léo) is also true. This hypothesis is naturally acceptable (for example, Léo was born one hour before Léa). Moreover, if the age of an individual x_0 is $a_0 < a$, Yng(x_0) is true. Then it can be easily proved by induction that *all* individuals are young. On the other hand, renouncing to threshold $\varepsilon > 0$, comes down to admitting that there exists individuals of distinct but arbitrarily close ages which should be placed in different categories (Yng and ¬ Yng). This is equally inacceptable.

The fuzzy logic proposed by Zadeh[138] at the intuitive level, and studied more formally by Goguen[139] obviates the paradox. See Baldwin and Guild[140] for a discussion. In order to do so, we let the extension of predicate "Yng" be no longer a set but a fuzzy set of ages, which corresponds to a function μ_{Yng} from A, the set of ages, to an ordered set $\mathcal{T}$, and such that

$$a' \geq a \Rightarrow \mu_{Yng}(a') \leq \mu_{Yng}(a)$$

which expresses that "the greater the age of an individual, the less young will this individual be." The truth degrees set, $\mathcal{T}$, is often [0,1], or a finite subset of this interval. $\mu_{Yng}(a)$ may be interpreted as the degree of "youngness" of age a, or more precisely, as the compatibility degree between a and the predicate Yng. $\mu_{Yng}(a)$ may thus be used to quantify the truth degree of formula Yng(a). It is clear that we have to turn to a multiple-valued logic, where truth degrees are no longer simply true, or false.

Now, the paradox is solved, since passing from Yng(Léa) to Yng(Léo), the truth degree slightly decreases. Goguen's work was given continuation at the syntactical and semantic level, particularly by Pavelka,[141] and Takeuti and Titani,[142] within theoretical frameworks relatively remote from Artificial Intelligence concerns.

B. Automated Reasoning in Fuzzy Logic

In the same time and independently, the intuitive semantics of vague predicates proposed by Zadeh[138] was largely developed,[143] and applied to the modelling of fuzzy "rules" and to reasoning from such rules[144,145,146] (see Dubois and Prade,[123] Chapter 4) for a more complete bibliography). These methods work directly in the semantics. For instance, the best-known fuzzy inference rule is called "generalized modus ponens" and can be formalized as

$$A'(x), (A(x) \Rightarrow B(x)) \vDash B'(x)$$

where A', A, B, B' are vague predicates, $\Rightarrow$ is the implication of a multivalued logic, $p \vDash q$ expresses that the truth degree of p is smaller than the truth degree of q, and more generally p, $p' \vDash q$ expresses that the truth value of q is lower-bounded by a function of the truth degrees of p and p'. In practice, we calculate the extension for B' in terms of those for A', A, and B by means of a numerical optimization procedure (which may be simplified). This calculation is done by means of the combination/projection principle[143] as follows:

(i) combine in a conjunctive manner the extension of A' with a fuzzy set resulting from a suitable combination of the extensions of A and B. Namely, keeping the same notation for predicates and their extensions, A and A' are fuzzy sets on a universe U and B is a fuzzy set on a universe V. Their membership functions are viewed as possibility distributions on U and V

whose combination yields a possibility distribution π on $U \times V$ defined by

$$\pi = \min(\mu_{A'}, \mu_A \Rightarrow \mu_B)$$

where $\Rightarrow$ is a function from $[0,1]^2$ to $[0,1]$ that expresses a multiple-valued implication; the minimum operation is sometimes generalized into a more general conjunctive operation

(ii) project the result of the combination on the universe of interest, here the one of B, i.e. compute

$$\mu_{B'}(v) = \sup_{u \in U} \pi(u,v) \quad \forall v \in V.$$

It is proved, in a general manner (e.g., Dubois and Prade[147,123]) that the extension for B' contains the one of B (for most of the implication functions), and that they draw aside the more A' and A differ. B' is in fact an approximation of B, sometimes pervaded with an uncertainty level. In particular, if $A'(x) = \neg A(x)$ then the uncertainty level is maximal (nothing can be deduced).

Beside these purely semantic approaches to the reasoning with vague predicates, other authors (Lee[148] and Giles,[149] for example) developed different extensions to the resolution principle with truth values in $[0,1]$. Nevertheless, the risk of confusion between truth value and uncertainty degree is rather high, and these notions seem to be more or less confused in subsequent works of computer scientists taking inspiration from Lee[148] in the development of fuzzy logic programming methods.

In fact, the calculation of the truth degree $t(\text{Yng}(\text{Léa}))$ of $\text{Yng}(\text{Léa})$ supposes that Léa's age a is precisely known, since $t(\text{Yng}(\text{Léa})) = \mu_{\text{Yng}}(a)$. When Léa's age is ill-known, we end up again in the framework of a logic of uncertainty, where we are led to capture the deficient knowledge of $t(\text{Yng}(\text{Léa}))$ by means of uncertainty degrees. In particular, truth degrees are compositional ($t(A(x) \wedge B(x))$ is a function of $t(A(x))$ and $t(B(x))$, and the same for all the connectives), while uncertainty degrees are not (for example, we only have $N(A(x) \vee B(x)) \geq \max(N(A(x)), N(B(x)))$, and $N(A(x) \vee B(x))$ is not a function of the necessities of the elementary propositions involved). In constrast, the logics of uncertainty can work on Boolean algebrae of classical formulae, whereas multiple-valued logics of vagueness must operate over poorer structures, necessary to keep their compositional character.[267]

In fact, the hypothesis of compositionality of the "coefficients" expresses an isomorphism between the algebra of propositions $\mathcal{P}$ and the set $\mathcal{C}$, where the coefficients take their value. But the Boolean algebras are never isomorphic to a completely ordered set of more than two coefficients. Consequently, compositional multiple-valued logics apply to algebras of non-Boolean propositions and cannot model uncertainty over a set of classical formulas.

C. Variants of Fuzzy Conditional Statements

Moreover, the semantics of rules where fuzzy predicates appear can vary according to the rule types. For instance $\text{Sdnt}(x) \Rightarrow \text{Yng}(x)$ will express that if x is a student, the possibility distribution which restricts the more or less possible values of his age is defined from the membership function μ_{Yng}. Here Sdnt is not a vague predicate. On the other hand, $Yng(x) \Rightarrow Sng(x)$ would rather mean: the younger someone is, the surer we are that he is single, that is something like

$$N(Sng(x)) \geq \mu_{Yng}(age(x)))$$

In certain situations these rules may operate in modus tollens form; i.e., $Sdnt(x) \Rightarrow Yng(x)$ will also be translated by "the less young someone is, the less possible it is that he is a student," i.e.,

$$\Pi(Sdnt(x)) \leq \mu_{Yng}(age(x))$$

whereas $Yng(x) \Rightarrow Sng(x)$ might mean that, should an individual not be single, the possibility distribution of his age corresponds to $\mu_{\neg Yng} = f(\mu_{Yng})$, where f is a function of $\mathcal{T}$ into $\mathcal{T}$ which inverts the ordering of elements; for example $\mu_{\neg Yng} = 1 - \mu_{Yng}$ if $\mathcal{T} = [0,1]$.

More generally, we can imagine rules of the form $A(x) \Rightarrow B(x)$ where A and B are vague predicates (it is not the case in our example), whose semantics would then be one of the followings

(I)   the more x is A, the more it is Λ that x is B
where $\Lambda \in \{$possible, probable, certain$\}$
(II)   the less x is B, the less it is Λ that x is A
(III)   the more x is A, the more x is B, or equivalently
the less x is B, the less x is A.

These type of rules are rather poorly expressed in classical logics, but are well-modelled in fuzzy logic using various multiple-valued connectives for combining μ_A and μ_B (see Prade[150] for rules of type (III) named "gradual" rules and Dubois and Prade[151] for other types of rules). All these rules have an implicit universal quantifier, i.e., $\forall x\ A(x) \Rightarrow B(x)$.

The treatment of these rules requires a formalization of their semantics in the form of the inequalities

(I) $t(A(x)) \leq g(B(x))$
(II) $g(A(x)) \leq t(B(x))$
(III) $t(A(x)) \leq t(B(x))$

where g is an uncertainty measure. These inequalities implicitly define conditional uncertainty measures which are obtained from resolving the implicit equations in these inequalities.[151]

Let us consider as an example the rule $\forall x\ Yng(x) \Rightarrow Sng(x)$, where Yng is a vague predicate meaning "the younger x, the more certain it is that x is single." This rule will be represented by means of a conditional possibility distribution π over $\mathcal{A} \times \{Sng, \neg Sng\}$ (where $\mathcal{A}$ is a set of ages over which it is possible to define the fuzzy set "Young" by the membership function μ_{Yng}), and π associates to a given age the maximal possibility degree of being single for a person of that age. Let us recall that $\mu_{Yng}(a)$ is the compatibility degree between the age and the idea of "young." This rule is of type II where g is a necessity measure, hence the inequality

$$\forall a, \mu_{Yng}(a) \leq N(Sng)$$

N depends on a and therefore corresponds to a possibility distribution over $\mathcal{A} \times \{Sng, \neg Sng\}$ satisfying the constraints

$\mu_{Yng}(a) \leq 1 - \pi(a, \neg Sng)$
$0 \leq \pi(a, Sng) \leq 1$ (absence of constraint over $N(\neg Sng)$)

Among the possibility distributions satisfying these constraints we naturally choose the least restrictive one (the one which authorizes the greatest possibility degrees). It is defined by

$$\forall a \in A, \pi(a, \neg Sng) = 1 - \mu_{Yng}(a), \quad \pi(a, Sng) = 1.$$

The conditional nature of the possibility distribution is related to the fact that the above rule is oriented. The first equality is justified by choosing for μ_{Yng} a decreasing characteristic function such that $\forall a \in \{a \mid \mu_{Yng}(a) = 1\}$ it is certain that an individual of age a is single ($\pi(a, \neg Sng) = 0$). This emphasizes the need for a contextual definition of "Young," since here, as soon as one reaches the legal age of marriage one ceases to be young with degree 1. The second equality expresses that one may be single at any age. This interpretation is compatible with the interpretation of the rule as a clause of the form $\neg Yng \vee Sng$ whose truth value for an individual x_0 of age a, whose marital status is known, is $\max(1 - t(Yng(x_0)), t(Sng(x_0)))$ with $t(Yng(x_0)) = \mu_{Yng}(a)$ and $t(Sng(x_0)) = 1$ if the person is single, and 0 otherwise. Let us note that in terms of the conditional possibility distribution, the uncertain clause (with no shade about Yng) ($\neg Yng(Léa) \vee Sng(Léa), \alpha$) is described by the following possibility distribution: $\pi(Yng, \neg Sng) = 1 - \alpha$; $\pi(Yng, Sng) = \pi(\neg Yng, Sng) = \pi(\neg Yng, \neg Sng) = 1$, where set $\mathcal{A}$ is reduced to $\{Yng, \neg Yng\}$.

It is clear that the vague nature of the predicates appearing in the rules is not directly related to the existence of exceptions. In particular the gradual rules are not rules with exceptions. But in rules of type (I), the uncertainty degrees in the conclusions (that is, the propensity to possess exceptions) are bounded by the truth degrees of the conditions.

D. Fuzzy Logic and Possibilistic Logic

A symbolic treatment of vague and uncertain information has been proposed,[128] in order to extend possibilistic logic to gradual predicates. In this case, we give up the excluded middle and the noncontradiction laws: $\forall x \; Yng(x) \vee \neg Yng(x)$ is no longer a tautology, we will only have $\forall a, \Pi(Yng(a) \wedge \neg Yng(a)) \leq 0.5$, $N(Yng(a) \vee \neg Yng(a)) \geq 0.5$. More generally, the *consistency degree* $\Pi(P \wedge Q)$ between two fuzzy predicates P and Q will be calculated from the extensions of these predicates (described by fuzzy sets). For instance, $P = $ "Young," and $Q = $ "Around 30 years old" (abbreviated by

"A30"), are defined by making use of membership functions μ_{Yng} and μ_{A30} into [0,1] and whose domain is a set of ages $\mathscr{A}$ (e.g. between 0 and 120 years). We then have, due to possibility theory (in accordance with the definition of the consistency degree $c(\mathscr{B})$ defined in Section VIII):

$$\Pi(P \wedge Q) = \sup_{a \in \mathscr{A}} \min(\mu_{Yng}(a), \mu_{A30}(a)).$$

In this way we calculate $\Pi(\text{Yng} \wedge \neg \text{Yng})$ with $\mu_{\neg Yng} = 1 - \mu_{Yng}$. Reasoning with vague knowledge using fuzzy predicates may be done in a symbolic manner, if we introduce these consistency degrees in the knowledge base. For instance, from the knowledge base

(Sdnt(Léa), 1); ($\neg$ Sdnt(Léa)$\vee$Yng(Léa), α_1); ($\neg$ Yng(Léa) $\vee$ Sng(Léa), α_2);
(Yng(Léa) $\vee \neg$ Yng(Léa), 0.5)   (Yng is a fuzzy predicate)

we deduce

(Sng(Léa), min(α_1, α_2, 0.5)).

It is thus possible to work with vague predicates such as Around-30-years-old(Léa) etc... (provided we calculate the consistency degrees between these facts and the other facts which concern age).

Fuzzy predicates can also be handled in possibilistic logic under the form of context dependent weights.[152] Namely, using the formalism proposed in Section VIII, the statement "the younger one is, the more certain it is that one is single" may be written down as a formula in possibilistic logic as ($\forall x$ Sng(x), $\mu_{Yng}(\text{age}(x))$), since $\pi(a, \neg \text{Sng}) = 1 - \mu_{Yng}(a)$ is equivalent to $N(\text{Sng}(x)) \geq \mu_{Yng}(\text{age}(x))$ with $a = \text{age}(x)$ and since π yields, by convention, a maximal possibility degree. We are now led to consider a weight whose value is no longer a constant, as it depends on a variable to be managed during unification. Let us note that the inequality may still be written in an equivalent manner, in the case of a crisp predicate $N(\forall x \text{ Sng}(x) \vee \neg \text{Yng}(x)) \geq \mu_{Yng}(\text{age}(x))$, as if Yng(x) is true for x then $\mu_{Yng}(\text{age}(x)) = 1$, while if Yng(x) is false, $\mu_{Yng}(\text{age}(x)) = 0$; this expresses the total certainty that young people (i.e., of age inferior to the legal age of marriage) are single.

E. Approximate Reasoning and Default Reasoning

Recently, Yager[153] has devised a semantic counterpart of default rules that, on small examples, produces results obtained by Reiter's logic. The idea is to interpret a default rule as a rule involving a possibility-qualified statement in its antecedent part, namely:

"if x is A and it is possible that y is B then z is C"

Now, "it is possible that y is B" is modelled by "$\Pi(B) = 1$," in turn interpreted as a fuzzy set B^+ of fuzzy sets, such as for any fuzzy set F,

$$\mu_{B^+}(F) = \sup_{v \in V} \min(\mu_B(v), \mu_F(v)) = \Pi(B \mid F).$$

The default rule is then interpreted as a fuzzy subset R of $U \times 2^V \times W$ defined by $R = \bar{A} \cup \bar{B}^+ \cup C$ with membership function

$$\mu_R(u, F, w) = \max(1 - \mu_A(u), 1 - \Pi(B \mid F), \mu_C(w)).$$

In the above expression u, v, and w respectively range on U, V, W, the universes where the extensions of A, B, C, respectively lie and the multiple-valued implication $\max(1 - a, b)$ is employed. Given some facts under the form "x is A'" and "y is B'," the combination/projection principle applied to μ_R, μ_A, $\mu_{\{B'\}}$ (the characteristic function of the singleton $\{B'\}$), gives "z is C'" such that

$$\mu_{C'}(w) = \max(\mu_C(w), \Pi(\bar{A} \mid A'), 1 - \Pi(B \mid B')).$$

Clearly when A is not fuzzy, $A' = A$ and $B' = V$ (unknown), the methodology inspired by the combination/projection principle leads to $C' = C$, since $\Pi(\bar{A} \mid A) = 1 - \Pi(B \mid V) = 0$. This default inference can be retracted if it is known that B' contradicts B later on, since then $\Pi(B \mid B') = 0$ and $C' = W$ (ignorance), i.e., the same behavior as with default logic is observed.

Dubois and Prade[1][29] have noticed that this approach to default reasoning do not separate default conclusions (i.e. those inferred when "y is B" is unknown) from established conclusions (those inferred when "y is B" is known). They have proposed to represent a default rule by means of standard rule (if x is A and y is B then y is C) together with default values attached to the part of the rule about which information is missing. This part corresponds to the explicit statement of exceptions (see Section VIII). With this view, default values are regarded as certainty-qualified propositions,[154] i.e., "y is B is α-certain", semantically equivalent to $\mu_{B'} = \max(\mu_B, 1 - \alpha)$ for α close to 1. Such default values can be dependent on context; for instance the default value is generated by the presence of the fact "x is A'" alone. In that case, given that x is A', the inference takes place as with standard fuzzy rules, but the conclusion becomes, due to the default value of y,

$$\mu_{C'}(w) = \max(\mu_C(w), 1 - \alpha, \Pi(\bar{A} \mid A'))$$

which remains uncertain even if $A' = A$ is not fuzzy, thus indicating the provisional character of the conclusion. However this approach requires a careful combination policy between default values and observed facts pertaining to the same variable, i.e., observed facts must inhibit the corresponding default values (that were meant only as a substitute to unavailable information) (see Section VIII). Besides there is the related problem of distinguishing between a default statement (a bird is assumed not to be a penguin, unless the contrary is explicitly stated) and an uncertain fact (uncertain evidence about a bird not being a penguin). In Yager's approach default statements are qualified by possibility and uncertain statements by degrees of certainty; in the other approach both are represented by the same conventions. Despite these difficulties, such works clearly indicate that default reasoning can be addressed in the set-theoretic and possibilistic framework of Zadeh's approximate reasoning; see also Yager[155] for a general set-theoretic perspective on default reasoning and Yager[156] for an integer-programming-based implementation of this approach.

F. Conclusion

Fuzzy logic concerns are distinct from those of the formalisms considered so far. It deals with a very particular aspect of the imperfection of information (the presence of vague predicates in the expression of knowledge), which other formalisms do not consider at all. Eventually, all the formalisms could be reconsidered with the addition of vague predicates. The inferential mechanisms of fuzzy logic rest on those of multiple-valued logics. They will therefore have the properties of these logics – properties which may vary according to the chosen logic. For example, contraposition holds for some multiple-valued implications, and does not hold for some others. Concludingly, the "orthogonal" character of fuzzy logic in relation to the concerns of other formalisms, and the existence of many systems having specific definitions and properties, renders of little relevance (and also too ambitious) a systematic analysis according to the comparison criteria proposed in this work, all the more so as certain notions evoked by these criteria should be redefined in the particular context of multiple-valued logics.

X. NUMERICAL QUANTIFIERS AND CONDITIONAL PROBABILITIES

A. Presentation

The proposition "Students are young" is sometimes understood as "Most of the students are young," where "most of" is seen as the linguistic expression of a numerical quantifier describing, in an approximate way, the proportion q_1 of students who are young. More generally, in this approach "The A's are B's" will be represented in the form of "$Q\ A(x)$ are $B(x)$," which will be precisely interpreted by a constraint limiting the cardinality of the extension of B relatively to the one of A, i.e.

$$\frac{|A \cap B|}{|A|} \in Q \quad (1)$$

with the following conventions: $A = \{x \in X \mid A(x) \text{ is true}\}$; $B = \{x \in X \mid B(x) \text{ is true}\}$; X = the set of considered objects; $|A|$ = the cardinality of A; Q = a set of possible values for a proportion (taking its value in [0,1]). In our example, X is a given set of individuals, and the first statement asserts that "Students are young," |Sdnt| is the number of students in X, |Sdnt ∩ Yng| = the number of young students in X, and Q represents "most of." There exists three ways of translating a quantifier like "most of" (or any other linguistic estimation), in terms of proportions:

(1) Q is a precise number between 0 and 1 (close to 1 in the case of "most of"); to think of always having such a number at hand may prove to be too optimistic.
(2) Q is an interval in the form of $[\underline{q}, \bar{q}] \subseteq [0,1]$; $\bar{q} = 1$ in the case of the quantifier "most of," interpreted as "at least a proportion $\underline{q}$."
(3) Q is a fuzzy interval, with membership function μ_Q taking values in $[0,1]$ (Zadeh[157]). $\mu_Q(p)$ evaluates to which the value p is in accordance with the idea of "most of" in our example. In particular, $\mu_Q(1) = 1$ (maximal conformity); $\mu_Q(0) = 0$ ("none" is not at all in accordance with "most of"), and $p \geq p' \Rightarrow \mu_Q(p) \geq \mu_Q(p')$ (the greater is p, the more it is in accordance with "most of"; see Figure 4(a)).

We note that representation 1 is a particular case of representation 2, which itself is a particular case of representation 3. In many cases the most realistic hypothesis seems to express "most of" in terms of an interval of proportions with boundaries which are ill-known, but rather close to 1, even if its identification might seem tricky in practice. Nevertheless, there exists empirical justifications and evaluation methods for the vague proportions.[158]

The knowledge granules e_i, $i = 1,4$ in the example are formalized as follows

$$e_1 : Q_1 \text{ Sdnt}(x) \text{ are Yng}(x) \; ; \; e_2 : Q_2 \text{ Yng}(x) \text{ are Sng}(x)$$
$$e_3 : Q_3 \text{ Sng}(x) \text{ are Yng}(x) \; ; \; e_4 : Q_4 \text{ Yng}(x) \text{ are Sdnt}(x)$$

where Q_1, Q_2, Q_3 translate the idea of "most of," but may disagree on the exact way of expressing it, since the meaning of "most of" is context-dependent. Q_4 corresponds to "part of," and is expressed by a proportion taking values strictly between 0 and 1, which might mean "around 25 %" in our example (see Figure 4(b)).

In Figure 2, and in practice, membership function μ_Q is linear by parts, which simplifies its identification. Fuzzy numbers calculus is indeed robust with respect to membership function variations.[123]

Reasoning from such numerically quantified general rules may be modeled as an optimization problem. We show here an approach to reason on such data, which although conceptually simple, should still be improved in practice. We will suppose for the sake of simplicity that quantifiers Q_i represent nonfuzzy intervals $[\underline{q}_i, \bar{q}_i]$. Here

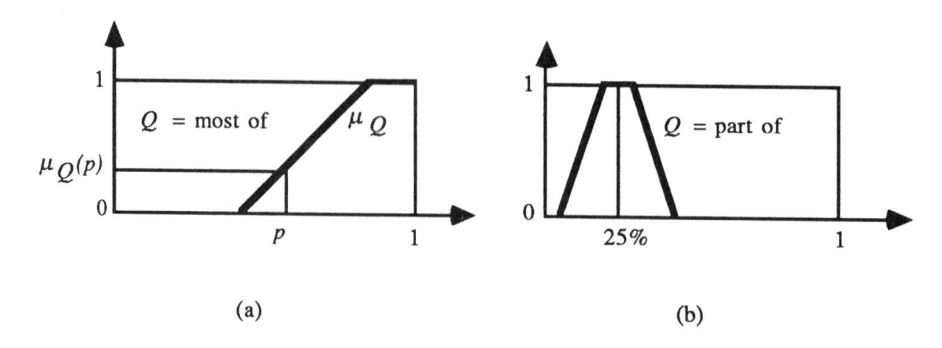

Figure 4. Fuzzy set representation of linguistic quantifiers.

three predicates are taken into account (Sdnt, Yng, Sng), i.e., $8 = 2^3$ situations should be considered, corresponding respectively to Sdnt ∧ Yng ∧ Sng, ¬ Sdnt ∧ Yng ∧ Sng, Sdnt ∧ ¬ Yng ∧ Sng, etc. Let us denote by x_{syg}, $s,y,g \in \{0,1\}$ the eight corresponding variables. For instance, x_{001} represents the proportion of non-students which are not young but single. In this case, $x_{syg} \in [0,1]$ and $\Sigma_{s,y,g \in \{0,1\}} x_{syg} = 1$. We have |Sdnt| = $x_{111} + x_{101} + x_{110} + x_{100}$; |Sdnt ∩ Yng| = $x_{110} + x_{111}$; etc. Then the statement e_1 "Q_1 Sdnt(x) are Yng(x)" is expressed by the two linear constraints

$$\underline{q_1}(x_{111}+x_{101}+x_{110}+x_{100}) \leq x_{110} + x_{111} \leq \bar{q}_1(x_{111}+x_{101}+x_{110}+x_{100}) \quad (L_1)$$

Once e_1, e_2, e_3, e_4 are represented by linear constraints L_1, L_2, L_3, L_4, we are able to answer all questions of the form "how many A's are B's?" "how many A's and B's are C's?" etc. In order to do so we will formally express the desired proportion q in the form of a rational fraction where variables x_{syg} appear, and we will successively carry out the maximization and minimization of q, in order to calculate its range $[\underline{q}, \bar{q}] = Q$. We will conclude "$Q$ A are B." For example, to the question "how many students are single?," the answer will be "Q Sdnt(x) are Sng(x)" with $Q = [\underline{q}, \bar{q}]$ such that $\underline{q}$ (resp. $\bar{q}$) is the minimal value (resp. maximal) taken by $\frac{|\text{Sdnt} \cap \text{Sng}|}{|\text{Sdnt}|}$, and induced by e_1, e_2, e_3, e_4 where

$$\underline{q} = \inf\{\frac{x_{101} + x_{111}}{x_{111} + x_{101} + x_{110} + x_{100}} \text{ under the constraints } (L_1)(L_2)(L_3)(L_4)\};$$

$$\bar{q} = \sup\{\frac{x_{101} + x_{111}}{x_{111} + x_{101} + x_{110} + x_{100}} \text{ under the constraints } (L_1)(L_2)(L_3)(L_4)\}.$$

This approach is systematically utilized by Paass,[159] in terms of probabilities.

In fact, in our example manipulations over set cardinality suffice to calculate $\underline{q}$ and $\bar{q}$ in a symbolic form (cf. Dubois et Prade[160]). We have the following bounds

$$\underline{q} = \underline{q}_1 \cdot \max(0, 1 - \frac{1 - \underline{q}_2}{\underline{q}_4}) \quad (2)$$

$$\bar{q} \leq \min(1, 1 - \underline{q}_1(1 - \frac{\bar{q}_2}{\underline{q}_4})) \quad (3)$$

Let us note that neither e_3 nor the upper bounds of Q_1 and Q_4 are used in the calculation. For instance, if Q_1 = at least 90 %, Q_2 = at least 90%, and Q_4 = between 20 and 30%, we find Q = at least 45%, which means that at least 45% of the students are single. In some situations the upper bound given by (3) can be improved owing to the equality proved by Dubois et al.[161]

$$\bar{q} = \min(1, 1 - q_1 + \frac{q_1 \cdot \bar{q}_2}{q_4}, \frac{\bar{q}_1 \cdot \bar{q}_2}{q_3 \cdot q_4}, \frac{\bar{q}_1 \cdot \bar{q}_2}{q_3 \cdot q_4}[1 - q_3] + \bar{q}_1) \quad (4)$$

This methodology is easily extended to the case of fuzzy quantifiers which express linguistic proportions.[157] In the example, relations (2–4) can be directly applied replacing the symbolic variables by fuzzy quantities and taking advantage of fuzzy arithmetic rules.[160] Fuzzy optimization techniques may be used in the general case of a set of rules with fuzzy quantifiers (cf. Dubois[162]).

This model of "Q A's are B's" can be directly extended to a quantification by means of conditional probabilities. Prob($B \mid A$) = α then expresses that when being an A (and nothing else) we have a probability α of being a B. Thus this does no longer correspond to assigning a probability weight α = Prob($\bar{A} \cup B$) to a clause, as in the case of logics of uncertainty. We are now very close to the conditional probabilistic logic of Adams,[163] which translates "A's are B's" by "Probability $P(B \mid A)$ is close to 1", i.e., $P(B \mid A) \geq 1 - \varepsilon$ where ε is very small. More generally, the representation of knowledge of the type "A's are B's" by the localization of the conditional probability $P(B \mid A)$ in an interval of the form $[\underline{q}, \bar{q}] \subseteq [0,1]$, is the base of Kyburg[164]'s works (see for example Kyburg[165] for an introduction).

B. Discussion

Point 0. In order to make this approach meaningful, it is necessary (at least conceptually) to be able to count the objects to which the rules refer. Such is the case in the example. This is not always so however, especially when the set X of objects, implicit in the rules, is ambiguous. Then we do not know how are we supposed to count. For instance, in the statement "most of the birds fly" it is not clear if X represents the set of birds species, the birds actually living on earth, the birds that I have seen till yesterday, etc. We do not really know how to establish the statistics on the birds that fly. The main reason is due to the fact that "to fly" is a typical property of birds, i.e., by definition, a bird is an animal likely to fly (with some exceptions). On the other hand, in the example employed here the concepts Student, Young, and Single have no semantic link between them: we *notice* that most of the students are young if they are counted in a given university town. This approach is clearly not very well-adapted to general rules expressing definitions with exceptions. Let us note that this problem arises only with quantifiers of the type "most of" (or their antonyms "very few of," etc...), that is when the objects to which the rules do not apply are exceptions, i.e., there are very few ones. However intermediary quantifiers (e.g., "part of") seem to be more systematically linked to statistical interpretations.

The numerical quantifier approach may handle fuzzy predicates (such as "Young," seen as a fuzzy set of ages), insofar as most of the cardinality properties are extended to fuzzy sets, provided that the set operations are conveniently defined, and that a scalar definition of fuzzy set cardinality is adopted.[157] See Yager[166] for the case when fuzzy set cardinality is a fuzzy interval of integers.

Cardinality properties are extended to the case of conditional probabilities, and "Q A's are B's" may also be interpreted as constraint over the conditional probability

$\text{Prob}(B \mid A) = \dfrac{\text{Prob}(B \cap A)}{\text{Prob}(A)}$. Let this constraint, denoted by $\text{Prob}(B \mid A) \in Q$, implicitly define a set of probability measures over X, and let $\mathcal{P}$ be such a set. Answering to a question comes down to calculating the upper and lower bounds of a probability which ranges on set $\mathcal{P}$ as in the case of the logics of uncertainty (Section VIII). These remarks emphasize the power of this approach when the objects which the rules refer to are not ambiguous.

Let us note that in certain cases, the expression "generally if A then B" might mean "A seldom occurs at the same time as non-B." Then this means that "generally" refers to the quantity $\dfrac{|\bar{A} \cup B|}{|X|} = 1 - \dfrac{|A \cap \bar{B}|}{|X|}$, and not to $\dfrac{|A \cap B|}{|A|}$. We are thus in the presence of an interpretation in terms of logical implication, as in Section VIII. It may be problematic, in practice, to choose between the two translations

"Among those that are A, most of them are B" ($\dfrac{|A \cap B|}{|A|} \in Q$)

or

"Among the items, only few are A without being B" ($\dfrac{|\bar{A} \cup B|}{|X|} \in Q$).

It is worth noticing that we may simultaneously have $\dfrac{|A \cap B|}{|A|} = 0$ (when $A \cap B = \emptyset$) and $\dfrac{|\bar{A} \cup B|}{|X|}$ close to 1 (it suffices that A contains very few elements of X). But, $\dfrac{|A \cap B|}{|A|} = 1 \Leftrightarrow \dfrac{|\bar{A} \cup B|}{|X|} = 1$ (provided that $A \neq \emptyset$!). Lastly, let us remark that in order to calculate $\dfrac{|A \cap B|}{|A|}$ it suffices to know the objects which are A while $\dfrac{|\bar{A} \cup B|}{|X|}$ supposes, moreover, that the objects which are not A are also known since $X = A \cup \bar{A}$. The problem of choosing between implication, and conditional probability belongs in fact to a larger discussion between probability and classical logic. (See Harper et al.[167] for a report on the controversy during the 1970s, and Goodman and Nguyen[168] for a possible solution to this controversy; see also Dubois and Prade[123-169] in the framework of possibility theory, where it is shown that the conditional certainty degree $N(A \mid B)$ coincide in many cases with $N(\bar{A} \cup B)$. The probabilistic logic proposed by Nilsson[126] uses $\text{Prob}(\bar{A} \cup B)$ rather than $\text{Prob}(B \mid A)$.

Remark: Conditional measures in belief functions theory

The semantic conflict between $\text{Prob}(A \mid B)$ and $\text{Prob}(\bar{A} \cup B)$ is likely to be avoided in the other numerical approaches to uncertainty. A nonprobabilistic counterpart of "Q A are B" may be expressed in the form of

"If A is true then (B is almost certain)"

This may be formally written down as $\forall x\ A(x) \rightarrow (g(B(x)) = \alpha)$, where g is a necessity measure $N(.\ |\ A)$, or a credibility measure $Bel(.\ |\ A)$. In the latter case, an evaluation $Pl(B\ |\ A) = \beta$ of the plausibility may also be known, with $\beta \neq 1$.

Let $\mathcal{F}$ be the set of focal elements characterizing the nonconditional belief function implicitly defined by $Bel(.\ |\ A)$, and m its basic probability. The set $\mathcal{F}_A$ of focal elements defined by conditioning by A is $\mathcal{F}_A = \{C \cap A\ |\ C \in \mathcal{F}\}$. $Bel(.\ |\ A)$ is then defined by: $m_A(B) = \Sigma_{C:A \cap C=B}\ m(C)$. That means that the masses previously allocated to the sets C such that $C \cap A = B$ are allocated to B, $\forall\ B \neq \emptyset$. It comes down to letting

$$Pl(A \cap B) = Pl(B\ |\ A) \cdot Pl(A)$$

with $Pl(B\ |\ A) = 1 - Bel(\bar{B}\ |\ A)$. The granule of knowledge $\forall x\ A(x) \rightarrow (Bel(B(x)) = \alpha, Pl(B(x)) = \beta)$ leads to the statement of the following constraints over Pl:

$$Pl(A \cap B) = \beta \cdot Pl(A)$$
$$Pl(A \cap \bar{B}) = (1 - \alpha) \cdot Pl(A)$$

These two equalities do not constrain $Pl(A)$, which we take as equal to 1 in order to express our complete ignorance in relation to A. We have then a single solution such that

$$m(\bar{A} \cup \bar{B}) = 1 - \beta,\ m(\bar{A} \cup B) = \alpha,\ m(X) = \beta - \alpha$$
(the latter term corresponds to ignorance)

This is what Smets[170] calls an "empty extension" of $Bel(.\ |\ A)$. It corresponds to leaving the intervals $[Bel(.), Pl(.)]$ as large as possible. We easily verify that

$$Bel(B\ |\ A) = Bel(\bar{A} \cup B) \qquad Bel(\bar{B}\ |\ A) = Bel(\bar{A} \cup \bar{B})$$

which reconciles conditionals with material implication. The case of possibility functions is treated in a analogous way, by posing $\beta = 1$. We find then the same semantics as that of $(\forall x\ A(x) \rightarrow B(x), \alpha)$ in possibility logic. On the other hand, the empty extension of a conditional belief measure does not correspond to the model of Chatalic et al.[136] presented in Section VIII-B.

Point 1. The approach by either precise, or imprecise numerical quantifiers is characterized by its capability of producing new general knowledge from given general knowledge. For example, we may link the two rules "Q_1 Sdnt(x) are Yng(x), and Q_2 Yng(x) are Sng(x) when $Q_2 = \forall$ and conclude that "Q_1 Sdnt(x) are Sng(x) is correct, when Q_1 is in the form $[q_1, 1]$ (or more generally μ_{Q_1} is monotonically increasing). By contrast, if $Q_2 \neq \forall$, nothing else can be concluded, i.e., we will conclude "Q Sdnt(x) are Sng(x)" with $Q = [0, 1]$, even if $Q_1 = \forall$. The cardinality laws state that even if all students are young, and that most of the young people are single, we do not generally know how many students are single, except if we have some information of the type "Q_4 Yng(x) are Sdnt(x))," where Q_4 is a sufficiently high proportion, as it was seen above.

In the case of an instantiated statement of the type "Léa is a student," if we ask for instance "Is Léa single?" it is necessary either

- to answer in the first place to the general question "are students single" and apply the answer to Léa, who is supposed to be a student chosen at random. For example, if we link in this way the two rules e_1 and e_2 with $Q_2 \neq \forall$, we will say that we do not know anything. But if we take e_4 into account we shall be able to conclude something;
- or to reason in an instantiated form directly. In this case "Léa is a student" will be translated by Prob(Sdnt(Léa)) = 1 (in terms of probability). Applying e_1 in the instantiated form Prob(Yng(Léa) | Sdnt(Léa)) ∈ $Q_1 = [q_1, \bar{q}_1]$ we will deduce Prob(Yng(Léa)) ≥ q_1; which by the application of e_2 (Prob(Sng(Léa) | Yng(Léa)) ∈ $Q_2 = [q_2, \bar{q}_2]$), will yield Prob(Sng(Léa)) ≥ $q_1 \cdot q_2$.

Contrary to the case of reasoning with non-instantiated rules, we find that Léa is single with a probability of at least $q_1 \cdot q_2$. In fact, in order to apply e_2 it must be supposed that Léa is a (female) young person *chosen at random*, which is false, since Léa is a student. This illustrates the problem, discussed by Kyburg,[164] of the choice of the good reference class (see also Loui[171] for instance). In the absence of any other information on the direct links between students and singles, or on the proportion of young people that are students, the conclusion "Léa is probably (≥ $q_1 \cdot q_2$) single" is *temporarily* valid; but this is only a default result which should be forgotten if a more specific piece of information should become available, for example, if we learn that "Q Sdnt(x) are Sng(x)." This problem is avoided if we do not instantiate; for example, if $Q_2 \neq \forall$, e_1 and e_2 yield: "[0,1] Sdnt(x) are Sng(x)," which, combined with "Q Sdnt(x) are Sng(x)," yields "([0,1] ∩ Q) Sdnt(x) are Sng(x)," i.e., "Q Sdnt(x) are Sng(x)."

Point 2. Rules of the form "Q A's are B's" are "of variable transitivity" in their noninstantiated form. More precisely we have seen that

"Q A's are B's," and "Q' B's are C's" yield "[0,1] A's are C's" if $Q' \neq \forall$

but

"Q A's are B's", and "$\forall$ B's are C's" yield "at least Q A's are C's"

In the first case, the completely unkown quantifier [0,1] expresses the absence of transitivity. Note the analogy of behavior between the implication of Delgrande (cf. Section VII-A) and the weak implication which represents "Q A's are B's" when $Q \neq \forall$. In the instantiated form these rules are transitive (with an attenuation effect due to the multiplication of proportions), but this transitivity is a little delusive since it furnishes only default information. More generally, cardinality laws (or conditional probabilities) provide the mechanism that permits to evaluate whether a form of transitivity holds or does not according to the values of the quantifiers present in the rules. For example, if e_1, e_2, and e_4 are given with $Q_1 = Q_2 =$ at least α%, and $Q_4 =$

at least $\beta\%$ the transitivity between e_1 and e_2 do not hold, due to (2), except when $\beta > 1 - \alpha$, and therefrom we deduce that at least $\dfrac{\alpha(\alpha + \beta - 1)}{\beta}$ of the young people are single. At this point the analogy with the implication of Delgrande, which is not supposed to deal with such subtleties, seems to come to an end.

N.B. Let us recall that $\text{Prob}(\bar{A} \cup C) \geq \max(0, \text{Prob}(\bar{A} \cup B) + \text{Prob}(\bar{B} \cup C) - 1)$. Thus a weakened transitivity subsists with the logical interpretation of the rules, when $\text{Prob}(\bar{A} \cup B) \geq \alpha$, $\text{Prob}(\bar{B} \cup C) \geq \beta$, and $\alpha + \beta > 1$.

Point 3. We remark the absence of the contraposition law for the rules "Q A's are B's" since such a rule is not intuitively equivalent to "Q $\bar{B}$'s are $\bar{A}$'s." Indeed, in the first case we deal with objects that are A and ignore all the properties of those that are not so. For example, "generally if Jean comes to the meeting, Mary does not" is not equivalent to "generally if Mary comes to the meeting, Jean does not" since it is possible that Mary only comes when Jean also comes, Jean comes very often and Mary nearly never. The numerical quantifiers approach respects this intuitive absence of contraposition of the general laws since $\dfrac{|A \cap B|}{|A|} \neq \dfrac{|\bar{A} \cap \bar{B}|}{|\bar{B}|}$, in terms of cardinality. There does not even exist a function f such that if "Q A's are B's" then "$f(Q)$ $\bar{B}$'s are $\bar{A}$'s", generally. On the other hand, if Q refers to $|\bar{A} \cup B| / |X|$, the contraposition law holds. We remark that the situation is analogous to that of default theory, where the normal defaults without prerequisites are contraposable, but not those with prerequisites.

Point 4. Another property of the nonclassical implication "Q A's are B's" is the one that we can suitably call its "nonmonotonicity." Indeed if "at least 75% of the students are single" nothing can be deduced, in general, on the proportion of young students who are single; thus we cannot say that this proportion is greater than or equal to 75%. Formally, from "Q A's are B's" we cannot deduce "$f(Q)$ A's and C's are B's" as soon as $Q \neq \forall$. This is analogous to what happens in conditional logic, where the weak implication is such that, if $A \Rightarrow B$ is a theorem, $A \wedge C \Rightarrow B$ is not necessarily so (see Section VII-A).

Likewise, knowing that "Q_1 A's are B's," "Q_2 C's are B's" generally nothing may be concluded about Q, such as "Q A's and C's are B's." If we calculate Q in terms of Q_1 and Q_2, we will find $Q = [0,1]$.

Nevertheless, numerical quantifier logic is monotonic in a sense that should be made precise. We have seen that each knowledge element of the form "Q A's are B's" implicitly defines a set of probability measures. Let $\mathcal{P}_i$, $i = 1,4$ be the set of probability measures induced by e_i, $i = 1,4$. The set induced by $\{e_1, e_2, e_3, e_4\}$ will be $\mathcal{P} = \cap_i \mathcal{P}_i$ which will determine the answer to a question such as "what is the value of Q in "Q Sdnt(x) are Sng(x)"?" where Q will be the interval limiting Prob(Sng(x) | Sdnt(x)). The addition of a piece of knowledge such as e_5 will transform $\mathcal{P}$ into $\mathcal{P} \cap \mathcal{P}_5$, and thus does nothing but shrink the interval Q of the proportions of singles among students. In this sense, the calculation of numerical quantifiers is monotonic, which assures it a certain modularity. Particularly, there exists an inconsistency from the moment that $\mathcal{P} = \emptyset$ (conflicting constraints).

Point 5. The approach described here copes as well with disjunctive pieces of information, and may represent knowledge elements such as e_5, i.e., "Q Sdnt(x) $\wedge$ Pnt(x) are Mrd(x) $\vee$ Chbt(x)." In order to calculate the possible values of Prob($C \mid A \cup B$) in function of those of Prob($C \mid A$), and Prob($C \mid B$) the same methodology is used, namely the one that exploits cardinality laws.

Point 6. It is clear that this approach permits the representation of an infinite number of different quantifiers: no matter which proportion, ill-known ones, vague ones, etc. The quantifiers $\forall$ and $\exists$ are found by letting $Q_i = \{1\}$, and $]0,1]$ respectively. Total ignorance is captured by $Q_i = [0,1]$ ("I do not know if the students are young," for example).

It is important to point out that the semantics of a logical sentence, to which a probability degree is attached, may be ambiguous. Therefore formula $\forall x\ A(x)$ may become Prob($A(x)$) = α in the sense that the proportion of the x's such that $A(x)$ is true is α; α is clearly a quantifier. But to the same formula with its universal quantifier, a probability degree Prob($\forall x\ A(x)$) = α, may be assigned, expressing a universal conjecture. In this case α may be a subjective probability (estimation of the confidence in the validity of formula $\forall x\ A(x)$). A "frequentist" interpretation of α in terms of proportions should thus refer to the models of $\forall x\ A(x)$, i.e., to the worlds in which *all* x make $A(x)$ true. When representing knowledge, it is important to choose between the two semantics. In this way Prob(Yng(x)) = α will rather express the fact that α% of the individuals are young, than an hesitation to affirm that all the individuals are young (Prob($\forall x$ Yng(x)) = α). We will remark that if x = Léa, Prob(Yng(x)) $\geq \alpha$, as well as Prob($\forall x$ Yng(x)) $\geq \alpha$ lead to the conclusion that Prob(Yng(Léa)) $\geq \alpha$.

Point 7. Given that the obtained conclusions are possibly pervaded with imprecision under the form of incompletely defined proportions, we may admit that this is a matter of multiple extensions, in the sense that each proportion or conditional probability attached to a conclusion, and compatible with that imprecision, may be seen as relative to an "extension" of the knowledge base. In order to choose between these "extensions," we may make use of supplementary "by default" hypotheses, which will reduce the bracketing of the proportion, or of the probability attached to a conclusion. We may even select a single number as in the Bayesian approach.

Point 8. Quantifier logic is modular as long as an added piece of information does not contradict the contents of the original data base, i.e., if $\mathcal{P}$ is a set of probabilities implicitly defined by that base, and $\mathcal{P}'$ is the set induced by a new piece of information p', we should have $\mathcal{P} \cap \mathcal{P}' \neq \emptyset$. Otherwise p' is inconsistent with the knowledge base. Nevertheless, the notion of inconsistency is here more flexible than that of classical logic. For example, Prob($A(x)$) $\in [0,\alpha]$ and Prob($\neg A(x)$) $\in [0,\beta]$ are not contradictory when $\alpha + \beta \geq 1$, whereas $A(x)$ and $\neg A(x)$ cannot be simultaneously present in a nonuncertain knowledge base.

Besides, the way we will use the approach is close to the one of a nonmonotonic calculation, because if we reason in the instantiated form, the obtained conclusions may be questioned by the addition of new pieces of information. For instance, if Léa is a student, we saw that we could reasonably think that she is single, i.e., Prob(Sng(Léa)) is higher than a certain bound (even though Prob(Sng(x) | Sdnt(x)) is usually unkown, as it was seen above). If we learn that Léa has children, Prob(Sng(Léa)) will be calculated by e_5 as being close to 0, and we can prove that this is the good answer, by noting that e_5 is more specific than e_1 and e_2.

In terms of general rules, this nonmonotonic phenomenon will not occur, though we shall find the same answer, for we no longer calculate Prob(Sng(x) | Sdnt(x)), but Prob(Sng(x) | Sdnt(x) ∧ Pnt(x)), i.e., we answer *another* question. The fact of not obtaining the same answer in the two cases is not surprising. The nonmonotonicity in the instantiated case comes from being interested in deducing the fact Sng(Léa), while in the noninstantiated case the formula to be "proved" carries its context in the form of a conditional (probability). In default logic terminology, we try to deduce a default whose prerequisite is Sdnt(x) ∧ Pnt(x), instead of inferring Sng(Léa). This type of manipulation is impossible in default logic.

Point 9. No mechanism for knowledge revision is provided, although necessary when an information element e_{n+1} added to a base $\{e_1 \ldots e_n\}$ contradicts that base in the sense that $\mathcal{P}_{n+1} \cap (\cap_{1 \leq i \leq n} \mathcal{P}_i)$ would be empty. We could imagine such a device based on the works about probability kinematics (e.g., Domotor[172]), or on recent proposals by Gärdenfors (see Section XV).

Point 10. We depict three ways of realizing the automatic resolution of the problems raised by this approach:

1. by the application of optimization techniques (based on linear programming), in order to obtain the intervals representing the desired quantifiers (see Paass[159] for example);
2. by means of constraint propagation methods, which use cardinality laws (or those of conditional probabilities); for example
Prob(A∩B|C)∈ [max(0,Prob(A|C)+Prob(B|C) - 1),min(Prob(A|C),Prob(B|C))], until a bracketing of the desired proportion is found. A method of this kind is used by Quinlan[173] in the system INFERNO but this method does not compute conditional probabilities. The repeated utilization of formulas (2) and (3)–(4) would belong to this kind of methods;
3. by trying to characterize a unique joint probability measure induced by the constraints expressing the knowledge. For example, by looking for a probability measure of maximal entropy respecting the constraints.[174] The Bayesian approach evoked in the next section obeys this philosophy.

Approach 1 employed in a brute force way is limited by combinatorial explosion, due to the enumeration of interpretations (n literals = 2^n possible cases for the attribution of truth values), to which probabilities to be calculated are associated. Nevertheless, it furnishes exact and reliable results (running the risk of being uninformative informative if the initial knowledge is too weak). Approach 2 has a better performance, at the expense of a loss of precision in the results; it proceeds by local advances and some more global constraints are neglected; however it makes the explanation of an obtained result possible. Approach 3 may be efficient but its results may be questionable for they will always be precise (due to the unicity hypothesis). It will provide a point-probability in the (maybe too large) interval which approach 1 would yield.

In the conditional logic of Adams,[163] where knowledge pieces of the form "the A's are B's" are translated into $P(B \mid A) \geq 1 - \varepsilon$, the author was able to introduce inference rules which permit the automation of reasoning from statements of this type. A knowledge base, called a theory, is then a pair $(\mathcal{F},\Delta)$, where $\mathcal{F}$ is a set of logical propositions (clauses in propositional logic) and Δ is a set of conditional expressions of the form $A \Rightarrow B$ whose interpretation, called ε-semantics, is $P(B \mid A) \geq 1 - \varepsilon$. Proposition C is "plausibly deduced" from $(\mathcal{F},\Delta)$, denoted by $\mathcal{F} \vdash_\Delta C$ if and only if $P(C \mid \mathcal{F}) \geq 1 - 0(\varepsilon)$ with $\lim_{\varepsilon \to 0} 0(\varepsilon) = 0$.
The three main inference rules in the logic of Adams are:

- "Triangularity" : from $A \Rightarrow B$ and $B \Rightarrow C$ deduce $A \wedge B \Rightarrow C$
- "Bayes" :   from $A \Rightarrow B$ and $A \wedge B \Rightarrow C$ deduce $A \Rightarrow C$
- "Disjunction" : from $A \Rightarrow B$ and $C \Rightarrow B$ deduce $A \vee C \Rightarrow B$

These rules are independently found in[43] (see Section II-C), where "natural" properties of nonmonotonic inference are investigated. Adams[163] shows that these three rules are sound and complete vis-à-vis the semantics of conditionals $A \Rightarrow B$. Pearl,[175] widely employs these results in order to build an inference system capable of producing all the plausible conclusions from a theory $(\mathcal{F},\Delta)$. He emphasizes the strong analogy existing between this system and the default logic of Reiter (see Section III), and tries to demonstrate that most of the inconveniences of this logic disappear. We may especially reason by case (Point 5) and answer general questions (i.e., to infer new "defaults") with the logic of Adams. In spite of the evident interest of this formalism, we may nevertheless remark that it is a logic of extreme probabilities, where only the numerical quantifiers close to either 1 or 0 are taken into account; it is not always possible to translate "the A's are B's" into "an overwhelming majority of A's are B's."

Recent works in the theory of measure-free conditionals[176] suggest that the three inference rules make sense for conditional objects without resorting to ε-semantics. There is some founded hope that a nonmonotonic logic in agreement with conditional logic eventually emerges.

XI. CAUSAL MODELS

The type of approach briefly considered in this section does not call for logical formalism, strictly speaking. It supports diagnosis models based on the exploitation of relations linking observations and causes, or in other words, of causes and effects, or specifically in the medical case, of symptoms and diseases. The presence of this section is justified by the fact that, in this type of application, we come across knowledge of the form "generally, the A's are B's" which expresses a probable or typical causality relation. What we try to express is that the fact of being an A causes (unless exceptional) the fact of being a B, as for example in the formula "overeating causes obesity."

In the first part, we present the Bayesian approach, which turns out to be well-adapted to diagnosis problems, using a causal interpretation of conditional probabilities. It is clear that we could present this approach as a variant of numerical quantifier logic, if we disregard this causal interpretation. On the other hand, the approaches evoked in the second part try to directly model the idea of causality in diagnosis reasoning processes.

A. Bayesian Approach

Bayesian approach to reasoning problems under uncertainty is related to the numerical quantifiers approach. Indeed, it models knowledge elements such as those above by making use of conditional probabilities. It differs by its concern for representing a causal link between variables, in accordance with the oriented nature of Bayesian networks. Let us note that in our test-example, the knowledge describes correlations and not causality relations themselves. The Bayesian approach supposes moreover that the available knowledge, whatever it is, permits the definition of *only one* probability measure, on the set of possible situations. This probability measure is considered as reasonable in the absence of further information.

This unicity asumption leads the Bayesians to formulate a certain number of requirements on the way of stating a problem, on the available data, and on the rule network structure. In return, the knowledge base computer treatment is considerably alleviated, and *local* propagation and combination processes may be validated. The reader should consult Pearl,[175] and Lauritzen and Spiegelhalter[177] for examples of local techniques. Here we will examine the types of hypothesis admitted by the Bayesian school and how such an approach adapts itself to the example.

1. Presentation

The simplest problem the Bayesian approach tackles is the following: given the probabilities $\text{Prob}(B \mid A)$ and $\text{Prob}(B \mid \bar{A})$, and the a priori probability $\text{Prob}(A)$, which expresses a priori knowledge on event A before any experiment, we observe B, and calculate the a posteriori probability $\text{Prob}(A \mid B)$ by means of Bayes theorem that reads

$$\text{Prob}(A \mid B) = \frac{\text{Prob}(B \mid A) \cdot \text{Prob}(A)}{\text{Prob}(B)} =$$

$$= \frac{\text{Prob}(B \mid A) \cdot \text{Prob}(A)}{\text{Prob}(B \mid A) \cdot \text{Prob}(A) + \text{Prob}(B \mid \bar{A}) \cdot (1 - \text{Prob}(A))}$$

In fact, by denoting $\lambda(B \mid A) = \dfrac{\text{Prob}(B \mid A)}{\text{Prob}(B \mid \bar{A})}$ called likelihood ratio and

$V(A) = \dfrac{\text{Prob}(A)}{\text{Prob}(\bar{A})}$ called a priori likelihood, we verify that the a posteriori likelihood

$V(A \mid B) = \dfrac{\text{Prob}(A \mid B)}{\text{Prob}(\bar{A} \mid B)}$ is obtained by $V(A \mid B) = \lambda(B \mid A) \cdot V(A)$. It is thus enough to know $\lambda(B \mid A)$ and $V(A)$ (or Prob(A)), in order to calculate Prob($A \mid B$). To determine whether Léa is young, given that she is single, we must know $\lambda(\text{Sng}(x) \mid \text{Yng}(x))$, i.e., the relative proportion of young single people to nonyoung single people. It is clear that the statement "most young people are single" is not sufficient to calculate $\lambda(\text{Sng}(x) \mid \text{Yng}(x))$, since it defines only the quantity Prob($\text{Sng}(x) \mid \text{Yng}(x)$) (supposing that "most" corresponds to a precise number). In order to calculate $\lambda(\text{Sng}(x) \mid \text{Yng}(x))$ we have either to have at hand a complementary statement such as "$Q \neg \text{Yng}(x)$ are $\text{Sng}(x)$," where $Q \in [0,1]$ or to directly translate the link between 'Young' and 'Single' by "there exists more ($\lambda > 1$), or less ($\lambda < 1$), or the same number $\lambda = 1$ of young single people as of nonyoung single ones."

Let us suppose that Léa is single, i.e., "Sng(Léa)." Let us further suppose that we know the *a priori* probability Prob(Yng(Léa)) that Léa (a person taken at random from the whole population) is young. From this we can deduce Prob(Yng(Léa) | Sng(Léa)) knowing that Léa is single. Let us note that this approach proceeds by belief revision, rather than by deduction. The *a priori* belief relative to Léa's youth is modified by the piece of information "Léa is single." Bayes theorem supposes that a priori belief always exists and is liable to be expressed by a probability measure.

This approach can be extended to the case where several rules converge towards a fact. For example, considering e_1 and e_3, we suppose that we know beforehand $\lambda(\text{Sdnt}(x) \mid \text{Yng}(x))$, $\lambda(\text{Sng}(x) \mid \text{Yng}(x))$, and Prob(Yng($x$)). Applying Bayes theorem with the sure facts Sdnt(Léa), and Sng(Léa), we calculate

$$V(\text{Yng}(\text{Léa}) \mid \text{Sng}(\text{Léa}) \wedge \text{Sdnt}(\text{Léa})) = \\ \lambda(\text{Sng}(\text{Léa}) \wedge \text{Sdnt}(\text{Léa}) \mid \text{Yng}(\text{Léa})) \cdot V(\text{Yng}(\text{Léa})).$$

But $\lambda(\text{Sng}(\text{Léa}) \wedge \text{Sdnt}(\text{Léa}) \mid \text{Yng}(\text{Léa}))$ must be calculated in terms of $\lambda(\text{Sng}(\text{Léa}) \mid \text{Yng}(\text{Léa}))$, and $\lambda(\text{Sdnt}(\text{Léa}) \mid \text{Yng}(\text{Léa}))$. It is here that the independence hypothesis Prob($A \cap B \mid C$) = Prob($A \mid C$) · Prob($B \mid C$) comes in: we suppose that C being ascertained, A and B become (statistically) independent. In the case of likelihood ratios we suppose that, given the fact of being young, there exists no relation between the fact of being a student, and the fact of being single (which may be questionable here); and likewise in the case of being no longer young, since $\lambda(A \mid B)$ does also depend on Prob($A \mid \bar{B}$). We then have

$$V(\text{Yng}(\text{Léa}) \mid \text{Sng}(\text{Léa}) \wedge \text{Sdnt}(\text{Léa})) = \\ V(\text{Yng}(\text{Léa})) \cdot \lambda(\text{Sng}(\text{Léa}) \mid \text{Yng}(\text{Léa})) \cdot \lambda(\text{Sdnt}(\text{Léa}) \mid \text{Yng}(\text{Léa})).$$

This approach is used in the expert system PROSPECTOR.[14] It has led to a controversy about the use of conditional independence hypotheses relatively to a fact and to its negation simultaneously; these hypotheses tend to seriously limit the reasoning capabilities and to overconstrain the set of probabilistic weights (see Bonissone[178] for an account of this debate).

Let us note that the use of conditional likelihood coefficients is interesting only in the case of binary variables (we consider only A and $\bar{A}$, etc.). Otherwise, we directly use the conditional probabilities without resorting to the conditional independence relative to the negation of facts (concerning the terms $\text{Prob}(A \cap B \mid \bar{C})$).

N.B. Smets[170] has generalized Bayes theorem to belief functions, with a hypothesis of the conditional independence type. See also Wierzchon.[179]

2. Discussion about Knowledge Representation

Point 0. This approach is directly applicable to the case of acyclic rule networks; in our case we obtain the following network

The difficulty in treating this network with the Bayesian approach comes from the existence of directed cycles $x \leftrightarrow y$, and $z \leftrightarrow y$. Thus the only cases that may be treated correctly by the standard approach are

(1) $x \rightarrow y \rightarrow z$; (2) $x \leftarrow y \leftarrow z$; (3) $x \leftarrow y \rightarrow z$; (4) $x \rightarrow y \leftarrow z$.

Networks 1), 2), and 3) correspond to the conditional independence hypothesis of x and z in relation to y, evident on network 3):

$$\text{Prob}(z \wedge x \mid y) = \text{Prob}(z \mid y)\text{Prob}(x \mid y)$$

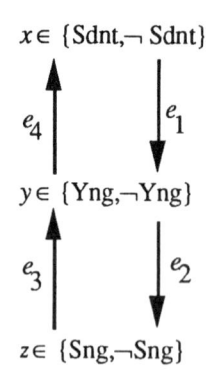

$x \in \{\text{Sdnt}, \neg \text{Sdnt}\}$

$e_4 \uparrow \qquad \downarrow e_1$

$y \in \{\text{Yng}, \neg \text{Yng}\}$

$e_3 \uparrow \qquad \downarrow e_2$

$z \in \{\text{Sng}, \neg \text{Sng}\}$

Figure 5. The network corresponding to a part of the test-example.

which is equivalent to $\text{Prob}(z \mid x \wedge y) = \text{Prob}(z \mid y)$ (network 1), and $\text{Prob}(x \mid z \wedge y) = \text{Prob}(x \mid y)$ (network 2). That means that if y is fixed, x and z are independent, for instance if a person is young, the fact of being a student has nothing to do with the fact of being single (a disputable hypothesis here, once again). In case (4), there is an implicit independence between x and z, $\text{Prob}(x \wedge z) = \text{Prob}(x) \cdot \text{Prob}(z)$.

These hypotheses (cf. Pearl[175]) are justified by affirming that if they did not hold we would have a network provided with another topology (for example, a direct link between x and z, given by the "expert." They allow to directly write the unique joint probability measure associated to the triple of binary variables (x, y, z), called probability function, that is

case (1) : $\quad$ Prob(x, y, z) = Prob$(z \mid y) \cdot$ Prob$(y \mid x) \cdot$ Prob(x)
case (2) : $\quad$ Prob(x, y, z) = Prob$(x \mid y) \cdot$ Prob$(y \mid z) \cdot$ Prob(z)
case (3) : $\quad$ Prob(x, y, z) = Prob$(x \mid y) \cdot$ Prob$(z \mid y) \cdot$ Prob(y)
case (4) : $\quad$ Prob(x, y, z) = Prob$(y \mid x) \cdot$ Prob$(y \mid z) \cdot$ Prob$(x) \cdot$ Prob(z).

Let us note that at least one *a priori* probability over one of the variables must be known. Once the joint probability function recovered (from the network), it is (theoretically) easy to answer any question, knowing (certain) facts relative to Léa, conditioning the joint probability function by these facts.

This approach has a very good performance when the graph associated to the knowledge base is a tree, or more generally when between any two nodes on the graph there exists only one path. When the graph is acyclic, we can come back to the preceding case by instantiating groups of variables in different ways and combining the corresponding results.[175] A more direct technique is proposed by Lauritzen and Spiegelhalter.[177] The absence of directed cycles is related to the causal interpretation of the network. If Prob$(A \mid B)$ measures the probability of B causing A, Prob$(B \mid A)$ will not be *a priori* specified, since A cannot cause B. Prob$(B \mid A)$ indeed evaluates to what extent A suggests B, and is more naturally a response of the model, not an input thereof. This causal interpretation is not present in our example. The existence of directed cycles, as in our example, makes the problem more tricky. The Bayesian approach actually consists of calculating Prob$(B \mid A)$ knowing Prob$(A \mid B)$, Prob$(A \mid \bar{B})$ and Prob(B). The existence of a cycle of length 2 comes down to *know* Prob$(A \mid B)$ and Prob$(B \mid A)$. If Prob(B) is also available there will be no degree of freedom left since

$$\text{Prob}(A \mid B)\text{Prob}(B) = \text{Prob}(B \mid A)\text{Prob}(A)$$

In this case, the numerical quantifiers approach (which does not forbid the use of *a priori* probabilities, viewed as further constraints) seems to be better adapted since it does not call for the conditional independence hypothesis nor for any causal interpretation. In that approach the use of *a priori* probabilities is facultative, while they are absolutely necessary in the Bayesian approach.

The essential part of works relative to the Bayesian approach concerns computation methods, and tries above all to find a way of decentralizing them without explicitly calculating the joint probability. See Lauritzen and Spiegelhalter[177] and Pearl[175] on this point. These works point out that Bayesian approach may be adapted to the modularity requirements of expert systems. But it does so at the price of an hypothesis that we may consider ill-adapted to the treatment of incomplete information in a nonnecessarily "causal" context.

The techniques using an uncertain knowledge representation based on belief functions,[120] and which combine the knowledge elements using Dempster rule (see Section VIII-B) generalize the local propagation methods developed by the Bayesian School. In particular, they also use network representation schemata (practically a particular type of hypergraphs called "Markov trees," e.g., Shafer et al.[180]), in order to express the knowledge base structure.

3. *Other Points of Discussion*

Bayesian approach shares many formal properties with the numerical quantifiers approach notably on points 2, 3, 4, 5, and 6, if we admit that Prob($B \mid A$) expresses a (causal) uncertain implication. However, it only furnishes particular answers bearing on the cases described with certainty (such as Yng(Léa), Sng(Léa),...). The unicity requirement of joint probability forbids any idea of multiple extension. Nevertheless this approach, when applicable, is very modular since new facts are easily integrated, showing a nonmonotonic behavior. For example, Prob(Sng(Léa) | Sdnt(Léa)) would be close to 1 if the fact Sdnt(Léa) was entered. The addition of Pnt(Léa) would lead to Prob(Sng(Léa) | Sdnt(Léa) ∧ Pnt(Léa)) close to 0. We can say that Bayesian approach supplies only default information likely to be modified later on. It is very well-adapted to an updating which changes the graph topology, due to its systematical rules for the construction of a joint probability. The revision process operates as long as the new piece of information remains partially coherent with the original knowledge. Otherwise, we cannot go any further. This approach is ill-adapted to the presence of cycles in the knowledge base since the causality notion is then absent and therefore does not allow preventing the presence of such cycles. Lastly, very efficient methods have been proposed for the treatment of queries.

B. Relational Approaches

Relational models make a distinction between a set m of manifestations which can be observed, and a set C of possible conclusions (causes). The "expert" knowledge is represented by means of a relation R defined over $C \times M$. By $(c,m) \in R$, we state that c is one of the possible causes of m, or more precisely, that m *may* occur (or *should* occur, according to certain authors) if cause c is present. Given a set of manifestations $M^+ \subseteq M$ observed in a given case, it is then a question of finding the possible causes of these manifestations (abductive reasoning). This is the approach proposed by Reggia and his colleagues,[181] who are more particularly interested in the minimal sets of causes that explain the set of observed manifestations. Reiter[182] discusses this model, in the framework of a logical formalization of diagnosis problems in the case of "should" relations. A similar relational model was previously developed, notably by Sanchez,[183] in the framework of fuzzy relations equations; the degree of association between cause and effect is encoded (in this case we estimate the certainty, rather than the possibility, that manifestation m occurs when cause c is present), as well as the intensity or the certainty of the presence of "observed" manifestations. The study of the solutions (when they do exist) of a fuzzy relation equation of the form $R \circ C^+ = M^+$, where C^+ represents an unknown (possibly fuzzy) set of causes, and $R \circ C^+$ the image of the fuzzy set C^+ by the fuzzy relation R, permits to determine

(i) the set of all causes whose manifestations coincide with or are included in

M^+

(ii) one or several smaller sets of causes (if they do exist) which explain all the manifestations of M^+.

We may complement the analysis[184] by considering

(iii) the set of causes that are *sufficient* individually to explain all the manifestations of M^+ (and possibly some other ones which would not have been observed yet)

(iv) the set of all the causes which explain at least a part of M^+.

The application of this type of approach to the example considered in the present work may seem artificial at first insofar as it does not deal with diagnosis problems strictly speaking. We may nevertheless consider as "manifestations" all the facts over which we are likely to have an information (in the example, "to be a student" and "to have children") and as possible "causes/diagnoses," those over which we may want to conclude (here, "to be single," or "to be married"). Let us consider, for instance, the graph of relation R depicted on Figure 6. Full lines indicate strong associations, dotted lines less strong ones, and the absence of lines weak or nonexisting associations. For example, the strong association "Student-Single," and the less strong association "Student-Married" indicate that students are more often single than married. Here the term "association" is used in a general sense since there does not exist a cause-effect relation in a link such as "Student-Single." From the graph above we will conclude that Léa is rather single than married, if all we know is that she is a student, and that she is rather married (or cohabitant) than single, if we know that she is a student and that she has a child; indeed in the latter case, considering Figure 6, the set $M^+ = \{Sdnt, Pnt\}$ is more compatible with Mrd (1 full line and 1 dotted line) than with Chbt (2 dotted lines), and more compatible with Chbt than with Sng (1 full line and no line at all). The intermediary term "Young" was not introduced in this (very) simplified model. In fact, the model requires that $M \cap C = \emptyset$; in more sophisticated systems however (Peng and Reggia[185]), it is possible to insert between M and C, sets whose elements will be linked by relations to the elements of M, and to those of C; this creates the possibility of "intermediary conclusions."

From the representation standpoint, this is an oriented approach, since M and C play different roles; if it is possible to express that students are single, on the other hand, it would not be possible to state that singles are students (if such were the case). There exists no simple way of representing a rule which presents a conjunction

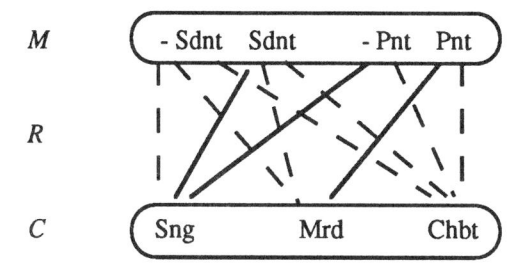

Figure 6. A tentative relational view of the test-example.

of elementary conditions such as, for instance, "Students who have children are married." The model allows the answering questions over a particular situation (described by M^+), but not general questions (even in the most sophisticated versions). The idea of looking for the minimal sets of causes to explain M^+, which permits the introduction of a kind of preference over several possible "extensions," may only be applied to problems where the C elements are not mutually exclusive (they are mutually exclusive in our example) and is not really interesting, except in the case of real diagnosis problems. The (very) limited representation capacity of this type of model is counter-balanced by its simplicity and, without any doubt, by its capacity of conveniently taking into account real diagnosis problems. It would be convenient, of course, to be able to distinguish more clearly between manifestations which are more or less certainly due to a given cause, and manifestations which may possibly accompany it.

XII. REASONING BY ANALOGY

Reasoning by analogy, in its most straightforward form, consists of inferring that what is true in a particular situation (or for a certain object) x_0 can (or should) still be so in another situation (or for another object) y_0 considered as similar to x_0 in other respects. This form of reasoning, simple in its principle, requires no knowledge of general laws which hold for all (or almost all) objects, but can generally lead to plausible conclusions only (i.e., which are not perfectly guaranteed). It takes an important place among commonsense reasoning techniques, as well as in scientific or artistic activity by allowing fruitful comparisons; see, for example.[186-187] Moreover, reasoning by analogy plays an important role among the learning processes and is employed to guide theorem proving. It will be considered here only from the viewpoint of our example.

The specificity of reasoning by analogy resides in the bringing together of two *particular* situations: it is inferred that a property will plausibly hold for object y_0, knowing that a similar property holds for object x_0, and, moreover, that objects x_0 and y_0 are similar from the point of view of a set of other properties. The conclusions have therefore no generality (Point 1). This may be pictured in the following way

$$\frac{P_1(x_0)/P'_1(y_0), \quad \ldots, \quad P_n(x_0)/P'_n(y_0)}{Q'(y_0)}$$
$$Q(x_0)$$

where P_i, and P'_i ($i = 1,\ldots,n$) are the elementary properties which are true for objects x_0 and y_0 respectively; properties P_i and P'_i are supposed to be identical or similar (in a more or less restrictive way according to the chosen approach) for all i; objects x_0 and y_0 are then said to be "analogous" (in the sense of properties P_i / P'_i). Moreover Q is a property which is true for x_0. Therefore reasoning by analogy consists of inferring that a property Q', identical or similar to Q, is satisfied by object y_0. In other words, $Q'(y_0)$ **must be to** $Q(x_0)$, **what the** $P'_i(y_0)$**'s are to** the $P_i(x_0)$'s. Mechanizations of reasoning by analogy have been proposed in Artificial Intelligence, notably in order to reproduce commonsense reasoning based on the comparison of situations[188] or for problem solving.[189] Reasoning by analogy goes beyond the usual framework of logics and, in fact, many criteria defined in the Introduction are meaningless here.

Reasoning by analogy does not directly apply to the example considered in this comparative study, since the available information is constituted in a good part of general laws such as "Students are young." We will thus suppose in the following that our knowledge is composed of a collection of examples referring to particular individuals. This type of knowledge, poorer than the general laws, is sometimes considered as a more natural form of "expertise," since more elementary. The following table sums up the available knowledge and substitutes to statements e_1–e_6. Table II indicates for each individual the properties that are true for him. The information contained in this table is coherent with statements e_1–e_6 in the sense that, for instance, all these students are young, and all young people, except Luc, are single. Learning mechanisms would permit the derivation of general laws such as e_1... e_6 from a greater amount of information of this type; see, for example.[190]

Knowing for instance that Wom(Léa), Sdnt(Léa), and Yng(Léa) what can be said of Léa's marital status? By analogy with Béa or Ida, we infer that Léa should be single. A question arises at this point. Which attributes should be considered in order to state that two cases are similar? If we disregard the professional status for instance, what is known of Léa's status is equally identical to Zoé's status, which again leads to the same conclusion. On the other hand, if sex is not taken into account, we will bring Léa closer to Béa, Ida, as well as to Léo or Luc; in the first three cases we infer by analogy that Léa is single, in the latter that she is cohabitant. Of course the similarities observed for different attributes are more or less relevant to the question. The fact that, according to a chosen analogy, we should be able to obtain different conclusions attests the brittleness of the conclusions obtained by this mode of reasoning. This resembles the possibility of existence of different extensions in different models of commonsense reasoning (Point 7). Once the attributes which are

Table II. Individual pieces of knowledge in relation with the test-example.

	Sex	Prof. Situa.	Age	Marital Situa.
Béa	Wom	Sdnt	Yng	Sng
Guy	Man	¬ Sdnt	¬Yng	Mrd
Ida	Wom	Sdnt	Yng	Sng
Léo	Man	Sdnt	Yng	Sng
Luc	Man	Sdnt	Yng	Chbt
Zoé	Wom	¬ Sdnt	Yng	Sng

used to establish the analogy are chosen we may, of course, regard the relative number of analogous situations which lead to a certain conclusion, as an evaluation of the plausibility of that conclusion. Therefore if sex is not considered, we will have in our example a plausibility of 3/4 that Léa is single. We may also only authorize the derivation of a conclusion if it is obtained no matter which is the analogous situation under consideration, i.e., if it there does not exist a known counter-example. Meanwhile the conclusions derived in both cases (numerical estimation of a plausibility or absence of a counter-example) could be questioned by the arrival of new pieces of information, that here means the description of new individuals' profile. In this sense reasoning by analogy is nonmonotonic (Point 4).

As emphasized by several authors (see, in particular, Bourrelly and Chouraqui[191]), we can trust reasoning by analogy all the more as the obtained conclusion is based on the existence of a dependency between the attributes used in the expression of the analogy and the attribute on which the conclusion bears. This is particularly true if the reasoning does not consider a large number of different examples, to which the situation that is enquired about might be similar. Thus, knowing that the weather in a given place is (largely) determined by its latitude and its situation with respect to the sea, we are able to conclude that the weather in Rome should be temperate, knowing that in Marseilles it is temperate (borrowing the example used by Bourrelly and Chouraqui[191]). In our student example, we may admit that the marital status depends (partially) on age, but that it does not have any relation to sex; in another context that might be not so.

In order to give a logical form to analogical reasoning it is necessary to postulate a dependency between the concerned attributes. This can be expressed by functional dependencies such as those employed in data bases (cf. Ullman[192] for example), i.e.,

$$\text{if } f_1(x) = f_1(y) \text{ and... and } f_n(x) = f_n(y) \text{ then } g(x) = g(y) \quad (1)$$

where $f_1, ..., f_n$, and g are functions (here, the attributes which apply to x and y). We express thus that if two objects have the same value for each attribute $f_1, ..., f_n$, then they have the same value for attribute g. Therefore, from (1) and $P_i(x_0)$, $P_i(y_0)$, for $i = 1, n$, $Q(x_0)$, where $P_i(x_0)$ is equivalent to $f_i(x_0) = a_i$, and Q is a property relative to the value of attribute g, it can be reasonably concluded that $Q(y_0)$ is true. Note that it is important to be able to establish for every i, $f_i(x) = f_i(y)$ (to do so, it is enough that the value of attribute f_i be precisely known for the considered objects), in order to be in a position to conclude. For instance, the functional dependency "if two cars are of the same trademark, type, and age, and have the same mileage, then they have the same price," will permit the determination of the price of a car from the price of a similar one, given that we are in a position to establish that the two cars are indeed similar (because the necessary information is available).

Davies and Russell[193] (see also Russell[194]) recently proposed a logical formalization of the reasoning by analogy, where beside dependencies of type (1), they can also express dependencies such as, for instance "knowing that x satisfies P_1, and knowing whether x satisfies P_2 or not, it can be concluded whether x satisfies Q or not." More generally, we may also express that if something is true for an object of a certain type, then it is true for all the objects of that type. The expression of such a dependency obviously permits us to conclude that an object of the concerned type satisfies Q (resp. $\neg Q$), from the moment that a similar object which satisfies Q (resp. $\neg Q$) is known.

Let us also mention the tentative approach by Polya,[16] who proposes the following inference scheme:

if	A and B are analogous	
and besides if	A is known to be true	(2)
then	B becomes more credible	

where A and B are propositions (this author does not believe however that the idea of analogy is completely definable in terms of classical logic).

Polya relates this inference scheme to the one that is, according to him, the basic scheme of the plausible reasoning of the abductive type (namely, given that A implies B, if B is true, A cannot become but more credible) by interpreting "A is analogous to B" as: there exists an implicant H common to A and B. The idea is that there exists a generalization H of propositions A and B, or in other words that A and B have a common foundation. Indeed,

if	H implies A	
since	A is true	
then	H is more credible	(plausible reasoning)
but	H implies B	
thus	B is also more credible	

(the credibility of A cannot increase less than that of H).

We can see that with another definition of analogy (even more disputable), namely that "A is analogous to B" if A and B have at least a common consequence C, we would still succeed in deriving (2) from the basic scheme of the plausible reasoning, and from modus ponens.

Without any doubt the implication, which underlies here the idea of analogy, does not correspond to material implication, since it would then suffice to let H be the contradiction (or C the tautology) to declare analogous any two propositions A and B. This shows the difficulty of a precise formalization of Polya's idea.

Polya's conception of analogy aims, in a certain way, to make more flexible the similarity required between the objects involved in the reasoning by analogy. In the preceding, similarity, often a simple identity, was evaluated in an all-or-nothing manner. Several authors (for example Coulon and David,[195] Farreny and Prade,[196] Stanfill and Waltz[197]) have introduced and, in different ways, used similarity degrees in reasoning by analogy, in order to weight the plausibility of the conclusions; more recently Collins and Michalski[198] have introduced similarity and dissimilarity degrees in the general framework they propose for plausible reasoning. In general, it is important to note that a weighted similarity may reflect two completely distinct ideas: it might be a question of estimating the proximity of two situations on which we possess precise information (the similarity is then closely related to the definition of distance), or else of evaluating the uncertainty over the identity of two situations for which we dispose solely of imprecise or vague information; of course these two points of view may be combined.

In fact, while it seems clear that there should exist a dependency between the concerned attributes so that reasoning by analogy leads to valuable conclusions, the dependencies formalized under the form (1) may seem to be too rigid. For instance, the climate of a region is not completely determined by its latitude, and its position with respect to the sea, even if they are very important factors, perhaps the most important ones. In our example, we may, for instance, make use of the following postulate, pervaded with uncertainty and imprecision: if two individuals are students, and are single or cohabitant, then it is almost certain that they are approximately of the same age. On the other hand it seems more risky to affirm that two young students, having approximately the same age are likely to have the same marital status. The latter rule would permit, however, the legitimation of both the conclusion that, Léa being a young student, she is likely to be single considering the status of Béa, Ida or Léo, and the conclusion that Léa is likely to be cohabitant if we relate to Luc's case. This dissonance between the conclusions is due to the fact that the table which constitutes our knowledge base is not coherent with the latter dependency rule. To avoid such an incoherence we could weaken the conclusion part of the dependency rule by a modality such as "possible." Reasoning by analogy would thus lead to less peremptory conclusions.

Imprecise or uncertain dependency rules may be expressed by

$$\text{if } R_1(f_1(x), f_1(y)) \text{ and} \ldots \text{ and } R_n(f_n(x), f_n(y)) \text{ then } S(g(x), g(y)) \qquad (3)$$

which generalizes (1). R_i and S can be fuzzy binary predicates corresponding to approximate and more or less flexible equalities. If we depart from the classical analogy schema, the R_i's may represent other forms of relations (for instance R_i is satisfied if $(f_i(x), f_i(y)) \in A^2$ where A is a subset of the domain of attribute f_i, or even R_i specifies a certain type of deviation between $f_i(x)$ and $f_i(y)$). Knowing the value of $g(x)$, and that the (more or less) possible values of the pair $(g(x), g(y))$ are restricted by the constraint expressed by the (fuzzy) predicate S, we can easily obtain the (fuzzy) subset restricting the (more or less) possible values of $g(y)$. The conclusion part of statement (3) permits us to express, for instance, that two second-hand cars of the same trademark (R_1), and of the same type (R_2), which have the same mileage approximately (R_3), and that are approximately of the same age (R_4), have close prices in general (S).

Given the pieces of information usually pervaded with imprecision and uncertainty, about the values of $f_1(x_0), f_1(y_0), \ldots, f_n(x_0), f_n(y_0), g(x_0)$, represented by the respective fuzzy sets $A_1(x_0), A_1(y_0), \ldots, A_n(x_0), A_n(y_0), B(x_0)$, we may then obtain the characteristic function of the fuzzy subset $B(y_0)$ which restricts the more or less possible values of $g(y_0)$, by

$$\mu_{B(y_0)} = \max(\mu_{S \circ B(x_0)}, 1 - \min_{i=1,n} N(R_i ; A_i(x_0) \times A_i(y_0))) \qquad (4)$$

where μ denotes the characteristic functions of the different fuzzy sets, and $S \circ B(x_0)$ the fuzzy set obtained by the composition of $B(x_0)$ with relation S, i.e.,

$$\mu_{S \circ B(x_0)}(t) = \sup_s \min(\mu_S(s,t), \mu_{B(x_0)}(s))$$

where s ranges in the domain of attribute g, and $N(R_i\,;\,A_i(x_0) \times A_i(y_0))$ denotes the necessity measure of fuzzy set R_i which represents, for instance, "to be similar to," knowing that the value of $(f_i(x_0), f_i(y_0))$ is restricted by the Cartesian product $A_i(x_0) \times A_i(y_0)$. This necessity (or certainty) degree is defined by

$$N(R_i\,;\,A_i(x_0) \times A_i(y_0)) = \inf_{u,v} \max(\mu_{R_i}(u,v), 1 - \min(\mu_{A_i(x_0)}(u), \mu_{A_i(y_0)}(v)))$$

where u and v cover the domain of attribute f_i; see (Dubois and Prade[123]) for justifications. Expression (4) asserts that the values outside $S \circ B(x_0)$ are only possible for $g(y_0)$, insofar as we are not completely sure that the condition part of (3) is perfectly satisfied (this certainty being estimated by $\min_{i=1,n} N(R_i\,;\,A_i(x_0) \times A_i(y_0))$). Formula (4) is in agreement with the following interpretation: "the more it is certain that the pair (x_0,y_0) satisfies the conditions of rule (3), the more it is certain that $S \circ B(x_0)$ effectively restricts the possible values of $g(y_0)$."

If instead of (3), we only have weaker rules of the kind "the more similar the values of attributes f_i, $i = 1,n$ for two items x and y, the more *possible* the (approximate) equality of $g(x)$ and $g(y)$," the relation (4) should be replaced by

$$\mu_{B(y_0)} = \min(\mu_{S \circ B(x_0)}, \min_{i=1,n} N(R_i\,;\,A_i(x_0) \times A_i(y_0))) \quad (5)$$

as suggested by Arrazola et al..[199] This means that the possibility that $g(y_0)$ is equal to a value t is bounded from above by the possibility that t is indeed a possible value for $g(x_0)$ and by the extent to which we are certain that the two items are similar according to the f_i's. The fuzzy set $B(y_0)$ obtained by (4) or by (5), depending on the kind of dependency rule we consider, is not necessarily the only set relative to possible values of attribute g for object y_0; this result may be combined with other conclusions obtained from other rules, or from considering other objects x for which we are also informed about the values of f_i and g. The way of combining partial conclusions will depend on the dependency rules: results given by (4) will be combined conjunctively (by a min opertion) while, the ones given by (5) will be combined disjunctively (by a max operation). Indeed here partial conclusions held as (somewhat) certain are to be understood as (flexible) constraints on the value of $g(y_0)$, such that *all* of which should be satisfied, while in case of partial conclusions held only as (somewhat) possible, nothing forbids a completely different conclusion to be also considered as possible, which explains why these conclusions are then combined disjunctively.[199]

Reasoning by analogy is based on the comparison of particular situations considered to be similar. Viewed in this way, it is conceptually simple, but it can only supply plausible solutions whose plausibility is often tricky to evaluate. The knowledge of dependency rules brings along a certain guarantee of rationality in the conclusions. But reasoning by analogy tends to lose its singularity as it gets closer to reasoning patterns which are valid in classical logic. In fact, these rules should be made flexible in certain cases in order to take into account the idea of similarity. Moreover, the conclusions derived from these rules will be, almost always incompletely certain, or even (more or less) possible only. Besides, when several reference examples are available from which analogical reasoning makes sense, we may still obtain notably different conclusions, insofar as the flexible dependency rules are liable to have exceptions, and that some among these examples do correspond to exceptions.

XIII. TRUTH-MAINTENANCE SYSTEMS

TMS (Truth-Maintenance System) and ATMS (Assumption-based Truth-Maintenance System) are systems concerned with the maintenance of coherence in a data base. TMS and ATMS are not primarily aimed at making inferences by themselves. Rather they record inferences transmitted to them by an external deduction system and they are in charge of the maintenance of the consistency of a set of assertions (here an assertion is an atomic formula without variable). They can handle nonclassical reasoning, since they allow for the management of assumptions, default values, and contradictions. TMS permits the expression of nonmonotonic expressions such as: "in the absence of P, deduce Q," and is well-adapted to default reasoning. ATMS permits us to explore different assumptions in parallel, and is better adapted to hypothetical reasoning.

A. TMS

1. Presentation

TMS[200] manages a set of assertions, also called the Base of Facts; it records the inferences that are transmitted to it by a deduction system in the form of pairs (assertion, justification); the contradictions detected by the deductive module are, in particular, transmitted to TMS in the form of pairs (CONTradiction, justification). TMS proceeds to calculate for each assertion a status satisfying the set of constraints described by the justifications. A justification may be seen as describing a reason to believe in the assertion.

A set of *justifications* is associated to each assertion i.e., a list (assertion, list of justifications) is made up. A justification for the assertion A is a set of assertions, called justifiers. A justification J is composed of IN-justifiers and OUT-justifiers. The elements of the Base of Facts are denoted by: (assertion, (list of justifications), status); a justification is denoted by: [St_1(assertion1), St_2(assertion2),..., St_k(assertionk)] with $St_i \in$ {IN,OUT}. From the assertion Bird(tweety) and the absence of the assertion Ostrich(tweety), it is possible to infer Flies(tweety); the justification of Flies(tweety) is [IN(Bird(tweety)), OUT(Ostrich(tweety))].

Consistent and well-founded assignment. Let L be an application, which to every assertion A associates a status IN or OUT. TMS looks for an assignment L ensuring a consistent and well-founded assignment. The status IN means "there exists at least one valid justification for the assertion, a reason to believe the assertion" and the status OUT "there exists no justification for the assertion." A *justification* is *valid* if its IN-justifiers are assertions having the status IN, and its OUT-justifiers are assertions having the status OUT. A justification may reduce to the empty set: then it is always valid. An assertion for which there exists an empty justification is called a *premise*. It has the status IN. An empty justification [∅] (in case of a premise) should not be mistaken for an empty list of justifications ( ): an assertion whose list of justifications is empty (it has no justification) has the status OUT. In the example, Sdnt(Léa) is a premise denoted by (Sdnt(Léa), ([∅]), IN); Rich(Léa) is an assertion without justification denoted by (Rich(Léa), ( ), OUT).

Assignment L is said to be *consistent* if and only if:

- for every assertion A in the Base of Facts, we have:
  $L(A)$ = IN if and only if there exists for A a valid justification; $L(A)$ = OUT otherwise.
- for every assertion CONT representing a contradiction, we have: L(CONT) = OUT (there exists no valid justification for this assertion).

An *assignment* is said to be *well-founded* if for every assertion there exists a chaining of valid justifications going back to premises, or to assertions with the status OUT. The notion of "well-founded" permits us to avoid having two assertions justifying each other. Thus if P is justified by ([IN(Q)]) and Q by ([IN(P)]) (if P then Q; if Q then P), the assignment $L(P)$ = IN, $L(Q)$ = IN is consistent but is not well-founded.

Representation of contradictions. The existence of a contradiction between two assertions P and Q is transmitted by the deductive module. A name is given to the contradiction, here ContraPQ. The contradiction is memorized in the TMS net in the form of two assertions:

- an assertion expressing the existence of the contradiction; it is an assertion of the type premise and has thus always the status IN:
  (ContraPQ, [(∅)])
- an assertion expressing the dependence links between the assertions participating in the contradiction:
  (CONT, [(IN(ContraPQ), IN(P), IN(Q))])

This assertion expresses that it is contradictory to have, at the same time, the existence of the contradiction ContraPQ, and P and Q justified. In a consistent assignment, the status of the assertion CONT should be OUT (see above).

Negation. Negation is not explicitly represented: P and $\neg P$ are represented by two distinct assertions P and not$P$; the deductive module can inform TMS of the existence of a contradiction between P and not$P$ as explained above: the two assertions cannot have the status IN at the same time. They may, however, both have the status OUT. Thus "Flies and notFlies are contradictory for tweety" is memorized in the net in the form of the two following assertions:

(Contraflies, [(∅)])
(CONT, [(IN(Contraflies), IN(Flies(tweety)), IN(notFlies(tweety)))]).

Representation of defaults. The inference "if A, and in the absence of information on B, deduce C" is transmitted to the TMS system in the form of the pair (assertion, justification): $(C, [IN(A), OUT(B)])$. In the following, such inferences will be called defaults. An assertion is called *hypothesis* if its valid justifications include OUT-justifiers. It is a default hypothesis. Upon the addition (or the withdrawal) of a justification to an assertion, the current assignment may become inconsistent; TMS undertakes to restore the consistency; for that it revises the status of the hypotheses; this is done by modifying the status of one of the OUT-justifiers of one of the hypotheses contributing to the contradiction. Let the Base of Facts be the following:

(Flies(tweety), ([IN(Bird(tweety)), OUT(Ostrich(tweety))]), IN)   *"hypothesis"*
(Bird(tweety), ([∅]), IN)   *"premise"*
(Ostrich(tweety), ( ), OUT)
(notFlies (tweety), ([∅]), IN)   *"premise"*

The assignment is consistent and well-founded.

Let us see the effects, on the assignment, of adding the piece of information "Flies and notFlies are contradictory for tweety." This is memorized in the form of two assertions:

(Contraflies, ([∅])) of status IN, since it is a premise
(CONT, [IN(Contraflies), IN(Flies(tweety)), IN(notFlies(tweety))]) whose status should be OUT in a consistent assignment.

The preceding assignment *is no longer consistent*; therefore it should be questioned. Flies(tweety) is a hypothesis since it is justified by the status OUT of Ostrich(tweety); to make the assignment consistent again, the status OUT of Ostrich(tweety) is forced into IN; then the status of Flies(tweety) becomes OUT and the assignment becomes consistent and well-founded. The justification of Ostrich(tweety) is composed of the assertions participating in the contradiction, here: IN(Bird(tweety)), IN(Contraflies), IN(notFlies(tweety)). The changing of status of one of the assertions is enough to "unjustify" the assertion Ostrich(tweety). This may be paraphrased as: knowing that tweety is a bird, which does not fly, and which cannot, at the same time, fly and not fly, it is justified to give up the hypothesis "tweety flies," considering that tweety is an Ostrich. The assignment obtained is again consistent and well-founded. See Figure 7.

(Flies(tweety), ([IN(Bird(tweety)), OUT(Ostrich(tweety))]), OUT)
(Bird(tweety), ([∅]), IN)   *"premise"*
(Ostrich(tweety), ([IN(Bird(tweety), IN(Contraflies), IN(notFlies(tweety))]), IN)
(notFlies(tweety), ([∅]), IN)   *"premise"*
(CONT,([IN(Flies(tweety)), IN(Contraflies), IN(notFlies(tweety))]),OUT)
   "contradiction"
(Contraflies, ([∅]), IN)

The management of the contradictions and their storage in the form of "nogoods," in order to avoid making choices already known as leading to contradictions,

REASONING UNDER INCOMPLETE INFORMATION 427

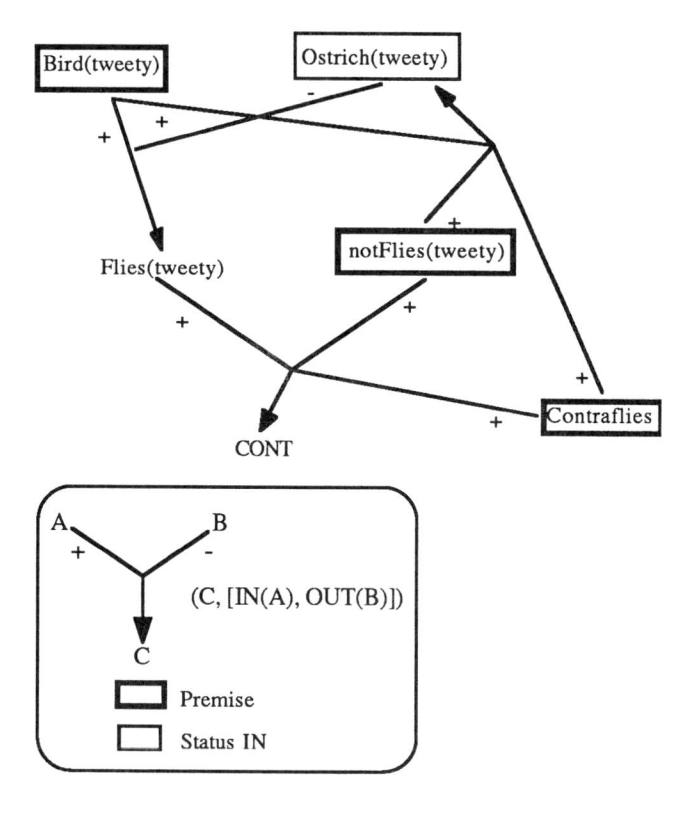

Figure 7. An example of consistent and well-founded assignment.

cannot be explained in detail here; see Doyle[200] or Charniak et al.[201] for a more detailed study.

Expression of normal defaults. The assertion "in the absence of information on P, deduce P" is expressible by $(P, [OUT(P)])$, but it is impossible to find a consistent assignment to it: this would come down to attempting to express that P is justifiable, if it is not justifiable. A normal default would rather be expressed by "in the absence of information on not$P$, deduce P."

Therefore, the default corresponding to statement 1 of our example, "students are young" may be expressed by:

$$\forall x \; Sdnt(x) \wedge OUT(notYng(x)) \rightarrow Yng(x)$$

If we apply this inference to Léa, we obtain the following pair (assertion, justification):

$$(Yng(Léa), [IN(Sdnt(Léa)), OUT(notYng(Léa))])$$

We note that the employed predicate notYng may be replaced by any other predicate representing the conditions of nonapplicability of the default:

$\forall x\ \text{Sdnt}(x) \wedge \text{OUT}(\text{ContinuingEducation}(x)) \wedge \text{OUT}(\text{Oldpeoplecourse}(x)) \rightarrow \text{Yng}(x)$

More generally, statement 1 may be expressed by:

$D1$: $\qquad \forall x\ \text{Sdnt}(x) \wedge \text{OUT}(ED1(x)) \rightarrow \text{Yng}(x)$
where $ED1$ represents the exceptions to statement $D1$.

TMS deals only with pairs (assertion, justification), which are transmitted to it by the deductive module; the language expressing the inferences is not specified by TMS; the translation of the statements below is given for information only
We may thus express the default statements of the test-example by:

$D1$: *"Students are young"*
$\qquad \forall x\ \text{Sdnt}(x) \wedge \text{OUT}(ED1(x)) \rightarrow \text{Yng}(x)$
$D2$: *"Young people are single"*
$\qquad \forall x\ \text{Yng}(x) \wedge \text{OUT}(ED2(x)) \rightarrow \text{Sng}(x)$
$D3$: *"Singles are young"*
$\qquad \forall x\ \text{Sng}(x) \wedge \text{OUT}(ED3(x)) \rightarrow \text{Yng}(x)$
$D5$: *"Students who have children are married"*
$\qquad \forall x\ \text{Sdnt}(x) \wedge \text{Pnt}(x) \wedge \text{OUT}(ED5(x)) \rightarrow \text{Mrd}(x)$

The inferences carried out by the deductive module are transmitted to TMS in the form of pairs (assertion, justification):

"Léa is a student" (Sdnt(Léa), [∅])
"$D1$ applies to Léa" (Yng(Léa), [IN(Sdnt(Léa)), OUT($ED1$(Léa))])
"$D2$ applies to Léa" (Sng(Léa), [IN(Yng(Léa)), OUT($ED2$(Léa))])
"$D3$ applies to Léa" (Yng(Léa), [IN(Sng(Léa)), OUT($ED3$(Léa))])
"$D5$ applies to Léa" (Mrd(Léa), [IN(Sdnt(Léa)), IN(Pnt(Léa)), OUT($ED5$(Léa))])
"Married and Single are contradictory"
$\qquad$(Contra1, [∅])
$\qquad$(CONTradiction, [IN(Mrd(Léa)), IN(Sng(Léa)), IN(Contra1)])

TMS calculates and proposes the following consistent and well-founded assignment:

L(Sdnt(Léa)) = IN; L(Yng(Léa)) = IN; L(Sng(Léa)) = IN; L(Contra1) = IN; L(Mrd(Léa)) = OUT; L(Pnt(Léa)) = OUT; L(ED1(Léa)) = OUT; L(ED2(Léa)) = OUT; L(ED5(Léa)) = OUT; L(CONT) = OUT. See Figure 8.

This assignment is the only possible one. We remark that, despite the existence of a cycle (due to $D2$ and $D3$), the assignment is well-founded: Yng(Léa) and Sng(Léa) are justified by Sdnt(Léa). If we further learn that "Léa has children," the (assertion, justification) pair: (Pnt(Léa), [∅]) is added; the status of Pnt(Léa) becomes IN, since Pnt(Léa) is a premise. TMS, when trying to assign the status IN to Mrd(Léa), detects a contradiction between Sng(Léa) and Mrd(Léa); it has the choice of questioning the status of $ED1$(Léa), that of $ED2$(Léa), or that of $ED5$(Léa). Three assignments are possible, corresponding to the following states of facts:

REASONING UNDER INCOMPLETE INFORMATION 429

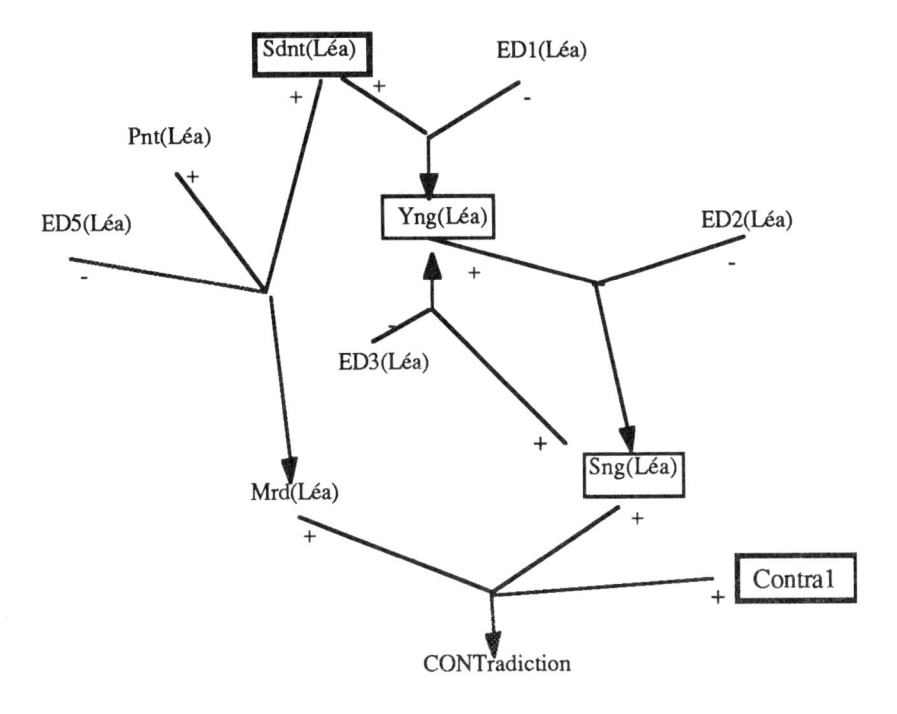

Figure 8. A consistent and well-founded assignment in the case of the test-example.

A1 : {Sdnt(Léa), Pnt(Léa), Mrd(Léa), *ED*1(Léa), Contra1},
A2 : {Sdnt(Léa), Pnt(Léa), Yng(Léa), Mrd(Léa), *ED*2(Léa), Contra1},
A3 : {Sdnt(Léa), Pnt(Léa), Yng(Léa), Sng(Léa), *ED*5(Léa), Contra1}

where *ED*1(Léa), *ED*2(Léa), and *ED*5(Léa) express that Léa is an exception to the default rules *D*1, *D*2, *D*5. Figure 9 corresponds to *A*2; the status of *ED*2(Léa) is forced to IN: in order to remove the contradiction, we have to suppose again that Léa is an exception to *D*2 "young people are single." We could also suppose that Léa is an exception to *D*1 "students are young" or to *D*5 "students who have children are married." The assignment proposed by TMS depends on the heuristics chosen.

Extension. Let us call extension the set of assertions to which TMS assigned the status IN. The three possible extensions for the preceding example are *A*1, *A*2, and *A*3. The extensions proposed by TMS correspond to the use of a maximal consistent set of defaults; extensions *A*1, *A*2, *A*3 correspond to the maximal noncontradictory sets of defaults {*D*2, *D*3, *D*5}, {*D*1, *D*3, *D*5}, {*D*1, *D*3, *D*2}. The set {*D*1, *D*2, *D*5} is contradictory.

TMS yields only *one* extension: the obtained extension depends on the heuristics chosen by the system, upon restoration of consistency, after the detection of contradictions (the order in which the inferences are transmitted also affects the result).

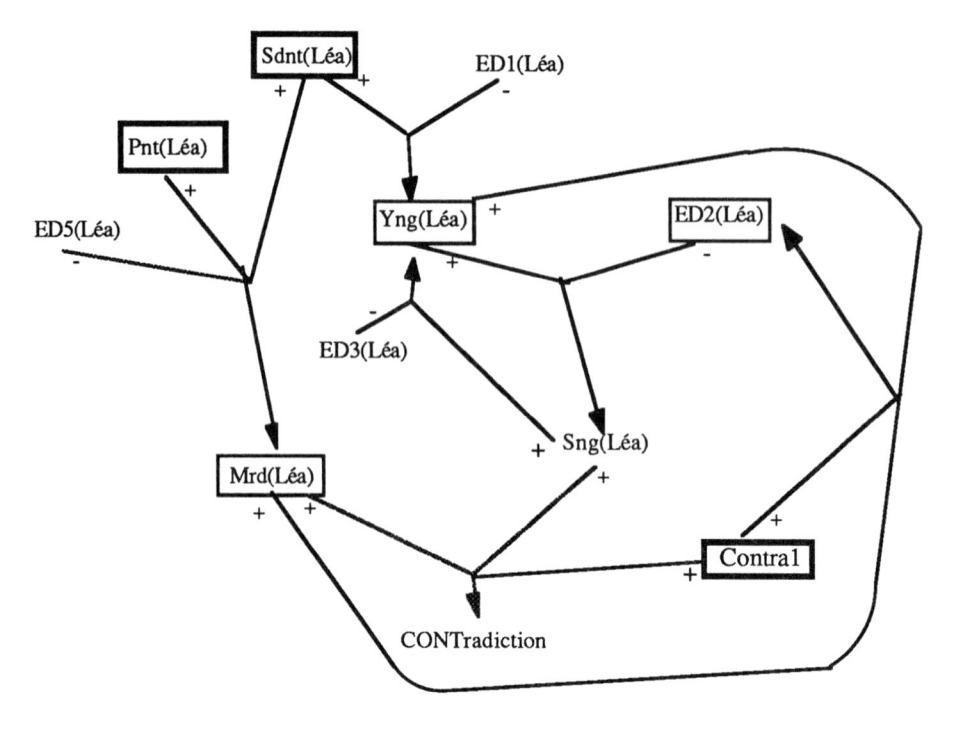

Figure 9. The assignment A2.

Expression of the disjunction. The material implication "all students who have children are married or cohabitants" may be expressed by the two defaults:

$D51$: $\quad \forall x\ \text{Sdnt}(x) \wedge \text{Pnt}(x) \wedge \text{OUT}(ED51(x)) \rightarrow \text{Mrd}(x)$
$D52$: $\quad \forall x\ \text{Sdnt}(x) \wedge \text{Pnt}(x) \wedge \text{OUT}(ED52(x)) \rightarrow \text{Chbt}(x)$

and the contradiction:

$$ED51(x) \wedge ED52(x) \rightarrow \text{CONTradiction}.$$

If Léa is a student and has children, we want to have Mrd(Léa) or Chbt(Léa); this is ensured by the contradiction: the exceptions to the defaults $D51$ and $D52$ may not have the status IN at the same time, and thus one of the two defaults will always be applicable. This represents a nonexclusive disjunction; in order to express the mutual exclusivity of the disjunction between Married and Cohabitant, it will be necessary to add the following contradiction: $\text{Mrd}(x) \wedge \text{Chbt}(x) \rightarrow \text{CONTradiction}$.

The assertion "students who have children are *generally* married or cohabitants" can be represented by the three defaults:

$D5$: $\quad \forall x\ \text{Sdnt}(x) \wedge \text{Pnt}(x) \wedge \text{OUT}(ED5(x)) \rightarrow \text{Mrd/Chbt}(x)$,
$D51$: $\quad \forall x\ \text{Mrd/Chbt}(x) \wedge \text{OUT}(ED51(x)) \rightarrow \text{Mrd}(x)$,
$D52$: $\quad \forall x\ \text{Mrd/Chbt}(x) \wedge \text{OUT}(ED52(x)) \rightarrow \text{Chbt}(x)$

the contradiction:

$$ED51(x) \wedge ED52(x) \rightarrow \text{CONTradiction}.$$

and $\quad\quad\quad\quad\quad$ Mrd(x) $\wedge$ Chbt(x) $\rightarrow$ CONTradiction to express the exclusion.

Remark: in case of nonexclusive disjunction, the proposed formula is a little too strong, since it contains the idea that, by default, the two terms of the disjunction shall be simultaneously true.

2. Comparison Criteria

Point 0: Representation issues – The pieces of information accepted by TMS are pairs (assertion, justification), where the assertions are instantiated atomic formulae; TMS permits the representation of inferences based on ignorance about the truth of an assertion by means of OUT-justifications, but does not propose, strictly speaking, a language to represent general statements with variables and quantifiers. The negation is not represented explicitly: this permits to acknowledge the difference between the absence of the justification of an assertion, and its negation; we may have no reason to believe P without having any reason to believe not$P$. This requires explicit addition of the contradiction $P \wedge$ not$P$ (and if needed the disjunction $P \vee$ not$P$). McAllester[202] proposes a truth-maintenance system employing a three-valued logic: each assertion may be true, false, or unknown (OUT). The negation is explicitly taken into account; on the other hand, it is impossible to justify P and not$P$ at the same time. The set of justifications is treated as a set of disjunctive propositional constraints.

Point 1: Generality / Particularity of the responses – TMS manages a set of assertions and proposes assignments only for the instanciated atomic formulae: it may only be used to answer questions concerning instanciated cases.

Points 2, 3, 4: Transitivity. Possibility of contraposition. Monotonicity – TMS only manages the inferences transmitted to it by the deductive module; it is not a logic, but a system for truth-maintenance. Strictly speaking there are no notions of implication and nonclassical inference. For this reason and for the one evoked in Point 1., questions 2, 3, and 4 are in fact meaningless.

Point 5: Taking disjunctive information into account – As it was previously seen on the example, disjunctive information may be expressed in the TMS formalism. The disjunction $A \vee B$ will be represented by the use of the predicate A/B, by the two defaults $D1$: OUT($ED1$) $\rightarrow A$, $D2$: OUT($ED2$) $\rightarrow B$, and the contradiction $ED1 \wedge ED2 \rightarrow$ CONT. If we add "generally A's are C's" and "generally B's are C's," all the extensions proposed by TMS will also contain C; TMS proposes only one extension and thus, for the same reason as above, nothing can be said about the validity of C.

Point 6: Quantifiers – Quantifiers like "most of," and "a part of" are not treated by TMS.

Point 7: Multiple extensions – TMS proposes only one extension; this extension depends on the heuristics used when questioning a hypothesis (in case of the detection of an inconsistency), as well as on the order in which the justifications are transmitted to it.

Point 8: Representation modularity – The representation language does not belong, strictly speaking, to TMS; it is thus difficult to treat this criterion.

Point 9: Effect of the updating – The possibility of updating is the essence of TMS, since its duty is to take into account, upon request, the pieces of information transmitted by the deductive module so as to analyze the effects of these pieces of information. This is done without recalculating the current assignment as a whole. The algorithm which calculates the assignment is based on the notion of data dependencies represented by the justifications; the algorithm provides for the addition but also for the suppression of a justification; the only necessary modifications are then carried out on the current assignment in order to restore its consistency; on the other hand, it is not possible to delete or to deny a premise. TMS should be considered as an efficient system permitting nonmonotonic reasoning, rather than as a system permitting belief revision (see Section XV).

Point 10: Complexity – Doyle[200] proposes an algorithm for the implementation of a system of the TMS type; the use of data dependencies[201,203] permits the handling of hypotheses and the management of the contradictions in an efficient manner. It employs the notion of "well-founded support" in order to improve performance: it does not recalculate the assignment at each updating step but is able to recognize when it tends to be no longer consistent and well-founded. TMS was employed for the implementation of nonmonotonic reasoning; Poole[50] uses TMS in this way in order to implement the default logic he proposes. The use of justifications in order to carry out an intelligent backtrack is found as early as in the EL system of (Stallman and Sussman[204]) (computer-based analysis of failures of electric circuits), which may be considered as one of the first "JTMS" or "Justification-based Truth Maintenance Systems." McAllester[202] proposed a system of the TMS type in which the assertions may take three truth-values: true, false or unknown; the justifications are expressed in the system in the form of disjunctions, and are seen as constraints which have to be satisfied.

The existence and the unicity of an extension are ensured when the justifications are monotonic (no OUT-justifier). It is no longer so in the presence of nonmonotonic justifications. A sufficient condition for the existence (respectively: the unicity) of an extension is the absence of odd (respectively: even) cycles in the justifications. While the algorithm of Doyle does not terminate in these pathological cases,[201] Goodwin[205] describes an algorithm that computes a well-founded assignment in polynomial time in many cases; it terminates by detecting odd loops or by giving an assignment. It can be proved that the class of TMS for which this algorithm terminates by providing a unique J-extension exactly corresponds to the class of effectively stratifiable logic programs, characterized by Bidoit and Froidevaux.[42] An effectively stratifiable logic program is a logic program that can be transformed into a stratifiable one (see Section II.B for the intuition underlying this notion), by means of elementary operations (analogous to Putnam-Davis transformations for sets of clauses), that preserve its default model semantics.

It is interesting to note that the translation of the example is done by resorting to supplementary abnormality predicates ($EDi(x)$); this use of supplementary predicates is very current and is found, in particular, in the form of abnormality predicates in (McCarthy[85]), and in the form of assertion predicates in Froidevaux[57] and Froidevaux and Kayser[56] or of the predicate APPL used by Brewka[206] in the framework of default logic; the naming of the defaults proposed by Poole[207] permits the expression of constraints between the defaults.

Morris[208,209] uses TMS in the treatment of the question raised by Hanks and McDermot,[210] relative to the expression of the "frame problem" (see Section XIV). The expression in default logics proposed by Hanks and McDermott[210] uses normal defaults. It leads to two extensions, one of which is contrary to our intuition. Morris shows that the expression of this problem using TMS, eliminates the intuitively noncorrect extension. He shows that the nonmonotonic justifications correspond to nonnormal defaults, and that the expression of the problem, with the help of nonnormal defaults, would also eliminate the undesirable extension. TMS permits, on the other hand, to take into account the addition of new pieces of information. Morris suggests thus that a variant to default logic is necessary in order to equip TMS with proper semantics. Also Brown and Shoham[211] and Inoué[212] are interested in the semantics of systems of the "JTMS" ("Justification-based Truth Maintenance Systems") type. A.L. Brown[213] proposes a multimodal logic called "logic of justified belief" which supplies a semantics to the different types of truth-maintenance systems. This connection can be exploited to set up an equivalence between a TMS and a logic program with negation in the premises. More precisely, if we translate the justifications of the form [IN(I), OUT(J)] → A (where $I = \{I_1, ..., I_n\}, J = \{J_1, ..., J_p\}$, $I_1, ..., I_n, J_1, ..., J_p$, A are propositions) of a TMS T into logic rules of the form $I_1 \wedge ... \wedge I_n \wedge \neg J_1 \wedge ... \wedge \neg J_p \to A$, we get a logic program Π_T such that M is a default model for Π_T iff the set of positive literals in M is a well-founded assignment for T.

There exists another way to establish a connection between default logic and TMS: this is through the correspondence introduced by Konolige between default logic and autoepistemic logic and a correspondence between autoepistemic logic and TMS.[214,215] These authors show that well-founded assignments of a TMS correspond to expansions of autoepistemic logic. The result is based on associating to an assertion A with its list $\{I_1, ..., I_n\}$ of IN-justifiers and its list $\{O_1, ..., O_m\}$ of out-justifiers the formula

$$\Box I_1 \wedge ... \wedge \Box I_n \wedge \neg \Box O_1 \wedge ... \wedge \neg \Box O_m \to A$$

of autoepistemic logic (the formulas $A, I_1, ..., I_n, O_1, ..., O_m$ are restricted to be atomic formulas). The precise versions (of assignments and expansions) involved in between TMS and autoepistemic logic are given in (Reinfrank, Dressler and Brewka[214] and Fujiwara and Honiden[215]).

B. ATMS

1. Presentation

ATMS (De Kleer[216-217-218]), as well as TMS, receives from a deductive module a set of pairs (assertion, justification). Whereas TMS calculates a status IN or OUT for each assertion, ATMS calculates, for each assertion, a label; this label represents the assumptions necessary and sufficient to validate an assertion. The first version of ATMS does not permit the use of OUT-justifications: it is more oriented towards hypothetical reasoning than towards reasoning by default: it is thus less-adapted to the proposed example.

A set of justifications, and a label are associated to an assertion. The elements of the Base of Facts are denoted by: (assertion, list of justifications, label). The *label* of an assertion A is a set of environments denoted by ($E1$, $E2$,..., Ep). An *environment* E is a set of basic assumptions denoted by [$H1$, $H2$,..., Hk]. A *basic assumption* H is an assertion specified as such by the user.

The deductive module may transmit pairs (contradiction, justification) to ATMS; the environments of a contradictory assertion are called *contradictory environments* or "no-good sets;" every superset of a contradictory environment is itself contradictory.

From a set of justifications, ATMS is responsible for calculating and updating the *label* of each assertion; it should be sound, complete, consistent, and minimal. The pairs (assertions, justifications) transmitted to ATMS by the deductive module correspond to (propositional) Horn clauses. Thus (Yng(Léa), [Sdnt(Léa)]) correspond to the clause $\neg$ Sdnt(Léa) $\vee$ Yng(Léa), and (CONT, [Mrd(Léa), Sng(Léa)]) to the negative clause $\neg$ Mrd(Léa) $\vee \neg$ Sng(Léa).

Let us call Σ the set of Horn clauses transmitted to ATMS. Let A be an assertion, with label $L(A)$: ($E1$, $E2$,..., Ep), with $Ei = (Hi1, Hi2,..., Hik)$. The label is said to be:

- sound if and only if $\forall Ei \in L(A)$, $\Sigma \vdash Hi1 \wedge Hi2 \wedge ... \wedge Hik \rightarrow A$.
- consistent if and only if $\forall Ei \in L(A)$, Ei is not contradictory.
- complete if and only if $\forall E'$ such that $\Sigma \vdash E' \rightarrow A$, $\exists Ei$ such that $Ei \subset E'$ and $Ei \in L(A)$.
- minimal if and only if there exits no $Ei \in L(A)$ and $Ej \in L(A)$ such that $Ej \subset Ei$.

An assertion having an empty justification is called a premise; its label reduces to an empty environment; it is denoted by ([∅]); this should not be confused with the assertion having an empty label denoted by ( ). An empty label may correspond to an assertion whose list of justifications is empty or to an assertion whose environments are all contradictory.

2. Treatment of the Example

The phrase "students are young" is expressed by:

$D1$: $\qquad \forall x \; \text{Sdnt}(x) \wedge D1(x) \rightarrow \text{Yng}(x)$

where $D1(a)$ is an assumption, meaning that the statement $D1$ applies to the individual a. The statements in the example may also be expressed by:

"Students are young" $\qquad \forall x \; \text{Sdnt}(x) \wedge D1(x) \rightarrow \text{Yng}(x)$
"Young people are single" $\qquad \forall x \; \text{Yng}(x) \wedge D2(x) \rightarrow \text{Sng}(x)$
"Singles are young" $\qquad \forall x \; \text{Sng}(x) \wedge D3(x) \rightarrow \text{Yng}(x)$
"Students who have children are married" $\forall x \; \text{Sdnt}(x) \wedge \text{Pnt}(x) \wedge D5(x) \rightarrow \text{Mrd}(x)$

ATMS only deals with pairs (assertion, justification) transmitted by the deductive module; the language for the expression of the inferences is not specified by ATMS; the translation of the above statements is given for information only. The inferences carried out by the deductive module are transmitted to ATMS in the form of pairs (assertion, justification):

"Léa is a student" (Sdnt(Léa), [∅])
"Léa has children" (Pnt(Léa), [∅])
"D1 applies to Léa" (Yng(Léa), [Sdnt(Léa), $D1$(Léa)]),
"D2 applies to Léa" (Sng(Léa), [Yng(Léa), $D2$(Léa)])
"D3 applies to Léa" (Yng(Léa), [Sng(Léa), $D3$(Léa)])
"D5 applies to Léa" (Mrd(Léa), [Sdnt(Léa), Pnt(Léa), $D5$(Léa)])
"Married and Single are contradictory"
 (CONTradiction, [Mrd(Léa), Sng(Léa)])

Once having the inferences done and transmitted to ATMS, the obtained labels are the following:

Sdnt(Léa) : ([∅]),
Pnt(Léa) : ([∅]),
Yng(Léa) : ([$D1$(Léa)]), obtained after the simplification of the label
 ([$D1$(Léa)], [$D1$(Léa), $D2$(Léa), $D3$(Léa)]),
Sng(Léa) : ([D1, D2]),
Mrd(Léa) : ([D5]).
CONT : ([D1, D2, D5]) [D1, D2, D5] is thus a contradictory environment.

The label of Yng(Léa) is calculated from its list of justifications: ([Sdnt(Léa), $D1$(Léa)], [Sng(Léa), $D3$(Léa)] obtained from statements 1 and 3. Let denote $D1$(Léa), $D2$(Léa), $D5$(Léa) by $D1$, $D2$, $D5$. The obtained label is ([$D1$], [$D1$, $D2$, $D3$]). But [$D1$] is "smaller" than [$D1$, $D2$, $D3$]. Due to the minimality property, the label is simplified into: ([$D1$]). If we add Sng(Léa) as a premise, the labels are recalculated and we obtain the following labels:

Sdnt(Léa) : ([∅]),
Pnt(Léa) : ([∅]),
Yng(Léa) : ([D1], [D3]),
Sng(Léa) : ([∅]),
Mrd(Léa) : ( ) obtained after the simplification of the label [D5].
CONT : ([D5])

[D5] is a new contradictory environment. But [D5] belongs to the environment of Mrd(Léa); due to the consistency property of the label, Mrd(Léa) is suppressed from the label which becomes empty.

Extension. ATMS calculates, for each assertion, all the noncontradictory and minimal environments that validates it. De Kleer calls *context* of a noncontradictory environment E the set of valid assertions in this environment, and thus having E, or a subset of E, in their label. Let us call extension the context of a maximal noncontradictory environment; in the preceding example, and before the addition of Sng(Léa), the maximal noncontradictory environments are [D1, D2, D3], [D1, D3, D5], and [D2, D3, D5]; they correspond to the three extensions: {Sdnt(Léa), Yng(Léa), Pnt(Léa), Sng(Léa)}, {Sdnt(Léa), Yng(Léa), Pnt(Léa), Mrd(Léa)}, and {Sdnt(Léa), Pnt(Léa), Mrd(Léa)}.

Expression of the disjunction. The disjunction expressed by "students who have children are either married or cohabitants" may be expressed by

$\forall x$ Sdnt$(x) \wedge$ Pnt$(x) \wedge D51(x) \rightarrow$ Mrd(x)
$\forall x$ Sdnt$(x) \wedge$ Pnt$(x) \wedge D52(x) \rightarrow$ Chbt(x)

but it is impossible to directly express that the environments containing neither $D51$, nor $D52$ are contradictory. This is due to the absence of OUT-justifications in ATMS.

3. Comparison Criteria

Point 0: Representation issues – The pieces of information accepted by ATMS are pairs (assertion, justification), where the assertions are instanciated atomic formulae; ATMS does not permit the representation of inferences based on ignorance about an assertion, but works on propositional assumptions specified as such to the system. As in TMS, negation is not explicitly represented.

Points 1, 2, 3, 4, 6. As TMS, ATMS is a truth-maintenance system, and the comments previously done for TMS also holds for ATMS on these four points.

Point 5: Taking disjunctive information into account – As seen in the example, disjunctive information may be expressed in the formalism of ATMS. The disjunction $A \vee B$ is expressed by two assumptions (or suppositions) HA and HB such that: $HA \rightarrow A$ and $HB \rightarrow B$. ATMS carries out a reasoning by case: the environments containing HA correspond to the cases where A is true, the environments containing *HB* correspond to those where *B* is true. On the other hand, due to the absence of the OUT-justification, it is not possible to express, in the basic formalism, that the environments containing neither *HA* nor *HB* are inconsistent. De Kleer[218] proposes, in order to overcome this drawback, the addition of the command "choose." Choose (*HA,HB*) directs the system to treat the environments containing neither *HA* nor *HB*, as inconsistent (or 'no-goods').

In presence of the statements "all the *A*'s are *B*'s," "all the *B*'s are *C*'s," the label of *C* is: ([*HA*], [*HB*]); it may be simplified to ([∅]), indicating thus that *C* is always true. In the presence of the statements: "generally the *A*'s are *C*'s" translated into: $A \wedge D1 \to C$, and "generally the *B*'s are *C*'s" translated into: $B \wedge D2 \to C$, the label of *C* is ([*HA,D1*], [*HB,D2*]), which cannot be simplified without supplementary information on *D*1 and *D*2.

Point 7: Multiple extensions – ATMS yields the set of environments validating an assertion; the extensions are not directly accessible, but may be calculated by considering the contexts corresponding to the maximal noncontradictory environments. De Kleer[218] discusses the usefulness of ATMS to represent defaults; he proposes the use of a control primitive "ignore(D1)"; it expresses a preference for the environments which do not contain the assumption D1.

Point 8: Modularity of the representation – The language of representation of the statements is not part of the ATMS system; it is thus difficult to speak about modularity.

Point 9: Effect of updating – The possibility of updating is the essence of ATMS: after each new justification transmitted by the deductive module, it updates, if needed, the labels of the assertions and ensures at every moment the properties of consistency, completeness, and minimality. The suppression of a justification is not, on the other hand, permitted in ATMS.

Point 10: Complexity – ATMS gave rise to implementations, in particular in the field of failure diagnosis (see, for example, De Kleer and Williams[219]). The efficiency is linked to the implementation of the union and intersection operations, and of tests of inclusion in the environments. De Kleer[217] proposes an implementation using Boolean tables. The approach of the ATMS type is close to the one proposed by Finger and Genesereth[220] and implemented in the system RESIDUE. Cayrol and Tayrac[221] propose a resolution strategy called CAT-correct and show how it may be used in order to implement an ATMS; they claim that the performance is significantly improved. Dressler[222] extends ATMS by permitting the use of nonmonotonic justifications. In Reinfranck et al.,[214] the so-called NM-ATMS-extensions are defined, and the existence of a one-to-one correspondence between these extensions and strongly grounded autoepistemic logic extensions (and hence default logic extensions under a suitable translation) is proved. The CAPRI system (Freitag and Reinfrank[223]) integrates the deductive module and the truth-maintenance system. Also CAPRI is capable of treating nonmonotonic justifications. It may be used either as a JTMS, based on justifications, or as a ATMS, based on assumptions.

Reiter and De Kleer[224] propose a formalization of the ATMS system. Let Σ the set of clauses transmitted to ATMS in the form of pairs (assertion, justification). We call support of a clause C every clause $S(C)$ such that we have $\Sigma \vdash S \vee C$ and that we do not have $\Sigma \vdash S$. To calculate the label of a unary clause α (reduced to a single literal) comes down to calculate the set of minimal supports of α: $\{S1, S2,..., Sn\}$. In ATMS, the supports are propositional clauses: the label of α is $(\neg S1, \neg S2,..., \neg Sn)$. A "prime implicant" * of Σ is defined as a clause PI such that:

– $\Sigma \vdash PI$
– for every proper subset PI' of PI, we do not have $\Sigma \vdash PI'$.

The label of an assertion α is then the set $\{E1, E2,..., Ep\}$, such that $\neg Ei \vee \alpha$ is a "prime implicant" of Σ. The problem comes thus down to calculate the set of "prime implicants" of a set Σ of propositional clauses. This formalization opens the way to a generalization of ATMS where Σ is not restricted to Horn clauses and the supports of the clauses are not propositional. Such a generalization is implemented in the inference engine SHERLOCK which calculates for a unary clause α, a set of hypothetical contexts CH such that $\Sigma \vdash \neg CH \vee \alpha$; the characteristics of this hypothetical contexts are specified in Cordier.[225,226] Inoué is also interested in hypothetical reasoning: in Inoué,[214] he compares the semantics of systems of the TMS or ATMS type; Inoué[227] reports on the APRICOT system, that captures hypothetical reasoning and is based on ATMS. Hypothetical reasoning is at the core of the works of Martins and Shapiro,[228] who describe the system MBR (or "Multiple Belief Revision"), whose aim is the representation and use of the beliefs of a set of agents. It differs from ATMS by a special implementation of inconsistent contexts, or "no-goods." Moreover, MBR is based on a logic described in Martins and Shapiro,[229] close to the logic of relevance. The formalization proposed by Reiter and De Kleer[224] shows, moreover, the strong links existing between ATMS and abductive reasoning. Cox and Pietrzycowski[230] employ a very similar formalization.

XIV. THEORIES OF ACTION AND THE FRAME PROBLEM

The temporal aspect of statements cannot be directly expressed in classical logic. At the language level, there exist no temporal operators. At the interpretation level, a structure is defined once and for all and cannot undergo any changes. In this section, we will consider certain problems associated with changes. We therefore propose to extend the example in order to illustrate these problems. Let us suppose that we want to represent the following facts and actions:

$e9$. Léa is pretty.
$e10$. Léa is single.

---

* "Prime implicant," the term used by De Kleer and Reiter, may seem to have been used in an improper way as PI is "implied" and not "implicant."

*e*11. Léa is enrolling at the university.
*e*12. Léa is living with someone at present, but I do not know if she is married.
*e*13. Léa is getting married.
*e*14. Léa has given birth to a child.
*e*15. Children live at the same place as their parents.

Unfortunately, describing the results of each of these actions does not suffice to describe the following state. One must also be able to derive the formulae which were true before the performance of the action and which remain true in the following state. For example, the color of an object does not change when the object is moved. When a person picks up an object from a table, the position of the table does not change, nor does the position of the other objects in the same room. It is not possible to derive that a formula remains true after the execution of an action, without using special axioms. But the problem is further complicated by the indirect changes caused by the performance of an action, which are generally not stated by the formula describing the results of the action (and cannot be), because they depend on the context in which the action is performed and are not true in all possible cases. For example, if someone pushes a bookcase around in a room, the bookcase and the books will move but not the other objects in the room.

The following problems associated with action performance can be identified [231-232]:

- the *qualification* problem, is concerned with the description of the results of action performance (see Ginsberg and Smith[233]),
- the *ramification* problem, is concerned with the possibility of deducing the indirect consequences of action performance (see McDermott[232]),
- the *frame* problem (McCarthy and Hayes[234]), has been identified as the problem of determining what facts do not change when an action is performed.

If we want to "solve" the ramification problem, i.e., if we want to avoid explicitly formulating *all* the consequences (the indirect ones, in particular) of the performance of an action, we formulate the minimal consequences of that action and use general rules to derive the indirect consequences. But Hanks and McDermott[235] have shown that we may then obtain states resulting from the performance of an action, which intuitively do not correspond to states likely to have resulted from that action. The problem of *multiple extensions* does not depend on the logic used. We may formulate the frame axioms in other formalisms (nonmonotonic logic, default logic, etc) and we generally obtain multiple extensions.

It is clear that these problems are linked, very generally speaking, to default reasoning: if an action produces a result *R*, then all the other facts which are not in *R* or which do not follow from it, do not necessarily change.

The frame problem was identified very early on, in Artificial Intelligence studies,[234,236,237,238] but no satisfactory solution had been provided so far. It has attracted new interest after the controversies set up by Hanks and McDermott,[210] who proposed to represent an action execution problem by circumscription and default logic, which yields a number of multiple extensions, only one of which is desired, the others being false (see Brown,[239] Brown and Park,[240] Schwind,[241] Ginsberg and Smith,[233,242] Georgeff,[243] Lifschitz[244] and Morris[209]).

In this section we will present two formalisms which propose solutions to the frame problem. One is based on *temporal logic*, and the other on situational calculus and circumscription.

A. A Temporal Logic of Change

Schwind[241,245] has proposed a formalism for action representation based on a temporal/modal logic. The idea of the formalism is very simple: It consists of a set of general laws, which are always true and cannot change, and of a set of situations, each described by a formula, liable to change. A change of situation is caused by an action, which may take place if certain conditions are satisfied. If the action is executable, then there exists one (or possibly many) following states in which the results are true. Changes may be represented as an ordered set of classical structures, where a structure S' follows a structure S if S' is one of the results of the application of an action on S. It turns out that the concept of Kripke-type structures[246,247] characterizing modal logics can be used to represent such changes. We may imagine such structures in the form of a tree or, more generally, as a graph of classical structures.

The logic of change ZK[241] is an extension of classical logic at the language level involving the addition of the temporal operator + and the modal operator □. + is an operator which formulates what is going to be true in all the states that immediately follow a state. +A is true in a state s, if A is true in all the states s' which immediately follow s. ZK may be semantically characterized in terms of Kripke structures.

The structure of the states defined by + is generally not linear. A state may therefore have several following and preceding states. With ZK, it is possible to make deductions about the possible following and preceding states. Let us consider a state s where a cube c is on a table t, which is expressed by the formula $On(c,t)$. Then a possible state s' preceding s is such that a person p has held c in s', which is expressed by $Hold(p,c)$. s resulted from the performance of the action "p lays c on t." Another possible state s'' preceding s is such that c already lies on t and s was obtained from s'' through another action. □ is the modal operator "necessary." □ is employed to express the fact that a formula is logically true. Consequently, the possibility operator ◊, which is equivalent to ¬□¬, expresses consistency. We are now going to see that this permits us to formulate a frame axiom at the language level without using meta-concepts.

1. The Modelling of Actions and the Frame Problem

An action is represented by a pair of formulae (P,R), where P describes the preconditions and R describes the results of an action. Given a structure K, an action (P,R) may be executed in a state s of K, if the preconditions P are true in s. If an action is executable in a state s then there exists a following state s' where its results R are true. In the ZK framework, Schwind[241] has proposed the following frame axiom (refering to an action (P,R)):

$$(E) \quad P \wedge p \wedge \Diamond(p \wedge R \wedge w) \to \neg \vdash\neg (p \wedge R \wedge w),$$

where w is a conjunction of formulae which contains the general laws of the underlying world (physical laws, social laws, etc), and p is any formula. Given that p was true in a situation in which the action was executed, we want to know whether p is always true after the execution, or if p contradicts one of the results of the action and thus can no longer be true. The consistency of p and R under the general conditions described by w is expressed by $\Diamond(p \wedge R \wedge w)$. $\Diamond(p \wedge R \wedge w)$ is true if $\neg(p \wedge R \wedge w)$ cannot be derived in ZK. If p is consistent with R under w it must remain true in each state resulting from the execution of (P,R), which is described by $\neg \vdash\neg (p \wedge R \wedge w)$. In w, we may also formulate causal relationships which prevent, by the requirement $\Diamond(p \wedge R \wedge w)$, the transfer of certain formulae into a following state.

The frame problem is not restricted to a certain theory but is, on the contrary, very general for all the logical theories of change. Another representation would consist of explicitly "indexing" each predicate with a state, by adding to it a supplementary place to indicate the state. For example, $On(a,b,s)$ is true if a is on b at the instant s. In this formulation the ability to deduce $A[s']$, if $A[s]$ is true and if s' is a state following s (by $A[x]$ we denote formula A which has an occurrence of the term x), should also be provided. It is clear that any reasoning which leads to solving the frame problem will be a nonmonotonic reasoning: provided that p is not affected by the execution of the action, p remains true in a following state if it was true before. Axiom (E) directly employs a formula $\Diamond F$ which is itself true if $\neg F$ cannot be deduced.

A model of action is defined by:

(i) a Kripke structure K, (i.e., a graph of classical structures),
(ii) a set of formulae true in each structure of K (general laws),
(iii) a set of actions, where each action is a pair of formulae of first order logic (P,R), where P describes the preconditions and R describes the result of the action,
(iv) a set of nonlogical axiom of the following form:
 – for each action (P,R), $P \wedge p \wedge \Diamond(p \wedge R \wedge w) \to \neg \vdash\neg (p \wedge R \wedge w)$ is a nonlogical axiom,
 – for each formula F, for which we do not have $w \vdash \neg F$, $\Diamond(w \wedge F)$ is a nonlogical axiom.

The example. The axiom of state change (E) is used in the following manner. Given a model of actions with the general laws w, a formula A characterizing a state, and an action (P,R) to be executed, then every formula A_1 characterizing the resulting state is deduced in the following manner: the propositional variable p of the axiom of state change

$$P \wedge p \wedge \Diamond(p \wedge R \wedge w) \to \neg \vdash\neg (p \wedge R \wedge w)$$

is instantiated by the largest sub-formula A' of A (in relation to R and w), such that non $\vdash \neg(A' \wedge R \wedge w)$, $A_1 = A' \wedge R$. The concept of "largest sub-formula of F in relation to G" needs of course to be defined: F' is the largest sub-formula of F in relation to G if and only if: $F \to F'$, and for all F'' such that $F \to F''$, and $F'' \to F'$ we have $G \wedge F' \leftrightarrow G \wedge F''$.

Example 1. We take the example given in the introduction and add the phrases $e9$ to $e15$ to it. The general law is the translation of $e7$, therefore

$$w = \neg(\text{Mrd}(x) \wedge \text{Chbt}(x)) \wedge \neg(\text{Sng}(x) \wedge \text{Chbt}(x)) \wedge \neg(\text{Mrd}(x) \wedge \text{Sng}(x))$$

Actions $e11$, $e12$, $e13$ and $e14$ are represented by

$a11.$ (true, Sdnt(Léa))
$a12.$ (Sng(Léa),Mrd(Léa) $\vee$ Chbt(Léa))
$a13.$ (Sng(Léa) $\vee$ Chbt(Léa), Mrd(Léa))
$a14.$ (true, Pnt(Léa))

('true' means that there exists no precondition), which yields the following state change axioms:

$A11.$ true $\wedge\, p \wedge \Diamond(w \wedge p \wedge \text{Sdnt}(\text{Léa})) \to \neg \vdash \neg\, (w \wedge p \wedge \text{Sdnt}(\text{Léa}))$
$A12.$ Sng(Léa) $\wedge\, p \wedge \Diamond(w \wedge p \wedge (\text{Mrd}(\text{Léa}) \vee \text{Chbt}(\text{Léa}))) \to$
    $\neg \vdash \neg\, (w \wedge p \wedge (\text{Mrd}(\text{Léa}) \vee \text{Chbt}(\text{Léa})))$
$A13.$ (Sng(Léa) $\vee$ Chbt(Léa)) $\wedge\, p \wedge \Diamond(w \wedge p \wedge \text{Mrd}(\text{Léa})) \to$
    $\neg \vdash \neg\, (w \wedge p \wedge \text{Mrd}(\text{Léa}))$
$A14.$ true $\wedge\, p \wedge \Diamond(w \wedge p \wedge \text{Pnt}(\text{Léa})) \to \neg \vdash \neg\, (w \wedge p \wedge \text{Pnt}(\text{Léa}))$

Let us assume that an initial state, characterized by $e9$ and $e10$, can be represented by the formula

$$C_1 = \text{Pty}(\text{Léa}) \wedge \text{Sng}(\text{Léa})$$

Let us apply action $a11$. We want to derive that if this action took place in state $s1$, represented by C_1, then there exists a result in a state characterized by a formula C_2 where the result of $a11$ is true:

$$C_1 \wedge w \to \neg \vdash \neg\, (C_2 \wedge w)$$

The deduction makes use of axiom $A11$ where p is instantiated with C_1 (true $\wedge\, q \leftrightarrow q$):

(1) Pty(Léa) $\wedge$ Sng(Léa) $\wedge\ \Diamond(w \wedge \text{Pty}(\text{Léa}) \wedge \text{Sng}(\text{Léa}) \wedge \text{Sdnt}(\text{Léa})) \to$
    $\neg \vdash \neg\, (w \wedge \text{Pty}(\text{Léa}) \wedge \text{Sng}(\text{Léa}) \wedge \text{Sdnt}(\text{Léa}))$

But we do not have: $\vdash \neg\, (w \wedge \text{Pty}(\text{Léa}) \wedge \text{Sng}(\text{Léa}) \wedge \text{Sdnt}(\text{Léa}))$.

(2) ◊(w ∧ Pty(Léa) ∧ Sng(Léa) ∧ Sdnt(Léa)) is thus a nonlogical axiom.
(3) Pty(Léa) ∧ Sng(Léa) → ¬⊢¬ (w ∧ Pty(Léa) ∧ Sng(Léa) ∧ Sdnt(Léa)) from (1) and (2).

The new state is therefore characterized by C_2 = Pty(Léa) ∧ Sng(Léa) ∧ Sdnt(Léa). The axiom of state change has thus permitted us to deduce that Léa is always pretty and single after her enrolment, but that now she is a student in addition. The result of that action was not contradictory with the state in which the action took place. Therefore, it is just purely and simply added to it. The largest sub-formula of C_1 consistent with w and Sdnt(Léa) is C_1. Let us now apply action a13 to state C_2. p in A13 is instantiated by C_2:

(4) (Sng(Léa) ∨ Chbt(Léa)) ∧ Pty(Léa) ∧ Sng(Léa) ∧ Sdnt(Léa) ∧
    ◊(w ∧ Pty(Léa) ∧ Sng(Léa) ∧ Sdnt(Léa) ∧ Mrd(Léa)) →
    ¬⊢¬ (w ∧ Pty(Léa) ∧ Sng(Léa) ∧ Sdnt(Léa) ∧ Mrd(Léa))

But we may deduce ⊢ ¬◊(w ∧ Pty(Léa) ∧ Sng(Léa) ∧ Sdnt(Léa) ∧ Mrd(Léa)) by necessitation of ⊢ ¬(w ∧ Pty(Léa) ∧ Sng(Léa) ∧ Sdnt(Léa) ∧ Mrd(Léa)). (4) is thus a tautology and nothing can be deduced therefrom. The largest sub-formula C' of C_2 such that w ∧ C' ∧ Mrd(Léa) is consistent, is Pty(Léa) ∧ Sdnt(Léa). With the instantiation of p by C', and using

(5) ◊(w ∧ Pty(Léa) ∧ Sdnt(Léa) ∧ Mrd(Léa)), we obtain
(6) C_2 ∧ w → ¬⊢¬ (w ∧ Pty(Léa) ∧ Sdnt(Léa) ∧ Mrd(Léa)).

In this example we were led to use axioms of the form ◊(w ∧ F). In a finite language it is possible to "generate" all these axioms. But for n propositional constants there exists a number to the order of 2^n of possibility axioms. It is out of the question, even in a domain as simple as the one described in our example, to consider manipulating all these axioms. But Lafon and Schwind[248] have demonstrated that it is not really necessary to use these axioms, and that we may obtain the states resulting from the execution of an action by using certain simple properties of a tableau-based theorem prover.[249]

2. The Deduction of the Resulting States by Means of a Tableau Prover

The prover based on semantic tableaus[250,251] proves a formula F by deducing a contradiction of ¬F. For ¬F a set of sets of formulae is built by applying a series of operations to ¬F. We may consider the prover as an application TP that makes a set of formulae correspond to a set of sets of literals called a tableau. For example, if a set in a tableau contains ¬(p ∨ q), this formula is replaced by the two formulae ¬p and ¬q. If a set contains p ∨ q, the set itself is replaced by two sets identical to the first one, but with p ∨ q replaced by p and q respectively. For example, TP({(a ∨ b) ∧ c}) = TP({a ∨ b, c}) = {{a,c},{b,c}}. A set is said to be closed if it contains a formula and its negation, a tableau is closed if each of its sets is closed. A formula F is a theorem, i.e., ⊢F, if and only if TP(¬F) is closed.

Let us note that $TP(F)$ corresponds to the disjunctive normal form of F where each of its elements correspond to the conjunction of its literals. Since $((A \wedge L \wedge \neg L) \vee B) \leftrightarrow B$ and $((A \wedge B) \vee A) \leftrightarrow A$, it is possible to eliminate from $TP(F)$ all the closed sets, and those containing another set of $TP(F)$. We call $TS(F)$ the image of F by TP after these simplifications. Let us equally note that $TP(\{F \wedge G\})$ is made up of all the unions of elements of $TP(\{F\})$ with the elements of $TP(\{G\})$:

$$TP(\{F \wedge G\}) = \{X \cup Y : X \in TP(\{F\}) \text{ and } Y \in TP(\{G\})\}$$

In the framework of the action model, we seek to deduce $A \wedge w \rightarrow \neg \vdash \neg (A' \wedge w \wedge R)$ if R is the result of the execution of an action (C,R). A' should be a subformula of A and if we want to solve the frame problem, i.e., if we want to keep the largest number of facts in the new state, we look for the maximal subformulae A' of A such that non $\vdash \neg (A' \wedge w \wedge R)$. But $\Diamond F$ is a nonlogical axiom if non $\vdash \neg F$, i.e., $TP(\{\neg \neg F\})$ is not closed. Let us then consider $TP(A \wedge R \wedge w)$. Then there exist two possible cases:

1st case: $TP(A \wedge R \wedge w)$ is not closed, then $\Diamond(A \wedge R \wedge w)$ by the definition of an action model, and the state resulting from the execution of the action is described by $A \wedge R$ (no conflict).

2nd case: $TP(A \wedge R \wedge w)$ is closed. The objective is to find the largest subformula of A, A' such that $TP(A' \wedge R \wedge w)$ is not closed. This can be achieved by "opening" the set $TP(\{A \wedge R \wedge w\})$ by eliminating the literals of A which are responsible for the contradictions (A is the only component of $A \wedge R \wedge w$, parts of which may be eliminated).

Example 2. We go on with example 1 by applying the action $a12$ to state C_1 and by reasoning in terms of the prover.

C_1 = Pty(Léa) $\wedge$ Sng(Léa)
$a12$. (Sng(Léa), Mrd(Léa) $\vee$ Chbt(Léa))

We therefore obtain

$TS(w) =$
  $\{\{\neg \text{Mrd(Léa)}, \neg \text{Chbt(Léa)}\}, \{\neg \text{Sng(Léa)}, \neg \text{Chbt(Léa)}\}, \{\neg \text{Mrd(Léa)}, \neg \text{Sng(Léa)}\}\}$
$TS(\{\text{Mrd(Léa)} \vee \text{Chbt(Léa)}\}) = \{\{\text{Mrd(Léa)}\}, \{\text{Chbt(Léa)}\}\}$
$TS(\{w \wedge (\text{Mrd(Léa)} \vee \text{Chbt(Léa)})\}) =$
  $\{\{\neg \text{Sng}(x), \neg \text{Chbt}(x), \text{Mrd(Léa)}\}, \{\neg \text{Mrd}(x), \neg \text{Sng}(x), \text{Chbt(Léa)}\}\}$
$TS(\{C_1\}) = \{\{\text{Pty(Léa)}, \text{Sng(Léa)}\}\}$
$TP(\{w \wedge (\text{Mrd(Léa)} \vee \text{Chbt(Léa)}) \wedge C_1\}) =$
  $\{\{\neg \text{Sng(Léa)}, \neg \text{Chbt(Léa)}, \text{Mrd(Léa)}, \text{Pty(Léa)}, \text{Sng(Léa)}\},$
  $\{\neg \text{Mrd(Léa)}, \neg \text{Sng(Léa)}, \text{Chbt(Léa)}, \text{Pty(Léa)}, \text{Sng(Léa)}\}\}$

This tableau is closed. There exists a possibility of opening it by eliminating Sng(Léa). The resulting state is then described by (Pty(Léa) $\wedge$ Mrd(Léa)) $\vee$ (Pty(Léa)

∧ Chbt(Léa)).

3. Multiple Extensions

Let us recall that, in order to deduce a formula A_1 characterizing a state resulting from the performance of an action (P,R) in a state A, the propositional variable p of the state change axiom

$$P \wedge p \wedge \Diamond(p \wedge R \wedge w) \rightarrow \neg \vdash \neg (p \wedge R \wedge w)$$

is instantiated by the largest subformula A' of A such that not $\vdash \neg(A' \wedge R \wedge w)$. And $A_1 = A' \wedge R$. But in general, there is more than one subformula which has this property. In terms of tables: $TP(\{A \wedge R \wedge w\})$ has more than one element, and thus there is more than one possibility of opening this tableau. And the following problems arise: which formula A' do we choose for the given action? How do we choose it? And are there possibly many plausible following states?

Example 3. Let us add the general law

$e16$. We cannot be student, married, and parent at the same time; which is translated by

$$f16.\ \neg\,(\mathrm{Mrd}(x) \wedge \mathrm{Pnt}(x) \wedge \mathrm{Sdnt}(x))$$

Let us consider

$$w1 = w \wedge f16$$

and let us apply the action $a14$ (true, Pnt(Léa))

$$p \wedge \Diamond(w \wedge p \wedge \mathrm{Pnt}(\mathrm{Léa})) \rightarrow \neg \vdash \neg (w \wedge p \wedge \mathrm{Pnt}(\mathrm{Léa}))$$

in the state described by

$$C3 = \mathrm{Pty}(\mathrm{Léa}) \wedge \mathrm{Sdnt}(\mathrm{Léa}) \wedge \mathrm{Mrd}(\mathrm{Léa}).$$

We then have

$TS(\{w1\}) = \{\{\neg\,\mathrm{Mrd}(\mathrm{Léa}), \neg\,\mathrm{Chbt}(\mathrm{Léa})\}, \{\neg\,\mathrm{Mrd}(\mathrm{Léa}), \neg\,\mathrm{Sng}(\mathrm{Léa})\}, \{\neg\,\mathrm{Sng}(\mathrm{Léa}),$
  $\neg\,\mathrm{Chbt}(\mathrm{Léa}), \neg\,\mathrm{Sdnt}(\mathrm{Léa})\}, \{\neg\,\mathrm{Sng}(\mathrm{Léa}), \neg\,\mathrm{Chbt}(\mathrm{Léa}), \neg\,\mathrm{Pnt}(\mathrm{Léa})\}\}$
$TS(\{w1 \wedge \mathrm{Pnt}(\mathrm{Léa})\}) = \{\{\neg\,\mathrm{Mrd}(\mathrm{Léa}), \neg\,\mathrm{Chbt}(\mathrm{Léa}), \mathrm{Pnt}(\mathrm{Léa})\}, \{\neg\,\mathrm{Mrd}(\mathrm{Léa}),$
  $\neg\,\mathrm{Sng}(\mathrm{Léa}), \mathrm{Pnt}(\mathrm{Léa})\}, \{\neg\,\mathrm{Sng}(\mathrm{Léa}), \neg\,\mathrm{Chbt}(\mathrm{Léa}), \neg\,\mathrm{Sdnt}(\mathrm{Léa}), \mathrm{Pnt}(\mathrm{Léa})\}\}$
  $= \{E1, E2, E3\}$
$TS(\{C3\}) = \{\{\mathrm{Pty}(\mathrm{Léa}), \mathrm{Sdnt}(\mathrm{Léa}), \mathrm{Mrd}(\mathrm{Léa})\}\} =_{df} \{E\}$
$TP(\{\{w1 \wedge \mathrm{Pnt}(\mathrm{Léa}) \wedge C3\}\}) = \{E1 \cup E, E2 \cup E, E3 \cup E\}$ which is closed.

The literals of E responsible for the contradiction are Mrd(Léa) in the first two sets, and Sdnt(Léa) in the third one. There are thus two possible ways of opening $TP(\{\{w1 \wedge Pnt(Léa) \wedge C3\}\})$. We eliminate either Mrd(Léa), or Sdnt(Léa). Given such a law, Léa has two possiblities: either she gets divorced or she abandons her studies.

The following example is that of an action which has two resulting states, one of which is absurd.

Example 4. Let us consider an instance of $e15$, Léo, Léa's son, lives in Marseilles if Léa lives there, he does not live in two different towns, and he lives either in Marseilles, or in Nice.

$$w2 = (Son(Léo,Léa) \wedge Lives(Léa,mars) \rightarrow Lives(Léo,mars)) \wedge$$
$$\neg (Lives(Léo,mars) \wedge Lives(Léo,nice)) \wedge$$
$$(Lives(Léo,mars) \vee Lives(Léo,nice))$$

Given the action "Léo moves to Nice": (true,Lives(Léo,nice)) and the initial state A_0 = Son(Léo,Léa) $\wedge$ Lives(Léa,mars), we obtain:

$TS(\{w\}) = \{\{Lives(Léo,mars), \neg Lives(Léo,nice)\},$
$\quad \{\neg Son(Léo,Léa), \neg Lives(Léo,mars),Lives(Léo,nice)\},$
$\quad \{\neg Lives(Léa,mars), \neg Lives(Léo,mars),Lives(Léo,nice)\}\}$
$TP(\{Lives(Léo,nice)\}) = \{\{Lives(Léo,nice)\}\}$
$TP(\{A_0\}) = TP(\{Son(Léo,Léa) \wedge Lives(Léa,mars)\}) = \{\{Son(Léo,Léa),$
$\quad Lives(Léa,mars)\}\}$

hence

$TS(\{w \wedge Lives(Léo,nice)\} = \{\{\neg Son(Léo,Léa), \neg Lives(Léo,mars), Lives(Léo,nice)\},$
$\quad \{\neg Lives(Léa,mars), \neg Lives(Léo,mars), Lives(Léo,nice)\}\}$
$TP(\{w \wedge Lives(Léo,nice) \wedge A_0\}) =$
$\quad \{\{\neg Son(Léo,Léa), \neg Lives(Léo,mars), Lives(Léo,nice),$
$Son(Léo,Léa), Lives(Léa,mars)\},$
$\quad \{\neg Lives(Léa,mars), \neg Lives(Léo,mars), Lives(Léo,nice), Son(Léo,Léa),$
$\quad Lives(Léa,mars)\}\}.$

$TP(\{w \wedge Lives(Léo,nice) \wedge A_0\})$ is closed. There are two possible ways of opening it, either by eliminating Son(Léo,Léa) in the first set, or by eliminating Lives(Léa,mars) in the second one. But the first resulting state is absurd, and only the second one is intuitively acceptable. Let us equally note that this example cannot be solved by specificity,[51] since the two predicates in question, Son(Léo,Léa), and Lives(Léa,mars) are symmetrical in w. Obviously, the problem of multiple resulting states (multiple extensions) is a nonlogical problem and cannot be solved, generally speaking, by logical means. In Example 3, we may equally realize that one of the resulting states is absurd, but it is not the general logical laws that tell us so.

4. The Comparison Criteria

The logic of actions is based on classical logic and does not contain the nonclassical implication (Points 2, 3, 4, 5). We may answer a question of general order as in classical logic (Point 1). We do not address the problem of representing quantifiers expressing "most of," etc. (Point 6). It is possible to obtain several resulting states and, *at the logic level,* all the extensions are accepted (Point 7). The representation of the base is not modular since it is classical (Point 8). The formalism is capable of managing the elimination and addition of information (Point 9). The use of a tableau prover supplies it with a simple means of treating questions. A state can always be obtained as a set of sets of literals, $TS(\{w \wedge A_i\})$. Each question Q is transformed by TS into a tableau $TS(\{Q\})$. Answering a question amounts to calculating $TP(\{w \wedge A_i \wedge Q\})$ by performing the union of sets (Point 10). With any given example, there always exist several possible translations. For example, we may eliminate the general rules in order to add new pieces of information to each state.

B. A Theory of Action Based on Circumscription

Lifschitz[244] proposes to formalize theories of action in the situational calculus framework.[234] Given that an action has a precondition and a result, he proposes the following formalization:

The language developed comprehends the following variable types: truth values v, actions a, situations s, and truth-valued facts f. In order to describe a theory of action, he employs the three following predicates:

Holds(f,s) is true if the fact f is true in the situation s.
Causes(a,f,v) is true if the action "a" has led the fact f to take the truth value v.
Precond(f,a) is true if the fact f is a precondition for the execution of the action a.
The axioms of each theory of action then include:
    (a1) (Success(a,s) $\wedge$ Causes(a,f,v)) $\rightarrow$ (Holds(f, result(a,s)) $\leftrightarrow v$ = true)
    (a2) $\neg$ Affects(a,f,s) $\rightarrow$ (Holds(f, result(a,s)) $\leftrightarrow$ Holds(f,s)),

where Success and Affects are defined predicates:

$$\text{Success}(a,s) \leftrightarrow \forall f(\text{Precond}(f,a) \rightarrow \text{Holds}(f,s))$$
$$\text{Affects}(a,f,s) \leftrightarrow \text{Success}(a,s) \wedge \exists v \, \text{Causes}(a,f,v).$$

(a1) expresses the fact that if the action "a" has attributed to fact f the truth value v, and if a is successful (i.e., if all the preconditions of a are true in situation s), then f is true in the resulting situation, if and only if v is true. (a2) inversely expresses that the facts f which are not "affected" by the execution of an action a (either one of the preconditions of the action is not true, or the action has not led the fact f to take the truth value v) are true in the resulting situation, if and only if they are true in the situation where a may be executed. (a1) permits us thus to solve the qualification problem: if a fact f becomes true by the performance of an action a (Causes(a,f,v)) and if this action is executable in a situation s (Succes(a,s)), then f is true in the resulting situation. ($a2$) permits us to solve the frame problem: the facts which are not affected by the execution of an action in a situation s remain true in the resulting situation, if and only if they were true in s. Circumscription (see Section V) is used in the following manner: Causes and Precond are circumscribed while varying the remaining predicate Holds. It is clear that this should permit us to derive $\neg$ Causes(a,f,v) (and thus $\neg$ Affects(a,f,v)) if the theory does not contain the formula Causes(a,f,v), which is needed in ($a2$).

Example. Let us formulate a simplified example where Léa, pretty and single, gets married.

$L1$. Holds(Pty(Léa), s_o)
$L2$. Holds(Sng(Léa), s_o)
$L3$. Causes(wedding,Mrd(Léa),true)
$L4$. Causes(wedding,Sng(Léa),false)
$L5$. Precond(Sng(Léa), wedding)
$L6$. Success(wedding, s) $\leftrightarrow$ $\forall f$(Precond(f, wedding) $\rightarrow$ Holds(f,s))
$L7$. Affects(wedding, f, s) $\leftrightarrow$ Success(wedding, s) $\wedge$ $\exists v$ Causes(wedding, f, v)
$L8$. Success(wedding, s) $\wedge$ Causes(wedding, f, v) $\rightarrow$
$\quad$ (Holds(f, result(wedding, s)) $\leftrightarrow$ v = true)
$L9$. $\neg$ Affects(wedding, f, s) $\rightarrow$ (Holds(f, result(wedding, s)) $\leftrightarrow$ Holds(f,s))
$L10$. T(Φ_{Causes}, $\Phi_{Precond}$; φ_{Holds}) $\wedge$
$\quad$ ($\forall x_1 \forall y_1 \forall z_1$ $\Phi_{Causes}(x_1, y_1, z_1) \rightarrow$ Causes(x_1, y_1, z_1)) $\wedge$
$\quad$ ($\forall x_2, \forall y_2$ $\Phi_{Precond}(x_2, y_2) \rightarrow$ Precond(x_2, y_2)) $\rightarrow$
$\quad$ ($\forall x_1 \forall y_1 \forall z_1$ Causes(x_1, y_1, z_1) $\rightarrow \Phi_{Causes}(x_1, y_1, z_1)$) $\wedge$
$\quad$ ($\forall x_2 \forall y_2$ Precond(x_2, y_2) $\rightarrow \Phi_{Precond}(x_2, y_2)$)

$T(\Phi_{Causes}, \Phi_{Precond} ; \varphi_{Holds})$ is the set of the formulae $L1$ to $L9$ in which Causes, Precond and Holds are replaced by Φ_{Causes}, $\Phi_{Precond}$ and φ_{Holds} respectively.

Let us show how Pty(Léa) remains true in the resulting state of the action of getting married by deriving Holds(Pty(Léa),result(wedding,s_o)) from $L1$,... $L10$.

By replacing the parameters $\Phi_{Causes}(x_1, y_1, z_1)$, $\Phi_{Precond}(x_2,y_2)$ and φ_{Holds} in the following manner:

(1) $\Phi_{Causes}(x_1, y_1, z_1) \leftrightarrow x_1$ = wedding $\wedge [(y_1$ = Mrd(Léa) $\wedge z_1$ = true) $\vee$
$\quad (y_1$ = Sng(Léa) $\wedge z_1$ = false)]
(2) $\Phi_{Precond}(x_2,y_2) \leftrightarrow x_2$ = Sng(Léa) $\wedge y_2$ = wedding
(3) $\varphi_{Istrue}(x_3,y_3) \leftrightarrow [x_3$ = Sng(Léa) $\wedge \neg \exists s'$ y_3 = result(wedding, s')]
$\quad \vee [x_3$ = Mrd(Léa) $\wedge \exists s'$ y_3 = result(wedding, s')]

and by using result(wedding, s) $\neq s_o$, false $\neq$ true, and more generally, all the inequalities between different terms, we obtain

(4) $\forall z_1 \neg$ Causes(wedding,Pty(Léa), z_1)
(5) $\neg \exists z_1$ Causes(wedding, Pty(Léa), z_1) $\vee \neg$ Success(wedding, Pty(Léa))
   (from (4))
(6) $\neg$ Affects(wedding, Pty(Léa), z_1) (de (4) and $L7$)
(7) Holds(Pty(Léa),result(wedding, s)) $\leftrightarrow$ Holds(Pty(Léa), s)
   (from (6) and $L9$ by modus ponens)
(8) Holds(Pty(Léa), result(wedding, s_o)) (from (7) and $L1$)

This rather impressive formalization allows to derive less facts than the one based on ZK. Let us note that it is very restricted in comparison with what we are able to express. An action may have only preconditions and results which are constants (possibly a conjunction, since it is possible to introduce several predicates Precond(f,a)), but no formulae with greater complexity (for example $f1 \vee f2$). Lifschitz proposes an alternative formulation where the results of the execution of an action may be terms, but this does not enable us to express a complex formula. In our example, only the actions $e11$ and $e14$ may be expressed by the formalism proposed by Lifschitz.

On the other hand, the ramification problem has not been solved. In the framework of this theory, we cannot "destroy" or "introduce" facts indirectly caused by the performance of an action. It is thus necessary to explicitly describe all the changes caused by an action. If Léa gets married, just formulating that she is married after the performance of this action does not suffice, it is also necessary to formulate that she is no longer single.

The multiple extension problem is solved since the theory has only one minimal model in which Causes and Precond are interpreted as in any minimal model.

No particular result is known on an implementation. What has been said about circumscription also applies here.

The theory of action proposed by Lifschitz, as well as ZK, presupposes that only those actions which took place at a given moment, cause changes and that nothing else happens in the world at the same time. Lifschitz and Rabinov[252] present a modification of the theory of action which allows for events ("miracles") occurring simultaneously with the actions that are described: if the properties of a new situation are inconsistent with the results of the execution of an action, unknown events can occur.

XV. REVISION THEORY

The modification of beliefs is an essential activity for men as well as for evolutionary systems. Given a knowledge base, we may distinguish three types of modifications:

(1) The expansion, namely the introduction of new pieces of information in the base without modifying the already existing information; consequently, inconsistencies might be introduced.
(2) The revision: in this case the introduction of new pieces of information in the base entails the modification of already existing pieces of information, for

example, the inconsistent pieces of information.
(3) The contraction: in this case a piece of information is taken from the set of the pieces of information of the base.

Let CONS be a relation of consequence on the formulae of a language, here the language of the classical logic of predicates. As it was seen in Section II-C this relation of consequence has the following properties:

- $A \subseteq \text{CONS}(A)$
- $\text{CONS}(\text{CONS}(A)) \subseteq \text{CONS}(A)$
- if $A \subseteq B$ alors $\text{CONS}(A) \subseteq \text{CONS}(B)$, where A and B are sets of formulae.

A theory T is a set of formulae closed for the deduction operation. Thus for each set of formulae A, $C(A)$ is the theory where the axiomatic base is A. T/B is the theory where the axiomatic base is that of T union B.

If we consider the knowledge bases as theories, we have to define what we understand by "result theory," the theory issued from having A added to, or withdrawn from, theory T (denoted by $T + A$, and $T - A$, respectively).

In order to define the result theory, Alchourron et al.[253] propose the following postulates, where A now denotes a formula:

(1) Postulates for the introduction of pieces of information
$A \in T + A$
$T + A = T / A$ if $\neg A \notin T$
$T + A$ is consistent, if A is consistent
$T + A = T + B$ if $A \vdash B$ and $B \vdash A$
$T - A = T \cap (T + \neg A)$
$T + (A \wedge B) \subseteq (T + A) / B$
$(T + A) / B \subseteq T + (A \wedge B)$ if $\neg B \notin T + A$

(2) Postulates for the withdrawal of pieces of information
$T - A \subseteq T$
$T - A = T$, if $A \notin T$ i.e., A is not deducible from T
$A \notin T - A$, if A is not a theorem
$T - A = T - B$ if $A \vdash B$ and $B \vdash A$
$T \subseteq (T - A) / A$
$T + A = (T - \neg A) / A$
$(T - A) \cap (T - B) \subseteq T - (A \wedge B)$
$T - (A \wedge B) \subseteq T - A$, if $A \notin T - (A \wedge B)$

It should be noted that the possibility of modifying theories is not, generally speaking, taken into account by a large part of the formalisms studied here.

Let us suppose that we have the following set of formulae:

Sdnt(Léa)
(Sdnt(Léa) → Yng(Léa)), where the symbol → is the classical implication,

which defines an axiomatic base of theory T. Let us further suppose that we get to learn that Léa is no longer young, i.e., $\neg$ Yng(Léa). If we add $\neg$ Yng(Léa) to T we will have an inconsistent theory, thus the revision of T by $\neg$ Yng(Léa) will be an operation of a certain complexity since the revision of a theory by a consistent formula yields a new consistent theory. With this objective in mind, we will determine what would be [T "less" Yng(Léa)]: the maximal sets contained in T from which Yng(Léa) is not derivable. In particular, we will have a set containing Sdnt(Léa) and another one containing Sdnt(Léa) $\rightarrow$ Yng(Léa).

The problem, as for the default logics, is to choose "within" the set of these maximal sets.

A first definition could be:

$$T + \neg \text{Yng (Léa)} = \text{CONS}(\{\cap \; [T \; \text{"less"} \; \text{Yng(Léa)}]\} \cup \{\neg \text{Yng(Léa)}\})$$

but in this case we obtain here a theory formed of solely the consequences of $\neg$ Yng(Léa). Another possibility is to define a selection γ which chooses a set within the various maximal sets (and thus the different theories which they determine). Therefore:

$$T + \neg \text{Yng(Léa)} = \text{CONS}(\{\gamma \; [T \; \text{"less"} \; \text{Yng(Léa)}]\} \cup \{\neg \text{Yng(Léa)}\})$$

But the problem now is to provide pertinent criteria for the definition of γ, which is far from being simple.

Recently Gärdenfors and Makinson[254] proposed a method for the revision and the contraction of theories, more constructive than the one presented above, based on an ordering on the facts which should be modified.

They show that a revision method verifies the precedently given postulate, if and only if there exists an ordering relation (denoted $\leq$ from now on), called "epistemic entrenchment"; $A \leq B$ means "A is less entrenched than (or as entrenched as) B." This relation satisfies the following properties:

> if $A \leq B$ and $B \leq C$ then $A \leq C$
> if $A \vdash B$ then $A \leq B$
> For each A and B, $A \leq A \wedge B$, or $B \leq A \wedge B$
> if T is a consistent theory, $A \notin T$ if and only if $A \leq B$ for each B
> if $B \leq A$ for each B, then $\vdash A$

Moreover, this ordering relation determines the priority according to which the revision may be carried out. We question the less entrenched facts first. Thus if $A \leq B$ then the updating of A has a higher priority. It is remarkable that the properties imposed on the epistemic entrenchment relation should be equivalent to the properties which characterize the qualitative certainty relations, which have as the only numerical counterpart the necessity measures considered in Section VIII, i.e., all set function N such that $\forall A, B, A \leq B \Leftrightarrow N(A) \leq N(B)$ is a necessity measure; see Dubois and Prade.[255] It seems natural, in fact, to reconsider first the less certain facts; this is in accordance with the treatment of the partially inconsistent knowledge bases delineated in Section VIII.

On the other hand, it is very difficult to define a semantics for the above considered operations of selection. On the contrary, for the other formalisms studied here, the semantics were well-established; for example, for the conditional logics where we dispose, in particular, of completeness theorems. Consequently, we may ask ourselves if these two approaches can be linked together; a natural way of accomplishing it is defined by the following relation:

$$(A \Rightarrow B) \in T \quad \text{if and only if} \quad B \in (T + A)$$

which is generally called the Ramsay principle. Gärdenfors[256] and Segerberg[257] show that the Ramsay principle and the postulates of Alchourron et al.[253] are incompatible. In other words, the modification of theories approach is much richer than the conditional logic approach; on the other hand, certain interesting properties of the conditional logic approach cannot be obtained, at least not as simply, in the modification of theories approach. In a more recent paper by Moreau,[258] it has been shown that this incompatibility is due to an additional condition on knowledge sets, namely that adding a formula to a knowledge set yields a knowledge set. Upon dropping this condition, "interesting" models (nontrivial models) can be found which satisfy the postulates of Alchourron et al. for + and the Ramsey principle.

Lastly, Gärdenfors[256] has also considered postulates for expansion, contraction and revision of probability functions.

XVI. A TENTATIVE CONCLUSION

It seems pointless to think that a single formalism would be capable of representing the multiple forms of commonsense reasoning. The variety of the approaches proposed is probably directly related to the large number of problems raised by the various forms of reasoning, although this variety may be partly due to the existence of various schools of thinking which are traditionally distinguished by the way they deal with these questions: the approaches following the mainstream of logic generally define a language with a syntax, a semantics, and inference rules, whereas the probabilistic approaches (or those involving other numerical formalisms) favour rules which manipulate axiomatically founded certainty degrees and an interpretation of these degrees based on clear conventions. We have already emphasized that with classical logic certain aspects of human reasoning cannot be easily realized, such as the temporary character of conclusions, the absence of a strong transitivity of inferences, the presence of uncertainty and of quantifiers other than "all..." and "there exists...," and the possibility of supporting conflicting conclusions (materialized by the existence of multiple extensions).

Against this background, several formalisms have been independently proposed although some subscribe to rather similar streams of thought. This work has shown that these formalisms tackle somewhat disparate aspects of human reasoning: for example, default logic adequately translates the idea of exception, autoepistemic logic is well-adapted to reasoning about what a given individual believes, and numerical formalisms are convenient tools for expressing shades of meaning, whether it be the quantification of uncertainty or the representation of vague predicates. In fact, since the approaches considered here handle rather different aspects of reasoning, the example, on which the comparative study is based, highlights their importance in a very unfair way. In particular, the example offers little opportunity to develop a fuller exposition of the types of reasoning treated by the approaches studied in sections IX, and from XI to XV. Nevertheless, the example, although it may seem elementary and restricted, appeared to us to be representative of the type of "commonsense knowledge" which we intend in practice to be the contents of knowledge bases. It is clear that our purpose was not to envisage the treatment of the sentences composing the example as an exercise in automatic analysis of natural language. But we hoped to go beyond the static analysis of "the A's are B's", which consists of making two usual sets correspond (the set of the A's and the set of the B's), in order to investigate the reasoning models implicitly attached to this type of statement.

In this work, a certain number of criteria of a technical nature have been proposed for purposes of comparison. They have permitted us to analyze and compare the different systems, in terms of their inferential properties. And above all, we have been able to evaluate the extent to which these nonclassical logics deviate from classical logic. In order to discuss in a completely satisfactory manner, in light of these criteria, the differences between the various formalisms examined here, it would be necessary to distinguish between certain variants of these formalisms, variants which may very well not have the same properties. Table III summarizes the criteria used to compare those approaches for which the criteria are most relevant, including classical logic.

In one way or another, the nonclassical formalisms tolerate forms of conflict which would lead to an inconsistency in classical logic, destroying any inferential capacity. This contributes to the improvement of modularity of the systems employing these formalisms. Certain systems have abandoned typical properties of classical logic such as the transitivity of the implication connective, its contraposition property and the monotonicity of the inference, in order to cope with the presence of exceptions in pieces of knowledge used by commonsense reasoning. This is particularly the case with default logic, circumscription, supposition-based logic, and numerical quantifiers. But these logics, except for default logic, retain reasoning by cases for treating disjunctive information.

Some systems are much closer to classical logic: for instance, possibilistic logic, remains monotonic on consistent knowledge bases and simply adds certainty degrees to predicate calculus; a form of nonmonotonicity appears when conflicting pieces of uncertain information are present. Delgrande's logic abandons the transitivity of implication (though, not completely) and not the transitivity of inference. Other systems, which realize causality notions, belief revision, or knowledge evolution, are of a different nature, though they relate to the problems of commonsense reasoning.

From the comparative study carried out in this work two philosophies of reasoning in the presence of incomplete information seem to emerge. The first one recommends supplanting the missing pieces of information by making supplementary hypotheses about them, before launching an often classical inference process. This approach is typically found in the closed world assumption (all that is not explicitly asserted to be true is considered to be false), the completion of data bases as defined by Clark,[32] as well as the logics of Brown[75] and Levesque[72] (see Section IV-C). It also applies to circumscription (all that is not known to be

Table III. Comparison of various logics according to criteria used in the study.

	Classical logic	Default logic	Modal logics of Doyle-McDermott and Moore	Circumscription	Logic of suppositions	Conditional logic of Delgrande	Possibilistic logic	Numerical quantifier logic	Bayesian approach	TMS of Doyle	ATMS of De Kleer	Logic ZK of Action
Answers to general questions	YES	NO	NO*	YES	YES	NO	NO*	YES	NO	NO	NO	YES
Transitivity of the inference the specific implication (weak)	YES	NO*	NO*	NO*	NO*	YES	YES	YES	YES	/	/	/
Monotonicity of the inference the specific implication (weak)	YES	/	NO*	NO*	NO	YES	/	/	/	/	/	/
Monotonicity of the inference the specific implication (weak)	YES	NO	NO	NO	NO	NO	YES	YES	YES	/	/	NO
Contraposition	YES	/	YES	YES	YES	NO	YES	NO	NO	/	/	/
Disjunctive information	YES	v	v	YES	NO*	NO	YES	NO	NO	/	/	/
Disjunctive information	YES	v	YES	YES	YES	YES	YES	YES	YES	v	v	YES
Non-classical quantifiers	NO	NO	NO	NO	NO	NO	NO	YES	YES	NO	NO	NO
Multiple extensions	NO	YES	YES	NO	YES	NO	NO	YES	NO	NO	NO	YES
Existence of revision procedures	NO	NO	NO	NO	NO	NO	YES (if partial inconsistency)	NO	YES (if partial inconsistency)	YES (heuristic)	YES	YES

A V indicates that the answer depends on the variant considered (for more detail, see the corresponding chapters). An asterisk (*) attached to "NO" indicates that the corresponding property holds under a weak form, even if it does not hold strictly speaking ; the sign / indicates that the property is meaningless in relation to the considered logic.

abnormal is considered *a priori* to be normal) as well as supposition-based logic (we make the maximum number of suppositions *a priori*) Bayesian reasoning is also of this type since we define a single *a priori* probability distribution by means of the principles of insufficient reason or of maximum entropy.

The second philosophy tends to adapt the language and/or the inferential mechanism to the incomplete character of the data. This may be done by modifying the notion of implication as in modal logics, by using special inference rules as in default logic, by concluding that what we do not succeed in demonstrating is false (negation as failure), or again by directly expressing uncertainty as in numerical logics whether in terms of certainty levels, or with the help of intermediate quantifiers between the universal and the existential quantifiers. This second philosophy covers, nevertheless, two conceptions of the reasoning question, depending on whether we allow inconclusiveness in certain cases, or not. For example, the numerical logics deductively propagate the incomplete character of the data, which contrasts with negation by failure, as well as with default logic when a strategy of choice between the extensions is added, where it is then always possible to answer questions in a clearcut manner.

It is beyond the ambition of Léa Sombé to choose between these two philosophies and to specify the properties that an "ideal" logic should satisfy, in the sense of each philosophy (according to the eleven criteria studied here, for instance). It is nevertheless necessary to consider another dichotomy: should we attempt to remedy the incomplete character of the data (the choice between doing this before starting the inference process, or during the inference, is essentially a question of strategy), or on the contrary should we accept the data such as they are. The first point of view is oriented towards decision-making and supposes it may be possible to revise the conclusions later, whereas the second one only discriminates between what is undoubtedly certain and what remains indeterminate on the basis of the available information, leaving to other considerations the responsibility of solving ambiguity.

The set of formalisms presented here attempts to provide a representative sample of current research in Artificial Intelligence on commonsense reasoning under incomplete information. This research offers new methodological perspectives for developing applications in domains such as automated systems for diagnosis or monitoring, knowledge base management, and specification of new programming languages. Other types of commonsense reasoning have not been considered here, such as qualitative reasoning which deals with symbolic reasoning about the behavior of (physical) systems usually described in a numerical manner,[259] or in another direction, variable-depth reasoning[260] which simultaneously manipulates several levels of description of statements. Additionally, there exist other logical formalisms which may contribute to the modeling of commonsense reasoning, for example the logic of "relevance",[261,262] paraconsistent logic,[263,264] or even quantic logic.[265,266]

Since the treatment of uncertainty in production systems partly motivated subsequent research on nonclassical logics, one may legitimately ask what might be the possible benefits of these logics for the expert systems technology. It seems, for example, that the logics of uncertainty provide a natural framework for the rigorous use of certainty factors (for example, Dubois and Prade[26]) the manipulation of which would be handled by calculation rules in accordance with a clear semantics. Likewise, the defaults in the logic of Reiter are very close to production rules where the certainty factor is replaced by the justification; the problem of the choice among several extensions replaces that of the combination of certainty factors attached to conflicting conclusions.

Interestingly enough, bridges between various approaches have been recently discovered, e.g., Konolige[48] (relation between default and autoepistemic logic), Konolige[101] (relation between autoepistemic logic and circumscription), Reinfrank et al.,[214] Fujiwara and Honiden[215] (relation between truth-maintenance and autoepistemic logic), Bidoit and Froidevaux[38,39,41] (relation between default logic, circumscription and stratified logic programming), Reiter,[99] Moinard[98] (relation between circumscription and predicate completion), Gelfond et al.[100] (relation between circumscription and negation as a failure). Besides, the fact that these new formalisms turn out to be more complementary than currently viewed suggests the possibility of hybridization, i.e., to envisage an association of some of them in order to cover the various facets of commonsense reasoning. An elementary example of this kind of combination is possibilistic logic which in its simplest form (where only lower bounds of necessity degrees, and no possibility degrees, are attached to the formulas) remains close to classical logic while dealing with uncertainty; moreover fuzzy logic and possibilistic logic, although very different (the former is truth-functional while the latter is *not* compositional with respect to all the connectives), can be jointly used for the treatment of uncertain information and vague predicates in a unified framework.[267] One might reconcile default logic and numerical models (for example, Neufeld and Poole[268] propose a nonnumerical formalism based on the theory of probability, Froidevaux and Grossetête[269] develop a graded default theory using necessity degrees in the sense of possibilistic logic). We may also think of associating a truth-maintenance system or a knowledge revision system with a nonmonotonic logic, or with a logic of uncertainty (see D'Ambrosio,[270] Laskey and Lehner,[271] Provan,[272] Dubois et al.[273] for various proposals of ATMS with uncertainty management using support logic programming,[22] Shafer belief functions or possibilistic logic), among other possibilities. More generally, it would be interesting to link together the notions of nonmonotonicity and revision in the context of evolutive data. Although the sections concerning the frame problem and the revision theory seem to be weakly related to the other ones through our example, some informal relations between them can be observed. In a more formal setting, recently D. Makinson and P. Gärdenfors[274] have found connections between the logic of theory change (alias belief revision) and nonmonotonic logics, by translating Gärdenfors postulates for belief revision[256] into the language of the nonmonotonic entailment. On the semantical side, one can somehow put such a work in a correspondence with Bell's[275] conditional logic approach to the preferential models characterization[88,89,91] of nonmonotonic logics.

There is also no doubt that the general trend in nonclassical inference is likely to evolve in the future according toward –and that is the lesson of this work– a global methodology, that seeks to relate a mosaic of approaches (which have often mutually ignored each other in the past) in order to favor the emergence of a more unified paradigm of reasoning under incomplete information.

Léa Sombé is indebted to Henri Farreny and Hervé Gallaire for their pertinent remarks on a first draft of this text, to Laurent Trilling, Chairman of the "Inference and Control" project of the PRC–GRECO in Artificial Intelligence, for his constant encouragement, and more generally to the PRC–GRECO for its support. Thanks are due to Bob Mercer who kindly proofread several sections of the manuscript. Léa Sombé specially thanks Agathe Lorente for her care in the realization of the final manuscript.

References

1. D. McDermott, "A critique of pure reason," *Computational Intelligence*, 3, 151–160 (1987).
2. H.J. Levesque (Ed.), Featured Issue of *Computational Intelligence*, 3, 149–237 (1987).
3. M. McLeish (Ed.), Featured Issue of *Computational Intelligence*, 4, 57–142 (1988).
4. P. Cheeseman, "An inquiry into computer understanding," *Computational Intelligence*, 4, 58–66 (1988).
5. M. Minsky, "A framework for representing knowledge," MIT Artificial Intelligence, Memo n° 306, 1974. Revised version in *The Psychology of Computer Vision*, Winston P. (Ed.), McGraw-Hill, New York, 1975, pp. 211–280.
6. T. Winograd, "Frame representations and the declarative procedural controversy," In *Representation and Understanding*, D. Bobrow and A.M. Collins (Eds.), Studies in Cognitive Science Series, Academic Press, New York, 1975.
7. P. Hayes, "In defense of logic," *Proc. 5th Inter. Joint Conf. on Artificial Intelligence (IJCAI 77)*, Cambridge, MA, 1977, pp. 559–565.
8. R. Turner, *Logics for Artificial Intelligence*, Ellis Horwood, Chichester, UK, 1984.
9. P. Smets, E.H. Mamdani, D. Dubois, and H. Prade (Eds.), *Non-Standard Logics for Automated Reasoning*, Academic Press, New York, 1988.
10. F.M. Brown, "A comparison of the commonsense and fixed point theories of nonmonotonicity," *Proc. of the 5th Nat. Conf. on Artificial Intelligence (AAAI-86)*, Philadelphia, 1986, pp. 394-400.
11. R. Lyndon, *Notes on Logic*, Van Nostrand, Princeton, New Jersey, 1967.
12. B.G. Buchanan and E.H. Shortliffe, *Rule-Based Expert Systems – The MYCIN Experiments of the Stanford Heuristic Programming Project*, Addison-Wesley, Reading, MA, 1984.
13. J. Pearl, "Embracing causality in default reasoning," *Artificial Intelligence*, 3 5, 259–271 (1988).
14. R. Duda, J. Gaschnig, and P. Hart, "Model design in the PROSPECTOR consultant system for mineral exploration," In *Expert Systems in the Micro-Electronic Age*, D. Michie (Ed.), Edinburgh, Scotland, Edinburgh Univ. Press, 1981, pp. 153–167.
15. L. Friedman, "Extending plausible inference," *Proc. 7th Inter. Joint Conf. on Artificial Intelligence*, Vancouver, BC, 1981, pp. 487–495.
16. G. Polya, *Mathematics and Plausible Reasoning – II: Patterns of Plausible Inference*, Princeton University Press, NJ, 1954. 2nd revised and augmented edition, 1968.
17. D.E. Heckerman, "Probabilistic interpretations for MYCIN's certainty factors," In *Uncertainty in Artificial Intelligence*, L. Kanal and J. Lemmer (Eds.), North-Holland, Amsterdam, The Netherlands, 1986, pp. 167–196.
18. P. Hajek, "Combining functions for certainty factors in consulting systems," *Int. J. Man-Machine Studies*, 2 2 , 59–67 (1985).
19. E. Rich, "Default reasoning as likelihood reasoning," *Proc. of the 3rd Nat.*

Conf. on Artificial Intelligence (AAAI-83), Washington, DC, Aug. 22-26, 1983, pp. 348–351.

20. M.L. Ginsberg, "Non-monotonic reasoning using Dempster's rule," *Proc. of the 4th Nat. Conf. on Artificial Intelligence (AAAI-84)*, Austin, TX, Aug. 6-10, 1984, pp. 126–129.

21. G. Soula, B. Vialettes, J.L. San Marco, X. Thirion, and M. Roux, "PROTIS: a fuzzy expert system with medical applications," In *Fuzzy Logic in Knowledge Engineering*, H. Prade and C.V. Negoita (Eds.), Verlag TÜV Rheinland, Köln, FRG, 1986, pp. 295–310.

22. J.F. Baldwin, "Support logic programming," *Int. J. of Intelligent Systems*, 1, 73–104 (1986).

23. P.P. Bonissone, S. Gan, and D. Decker, "RUM: a layered architecture for reasoning with uncertainty," *Proc. of the 10th Inter. Joint Conf. on Artificial Intelligence (IJCAI-87)*, Milano, Italy, 1987, pp. 891–898.

24. H. Farreny, H. Prade, and E. Wyss, "Approximate reasoning in a rule-based expert system using possibility theory: a case study," *Proc. 10th World IFIP Cong.*, Dublin, Sept. 1-5, Information Processing'86 (H.J. Kugler, ed.), North-Holland, Amsterdam, The Netherlands, 1986, pp. 407-413.

25. L. Godo, R. López de Mántaras, R. Sierra, and A. Verdaguer, "Managing linguistically expressed uncertainty in MILORD – Application to medical diagnosis," *Proc. 7th Inter. Workshop on Expert Systems and their Applications*, Avignon, France, 1987, published by EC2, Nanterre, France, pp. 571–596.

26. D. Dubois and H. Prade, "Handling uncertainty in expert systems: pitfalls, difficulties, remedies," Tech. Report (L.S.I., Univ. P. Sabatier, Toulouse), n° 311. Also in *The Reliability of Expert Systems*, E. Hollnagel (Ed.), Ellis Horwood, Chichester, UK, 1989, pp. 64-118.

27. P.R. Cohen and M.R. Grinberg, "A theory of heuristic reasoning about uncertainty," *The AI Magazine*, 17–24 (1983).

28. J. Fox, "Three arguments for extending the framework of probability," In *Uncertainty in Artificial Intelligence*, L.N. Kanal and J.F. Lemmer (Eds.), North-Holland, Amsterdam, The Netherlands, 1986, pp. 447–458.

29. O. Gascuel, J. Charlet, and B. Mari, "Le système LEZARD: un travail expérimental sur le raisonnement incertain en médecine," *Proc. of the 5th Inter. Worhshop on Expert Systems and Their Applications*, Avignon, France, published by ADI, 1985, pp. 1203–1217.

30. J.G. Ganascia, "Raisonnement incertain ou incertitude sur le raisonnement," *Actes Conf. Cognitiva*, Paris, France, June 4-7, 1986, pp. 633–638.

31. P.R. Cohen, D. Day, J. De Lisio, M. Greenberg, R. Kjeldsen, D. Suthers, and P. Berman, "Management of uncertainty in medicine," *Int. J. Approximate Reasoning*, 1, 103–116 (1987).

32. K.L. Clark, "Negation as failure," In *Logic and Data Bases*, H. Gallaire and J. Minker (Eds.), New York, 1978, pp. 293–322.

33. J.C. Shepherdson, "Negation as failure: a comparison of Clark's completed data base and Reiter's closed world assumption," *J. of Logic Programming*, 1, 51–79 (1984).

34. J.W. Lloyd, *Foundations of Logic Programming*, 2nd edition, Springer-Verlag, New York, 1987.

35. R.K. Apt, H. Blair, and A. Walker, "Towards a theory of declarative knowledge," *Workhop on Foundations of Deductive Databases and Logic Programming*, 1986, pp. 546–628. (Also in Minker, 1988).[37]

36. T.C. Przymusinski, "On the semantics of stratified deductive databases," *Workshop on Foundations of Deductive Databases and Logic Programming*, 1986, pp. 433–443. Also in (Minker, 1988).[37]

37. J. Minker (Ed.), *Foundations of Deductive Databases and Logic Programming*, Morgan Kaufmann, Menlo Park, CA, 1988.

38. N. Bidoit and C. Froidevaux, "Minimalism subsumes default logic and circumscription in stratified logic programming," *Proc. of IEEE Conf. on Logic in Computer Science (LICS-87)*, Ithaca, NY, 1987, pp. 89–97.
39. N. Bidoit and C. Froidevaux, "General logical databases and programs: default logic semantics and stratification,"*Information and Computation*, to appear.
40. M. Gelfond and V. Lifschitz, "The stable model semantics for logic programming," *15th Inter. Conf. on Logic Programming*, 1988.
41. N. Bidoit and C. Froidevaux, "More on stratified default theories," *Proc. of Europ. Conf. on Artificial Intelligence (ECAI-88)*, München, Germany, 1988, pp. 492–494.
42. N. Bidoit and C. Froidevaux, "Negation by default and non-stratifiable logic programs," In *Theoretical Computer Science*, Special Issue on Research in Deductive Databases, to appear. Also in Tech. Report (L.R.I., Univ. Paris-Sud), n° 437, 1988.
43. D.M. Gabbay, "Theoretical foundations for non-monotonic reasoning in expert systems," In *Logics and Models of Concurrent Systems*, K.R. Apt (Ed.), Springer-Verlag, Berlin, 1985, pp. 439–457.
44. R. Reiter, "A logic for default reasoning," *Artificial Intelligence*, 13, 81–132 (1980).
45. W. Lukaszewicz, "Two results on default logic," *Proc. of Inter. Joint Conf. on Artificial Intelligence (IJCAI-85)*, Los Angeles, CA, 1985, pp. 459–461.
46. W. Lukaszewicz, "Considerations on default logic: an alternative approach," *Computational Intelligence*, 4, 1–16 (1988).
47. P. Besnard, *An Introduction to Default Logic*, Springer–Verlag, Berlin, 1989.
48. K. Konolige, "On the relation between default and autoepistemic logic," *Artificial Intelligence*, 35, 343–382 (1988). See also "Errata," *Artificial Intelligence*, 41, 115 (1989).
49. D. Touretzky, "Implicit ordering of defaults in inheritance systems," *Proc. of Amer. Assoc. for Artificial Intelligence Conf. (AAAI-84)*, 1984, pp. 322–325.
50. D. Poole, "On the comparison of theories; preferring the most specific explanation," *Proc. of the 9th Inter. Joint Conf. on Artificial Intelligence (IJCAI-85)*, Los Angeles, CA, 1985, pp. 144–147.
51. Y. Moinard, "Donner la préférence au défaut le plus spécifique," *Actes 6ème Congrés AFCET-INRIA Reconnaissances des Formes et Intelligence Artificielle*, Antibes, France, 1987, pp. 1123–1132.
52. D.W. Etherington, "Formalizing non-monotonic reasoning systems," *Artificial Intelligence*, 31, 41–85 (1987).
53. R. Reiter and G. Criscuolo, "On interacting defaults," *Proc. of Inter. Joint Conf. on Artificial Intelligence (IJCAI-81)*, Vancouver, BC, 1981, pp. 270–276.
54. D.W. Etherington and R. Reiter, "On inheritance hierarchies with exceptions," *Proc. of Amer. Assoc. for Artificial Intelligence Conf. (AAAI-83)*, Washington, DC, 1983, pp. 104–108.
55. D.W. Etherington, *Reasoning with Incomplete Information: Investigations of Non-Monotonic Reasoning*, Research Notes in Artificial Intelligence, Pitman, 1987.
56. C. Froidevaux and D. Kayser, "Inheritance in semantic networks and default logic," In *Non-Standard Logics for Automated Reasoning*, P. Smets, A. Mamdani, D. Dubois, and H. Prade (Eds.), Academic Press, London, UK, 1988, pp. 179–212.
57. C. Froidevaux, "Taxonomic default theory," *Proc. of Europ. Conf. on Artificial Intelligence (ECAI-86)*, Brighton, 1986, pp. 123–129.
58. P. Besnard, R. Quiniou, and P. Quinton, "A theorem prover for a decidable subset of default logic," *Proc. of the 3rd Amer. Assoc. for Artificial Intelligence Conf. (AAAI-83)*, Washington, D.C., 1983, pp. 27–30.
59. C.B. Schwind, "A tableaux-based theorem – prover for a decidable subset of default logic," To appear in *Proc. 10th Inter. Conf. on Automated Deduction*

(CADE-10), 1990.
60. D. McDermott and J. Doyle, "Non-monotonic logic I," *Artificial Intelligence*, **13**, 41–72 (1980).
61. M. Davis, "The mathematics of non-monotonic reasoning," *Artificial Intelligence*, **13**, 73–80 (1980).
62. D. McDermott, "Nonmonotonic logic II," *J. Assoc. for Comp. Mach.*, **29**, 33–57 (1982).
63. D.M. Gabbay, "Intuitionistic basis for non-monotonic logic," *Proc. 6th Conf. on Automated Deduction*. Lecture Notes in Computer Sciences, Vol. 38, Springer-Verlag, Berlin, 1982, pp. 260–273.
64. M.R.B. Clarke and D. Gabbay, "An intuitionistic basis for non-monotonic reasoning," In *Non-Standard Logics for Automated Reasoning*, P. Smets, E.H. Mamdani, D. Dubois, and H. Prade (Eds.), Academic Press, New York, 1988, pp. 163–178.
65. M.R.B. Clarke, "Intuitionistic non-monotonic reasoning – Further results," *Proc. 9th Europ. Conf. on Artificial Intelligence (ECAI 88)*, München, Germany, 1988, pp. 525–527.
66. R. Moore, "Semantical considerations on nonmonotonic logic," *Artificial Intelligence*, **25**, 75–94 (1985).
67. R. Moore, "Autoepistemic logic," In *Non-Standard Logics for Automated Reasoning*, P. Smets, E.H. Mamdani, D. Dubois, and H. Prade (Eds.), Academic Press, London, UK, 1988, pp. 105–136.
68. B.F. Chellas, *Modal Logic: an Introduction*, Cambridge University Press, Cambridge, MA, 1980.
69. I. Niemelä, "Decision procedure for autoepistemic logic," *Proc. 9th Conf. on Automated Deduction*, Argonne, IL, 1988. Lecture Notes in Computer Science, Vol. 310, Springer-Verlag, 676–684.
70. W. Marek and M. Truszczynski, "Relating autoepistemic and default logic," *Proc. of the 1st Inter. Conf. on Knowledge Representation*, Toronto, 1989, 276–288.
71. J.Y. Halpern and Y. Moses, "Toward a theory of knowledge and ignorance," In *Logic and Models of Concurrent Systems*, K. Apt (Ed.), Springer-Verlag, Berlin, 1985, pp. 459–476.
72. H.J. Levesque, "All I know: an abridged report," *Proc. 6th National Conf. on Artificial Intelligence (AAAI-87)*, Seattle, WA, 1987, pp. 426–431.
73. P. Bieber, "Aspects épistémiques des protocoles cryptographiques", Doctoral dissertation, Univ. P. Sabatier, Toulouse, 1989.
74. P. Bieber and L. Fariñas del Cerro, "A monotonic logic for non-monotonic reasoning", Report IRIT, Univ. P. Sabatier, Toulouse, France, 1989.
75. F.M. Brown, "A commonsense theory of non-monotonic reasoning," *Proc. 8th Conf. on Automated Deduction (CADE-8)*, Oxford. Lecture Notes in Computer Sciences, Vol. 230, Springer-Verlag, New York, 1986, pp. 209–228.
76. J.Y. Halpern and M.O. Rabin, "A logic to reason about likelihood," *Artificial Intelligence*, **32**, 379–405 (1987).
77. G.E. Hughes and M.J. Cresswell, *An Introduction to Modal Logic*, Methuen, London, UK, 1968.
78. D. Dubois, H. Prade, and C. Testemale, "In search of a modal system for possibility theory," *Proc. of the Europ. Conf. on Artificial Intelligence (ECAI-88)*, Münich, Germany, 1988, pp. 501–506.
79. A.M. Frisch and P. Haddawy, "Probability as a modal operator," *Proc. 4th Workshop on Uncertainty in Artificial Intelligence*, Univ. of Minnesota, MN, 1988, pp. 109–118.
80. R. Fagin and J.Y. Halpern, "Reasoning about knowledge and probability: preliminary report," *Proc. of the 2nd Conf. on Theoretical Aspects of Reasoning about Knowledge*, M.Y., Vardi (Ed.), Pacific Grove, CA, March 7-9, 1988, pp. 277–293.

81. E.H. Ruspini, "Epistemic logics, probability, and the calculus of evidence," *Proc. of the 10th Inter. Joint Conf. on Artificial Intelligence (IJCAI 87)*, Milan, Italy, August 23-28, 1987, pp. 924–931.

82. F. Bacchus, "Statistically founded degrees of belief," *Proc. of the 7th Biennial Conf. of the Canadian Society for Computational Studies of Intelligence (CSCSI'88)*, R. Goebel, Ed., Edmonton, Alberta, Canada, June 6–10, 1988, pp. 59–66.

83. R. Reiter, "On closed world databases," In *Logic and Databases*, H. Gallaire and J. Minker (Eds), Plenum Press, New York, 1978, pp. 55–76.

84. J. McCarthy, "Circumscription – A form of nonmonotonic reasoning," *Artificial Intelligence*, 1 3 , 27–39 (1980).

85. J. McCarthy, "Applications of circumscription to formalizing commonsense knowledge," *Artificial Intelligence*, 2 8 , 89–116 (1986).

86. D.W. Etherington, R. Mercer, and R. Reiter, "On the adequacy of predicate circumscription for closed-world assumption," *Computational Intelligence*, 1, 11–15 (1985).

87. Y. Moinard, "Contribution à l'étude de la circonscription," Thesis, Université de Rennes 1, France, 1988.

88. P. Besnard and P. Siegel, "The preferential models approach to non monotonic logics," In *Non-Standard Logics for Automated Reasoning*, P. Smets, A. Mamdani, D. Dubois, and H. Prade, (Eds.), Academic Press, London, 1988, pp. 137–161.

89. Y. Shoham, *Reasoning about Change*, MIT Press, Cambridge, UK, 1988. See also "A semantical approach to non-monotonic logic," *Proc. of the 10th Inter. Joint Conf. on Artificial Intelligence (IJCAI-87)*, Milano, Italy, 1987, pp. 388–392.

90. G. Bossu and P. Siegel, "Nonmonotonic reasoning and databases," *Proc. Workshop Logical Bases for Data Bases*, Toulouse, France, December 1982. In *Advances in Data Bases Theory*, H. Gallaire, J. Minker, and J.M. Nicolas (Eds.), Plenum Press, New York and London, 1984, pp. 239–284.

91. G. Bossu and P. Siegel, "Saturation, nonmonotonic reasoning and closed-world assumption," *Artificial Intelligence*, 2 5 , 227-260 (1985).

92. D. Perlis and J. Minker, "Completeness results for circumscription," *Artificial Intelligence*, 2 8 , 29–42 (1986).

93. P. Besnard, "The completeness problem for first order circumscription," *Proc. AISB Conf.*, Univ. of Sussex, April 17–21, 1989, pp. 71–78. See also "The importance of open and recursive circumscription" (with R. Mercer and Y. Moinard), *Artificial Intelligence*, 3 9 , 251–262 (1989).

94. P. Siegel, "Représentation et utilisation de la connaissance en calcul propositionnel," Thèse de Doctorat d'Etat en Informatique, Univ. d'Aix-Marseille II, France, Juillet 1987.

95. S. Jeannicot, L. Oxusoff, and A. Rauzy, "Evaluation sémantique : une propriété de coupure pour rendre efficace la procédure de Davis et Putnam," *Revue d'Intelligence Artificielle* (Hermès), 2, 41-60 (1988).

96. V. Lifschitz, "Closed-world databases and circumscription," *Artificial Intelligence*, 2 7 , 229–235 (1985).

97. D.W. Etherington, "Relating default logic and circumscription," *Proc. 10th Inter. Joint Conf. on Artificial Intelligence (IJCAI 87)*, Milano, Italy, 1987, pp. 489–494.

98. Y. Moinard, "Predicate completion is equivalent to pointwise circumscription (sometimes)," *Proc. Inter. Conf. on Logic Programming*, Seattle, WA, 1988, pp. 1097–1105.

99. R. Reiter, "Circumscription implies predicate completion (sometimes)," *Proc. National Conf. on Artificial Intelligence (AAAI-82)*, Pittsburgh, PA, 1982, pp. 418–420.

100. M. Gelfond, H. Przymusinska, and T. Przymusinski, "On the relationship

between circumscription and negation as failure," *Artificial Intelligence*, **38**, 75–94 (1989).

101. K. Konolige, "On the relation between autoepistemic and circumscription, (Preliminary Report)", *Proc. of the 11th Inter. Joint Conf. on Artificial Intelligence (IJCAI-89)*, Detroit, MI, 1989, pp. 1213-1218.

102. P. Besnard and P. Siegel, "A framework for logics of 'suppose' and 'admit'," *Europ. Workshop on Logical Methods in Artificial Intelligence (JELIA 88)*, Roscoff, France, June 1988, pp. 65–68 (available from LIUC, Univ. of Caen, France). See also "Supposition-based logic for automated nonmonotonic reasoning," *Proc. of the 9th Conf. on Automated Deduction*, Argonne, IL, May 1988, pp. 592–601.

103. P. Siegel, "A modal language for non-monotonic logic," *Workshop on Nonmonotonic Reasoning (Esprit Bas. Res. Action DRUMS : Defeasible Reasoning and Uncertainty Management Systems)*, Marseille, Feb. 24-28, 1990.

104. Z. Pawlak, "Rough sets," *Int. J. Comp. Inform. Scien.*, **6**, 205–218 (1981).

105. Z. Pawlak, "Rough classification," *Int. J. Man-Machine Studies*, **20**, 469–485 (1984).

106. R.F. Stalnaker, "A theory of conditionals," In *Studies in Logical Theory*, N. Rescher (Ed.), Basil Blackwell, Oxford, UK, 1968, pp. 98–112.

107. J.P. Delgrande, "A first-order conditional logic for prototypical properties," *Artificial Intelligence*, **33**, 105–130 (1986).

108. J.P. Delgrande, "An approach to default reasoning based on a first-order conditional logic: revised report," *Artificial Intelligence*, **36**, 63–91 (1988).

109. D. Nute, "Non-monotonic reasoning and conditionnals," ACMC Research Report (Univ. of Georgia) n° 01-0002, 1984.

110. D. Nute, "Defeasible reasoning and decision support systems," *Decision Support Systems*, **4**, 97–110 (1988).

111. E. Orlowska and Z. Pawlak, "Expressive power of knowledge representation systems," Institute of Computer Science, Polish Academy of Sciences, Warsaw, Report 432, 1981.

112. E. Orlowska and Z. Pawlak, "Representation of non-deterministic information," *Theoretical Computer Science*, **29**, 27-39 (1984).

113. L. Fariñas del Cerro and E. Orlowska, "DAL, a logic for data analysis," *Theoretical Computer Science*, **36**, 251–264 (1985).

114. J. Łoś, "Semantic representations of the probability of formulas in formalized theories," *Studia Logica*, **14**, 183–194 (1963).

115. J.E. Fenstad, "Representations of probabilities defined on first order languages," In *Sets, Models and Recursion Theory*, J.N. Crossley (Ed.), North-Holland, Amsterdam, The Netherland, 1967, pp. 156–172.

116. R. Carnap, *Logical Foundations of Probability*, Routledge & Kegan Paul, London, U.K., 1950.

117. M.H. Van Emden, "Quantitative deduction and its fixpoint theory," *J. of Logic Programming*, 3, 37–53 (1986).

118. V.S. Subrahmanian, "Towards a theory of evidential reasoning in logic programming," *Logic Colloquium'87 (Europ. Summer Meeting of the Association of Symbolic Logic)*, Granada, Spain, 1987.

119. V.S. Subrahmanian, "Intuitive semantics for quantitative rule sets," *Proc. 5th Inter. Conf./Symp. on Logic Programming*, K.A. Bowen and R. Kowalski (Eds.), MIT Press, Cambridge, MA, 1988, pp. 1036–1053.

120. G. Shafer, *A Mathematical Theory of Evidence*, Princeton Univ. Press, Princeton, NJ, 1976.

121. B. Duval and Y. Kodratoff, "Automated deduction in an uncertain and inconsistent data basis," *Proc. of the 7th Europ. Conf. on Artificial Intelligence (ECAI'86)*, Brighton, July 21-25, 1986, pp. 101–108.

122. L.A. Zadeh, "Fuzzy sets as a basis for a theory of possibility," *Fuzzy Sets and Systems*, **1**, 3–28 (1978).

123. D. Dubois and H. Prade (with the collaboration of Farreny H., Martin-Clouaire R., and Testemale C.), *Théorie des Possibilités - Applications à la Représentation des Connaissances en Informatique*, Masson, Paris (1st edition, 1985; 2nd revised and augmented edition, 1987). English version: *Possibility Theory - An Approach to Computerized Processing of Uncertainty*, Plenum Press, New York, 1988.
124. M. Cayrol, H. Farreny, and H. Prade, "Fuzzy pattern matching," *Kybernetes*, **11**, 103–116 (1982).
125. D. Dubois and H. Prade, "Necessity measures and the resolution principle," *IEEE Trans. on Systems, Man and Cybernetics*, **17**, 474–478 (1987).
126. N.J. Nilsson, "Probabilistic logic," *Artificial Intelligence*, **28**, 71–87 (1986).
127. D. Dubois, J. Lang, and H. Prade, "Advances in automated reasoning using possibilistic logic," Extended abstract, *Preprints of Europ. Workshop on Logical Methods in Artificial Intelligence (JELIA 88)*, Roscoff, France, June 27-30, 1988, pp. 95–99 (available from LIUC, Univ. of Caen, France). Augmented version in Tech. Report, n° 304 (LSI, Univ. P. Sabatier, Toulouse, France), 1988.
128. D. Dubois and H. Prade, "Resolution principles in possibilistic logic," In Tech. Report L.S.I. (Univ. P. Sabatier, Toulouse), n° 297, 1988. Also in *Int. J. of Approximate Reasoning*, 4, 1–21 (1990).
129. D. Dubois and H. Prade, "Default reasoning and possibility theory," *Artificial Intelligence*, **35**, 243–257 (1988).
130. D. Dubois, J. Lang, and H. Prade, "Theorem proving under uncertainty - A possibility theory-based approach," *Proc. of the 10th Inter. Joint Conf. on Artificial Intelligence (IJCAI-87)*, Milano, Italy, 1987, pp. 984–986.
131. B. De Finetti, "La prévision, ses lois logiques et ses sources subjectives," Ann. Inst. H. Poincaré 7, 1937, translated by H. Kyburg Jr., in *Studies in Subjective Probability*, H. Kyburg Jr. and H. Smokler (Eds.), Wiley, New York, 1937, pp. 95–158.
132. B.N. Grosof, "An inequality paradigm for probabilistic knowledge - The logic of conditional probability intervals," In *Uncertainty in Artificial Intelligence*, L.N. Kanal and J.F. Lemmer (Eds.), North-Holland, Amsterdam, The Netherlands, 1986, pp. 259–275.
133. E.W. Adams and H.P. Levine, "On the uncertainties transmitted from premises to conclusions in deductive inferences," *Synthese*, **30**, 429–460 (1975).
134. D. Dubois and H. Prade, "The principle of minimum specificity as a basis for evidential reasoning," In *Uncertainty in Knowledge-Based Systems*, B. Bouchon and R.R. Yager (Eds.), Proc. Inter. Conf. Inform. Proces. & Management of Uncertainty in Knowledge-Based Systems, Paris, Springer-Verlag, New York, 1987, pp. 75-84.
135. R.R. Yager, "Reasoning with uncertainty for expert systems," *Proc. of the 9th Inter. Joint Conf. on Artificial Intelligence (IJCAI 85)*, Los Angeles, CA, August 18-23, 1985, pp. 1295–1297.
136. P. Chatalic, D. Dubois, and H. Prade, "An approach to approximate reasoning based on the Dempster rule of combination," *Int. J. of Expert Systems, Research and Applications*, 1, 67–85 (1987).
137. L.A. Zadeh, "Review of 'A mathematical theory of evidence' (G. Shafer)," *The AI Magazine*, 5, 81–83 (1984).
138. L.A. Zadeh, "Fuzzy sets," *Information and Control*, 8, 338–353 (1965).
139. J. Goguen, "The logic of inexact concepts," *Synthese*, **19**, 325–373 (1969).
140. J.F. Baldwin and N.C.F. Guild, "The resolution of two paradoxes by approximate reasoning using a fuzzy logic," *Synthese*, **44**, 397-420 (1980).
141. J. Pavelka, "On fuzzy logic – I: Many-valued rules of inference; II: Enriched residuated lattices and semantics of propositional calculi; III: Semantical completeness of some many-valued propositional calculi," *Zeitschr. f. math. Logik und Grundlagen d. Math.*, **25**, 45-72; 119-134; 447-464 (1979).

142. G. Takeuti and S. Titani, "Intuitionistic fuzzy logic and intuitionistic fuzzy set theory," *J. of Symbolic Logic*, **49**, 851–866 (1984).
143. L.A. Zadeh, "A theory of approximate reasoning," In *Machine Intelligence 9*, J.E. Hayes, D. Mitchie, and L.I. Mikulich (Eds.), Elsevier, 1979, pp. 149–194.
144. E.H. Mamdani, "Application of fuzzy logic to approximate reasoning using linguistic systems," *IEEE Trans. on Computers*, **26**, 1182–1191 (1977).
145. R.R. Yager, "Approximate reasoning as a basis for rule-based expert systems," *IEEE Trans. on Systems, Man & Cybernetics*, **14**, 636–643 (1984).
146. E. Trillas and L. Valverde, "On mode and implication in approximate reasoning," In *Approximate Reasoning in Expert Systems*, M.M. Gupta, A. Kandel, W. Bandler, and J.B. Kiszka (Eds.), North-Holland, Amsterdam, The Netherlands, 1985, pp. 157–166.
147. D. Dubois and H. Prade, "Fuzzy logics and the generalized modus ponens revisited," *Cybernetics & Systems*, **15**, 293–331 (1984).
148. R.C.T. Lee, "Fuzzy logic and the resolution principle," *J. of the Association for Computing Machinery*, **19**, 109–119 (1972).
149. R. Giles, "Resolution logic for fuzzy reasoning," *Proc. of the 15th IEEE Inter. Symp. for Multiple-Valued Logic*, Kingston, Ontario, BC, 1985, pp. 60–67.
150. H. Prade, "Raisonner avec des règles d'inférence graduelle – Une approche basée sur les ensembles flous," *Revue d'Intelligence Artificielle*, 2(2), 29–44 (1988).
151. D. Dubois and H. Prade, "A typology of fuzzy "if... then..." rules," *Proc. of the 3rd Inter. Fuzzy Systems Association (IFSA) Congress*, Seattle, WA, Aug. 6-11, 1989, pp. 782-785.
152. D. Dubois, J. Lang, and H. Prade, "Automated reasoning using possibilistic logic: semantics, belief revision and variable certainty weights," *Preprints of the 5th Workshop on Uncertainty in Artificial Intelligence*, Windsor, Ontario, Aug. 18-20, 1989, pp. 81–87. Also in: Tech. Report IRIT/90-2/R (IRIT, Univ. P. Sabatier, Toulouse, France), 1990.
153. R.R. Yager, "Using approximate reasoning to represent default knowledge," *Artificial Intelligence*, **31**, 99–112 (1987).
154. H. Prade, "Reasoning with fuzzy default values," *Proc. of the Inter. Symp. on Multiple-Valued Logic*, Kingston, Ontario, 1985, pp. 191–197.
155. R.R. Yager, "A generalized view of non-monotonic knowledge : a set-theoretic perspective," *Int. J. of General Systems*, **14**, 251-265 (1988).
156. R.R. Yager, "A mathematical programming approach to inference with the capability of implementing default rules," *Int. J. Man-Machine Studies*, **29**, 685-714 (1988).
157. L.A. Zadeh, "Syllogistic reasoning in fuzzy logic and its application to usuality and reasoning with dispositions," *IEEE Trans. on Systems, Man and Cybernetics*, **15**, 754–763 (1985).
158. A. Rapoport, T.S. Wallsten, and J.A. Cox, "Direct and indirect scaling of membership functions of probability phrases," *Mathematical Modelling*, 9, 397–417 (1987).
159. G. Paass, "Probabilistic logic," In *Non-Standard Logics for Automated Reasoning*, P. Smets, E.H. Mamdani, D. Dubois, and H. Prade (Eds.), Academic Press, New York, 1988, pp. 213–251.
160. D. Dubois and H. Prade, "On fuzzy syllogisms", *Computational Intelligence*, 4(2), 171–179 (1988).
161. D. Dubois, H. Prade, and J.M. Toucas, "Inference with imprecise numerical quantifiers," *3rd Polish Symp. on Fuzzy Sets and Interval Analysis in Pure and Applied Mathematics*, Poznan, Poland, Sept. 20-23, 1989. To appear in *Intelligent Systems: State of the Art and Future Directions*, Z. Ras and M. Zemankova (Eds.), Ellis Horwood Ltd, Chichester.
162. D. Dubois, "Linear programming with fuzzy data," In *Analysis of Fuzzy Information – Vol. 3: Applications in Engineering and Science*, J.C. Bezdek (Ed.), CRC Press, Boca Raton, FL., 1987, pp. 241–263.

163. E.W. Adams, *The Logic of Conditionals*, D. Reidel, Dordrecht, 1975.
164. H.E. Kyburg, Jr., *The Logical Foundations of Statistical Inference*, Reidel, Dordrecht, The Netherland, 1974.
165. H.E. Kyburg, Jr., "Knowledge", In *Uncertainty in Artificial Intelligence 2*, J.F. Lemmer and L.N. Kanal (Eds.), North-Holland, Amsterdam, The Netherland, 1988, pp. 263-272.
166. R.R. Yager, "Quantified propositions in a linguistic logic," *Int. J. Man-Machine Studies*, **19**, 195-227 (1983).
167. W.L. Harper, R. Stalnaker, and G. Pearce (Eds.), *Ifs. Conditionals, Beliefs, Decision, Chance and Time*, D. Reidel Dordrecht, The Netherlands, 1981.
168. I.R. Goodman and H.T. Nguyen, "Conditional objects and the modeling of uncertainties," In *Fuzzy Computing*, M.M. Gupta and T. Yamakawa (Eds.), North-Holland, Amsterdam, The Netherland, 1988, pp. 119-138.
169. D. Dubois and H. Prade, "The logical view of conditioning and its application to possibility and evidence theories," *Int. J. of Approximate Reasoning*, **4**, 23-46 (1990).
170. P. Smets, "Belief functions," In *Non-Standard Logics for Automated Reasoning*, P. Smets, E.H. Mamdani, D. Dubois, and H. Prade (Eds.), Academic Press, New York, 1988, pp. 253-277.
171. R. Loui, "Computing reference classes," In *Uncertainty in Artificial Intelligence 2*, J.F. Lemmer and L.N. Kanal (Eds.), North-Holland, Amsterdam, The Netherland, 1988, pp. 273-289.
172. Z. Domotor, "Probability kinematics, conditionals and entropy principles," *Synthese*, **63**, 75-114 (1985).
173. J.R. Quinlan, "INFERNO: a cautious approach to uncertain inference," *The Computer Journal*, **26**, 255-269 (1983).
174. P. Cheeseman, "A method of computing generalized Bayesian probability values for expert systems," *Proc. of the 8th Inter. Joint Conf. on Artificial Intelligence (IJCAI-83)*, Karlsruhe, Germany, Aug. 8-12, 1983, pp. 198-202.
175. J. Pearl, *Probabilistic Reasoning in Intelligent Systems: Networks of Plausible Inference*, Morgan Kaufmann, San Mateo, CA, 1988.
176. D. Dubois and H. Prade, "Measure-free conditioning, probability and non-monotonic reasoning," *Proc. of the 11th Inter. Joint Conf. on Artificial Intelligence (IJCAI-89)*, Detroit, MI, Aug. 20-25, 1989, pp. 1110-1114.
177. S.L. Lauritzen and D.J. Spiegelhalter, "Local computations with probabilities on graphical structures and their applications to expert systems," *J. Roy. Statist. Soc. B*, **50**, 157-224 (1988).
178. P.P. Bonissone, "Plausible reasoning," In *Encyclopedia of Artificial Intelligence*, S. Shapiro, (Ed.), Wiley, 1987, pp. 854-863.
179. S.T. Wierzchon, "An inference rule based on Sugeno measure," In *Analysis of Fuzzy Information – I: Mathematics and Logic*, J.C. Bezdek (Ed.), CRC Press, Boca Raton, FL, 1987, pp. 85-96.
180. G. Shafer, P.P. Shenoy, and K. Mellouli, "Propagating belief functions in qualitative Markov trees," *Int. J. of Approximate Reasoning*, **1**, 349-400 (1987).
181. J.A. Reggia, D.S. Nau, and P.Y. Wang, "A formal model of diagnostic inference – Problem formulation and decomposition," *Information Sciences*, **37**, 227-256 (1985).
182. R. Reiter, "A theory of diagnosis from first principles," *Artificial Intelligence*, **32**, 57-95 (1987).
183. E. Sanchez, "Solutions in composite fuzzy relation equations: application to medical diagnosis in Brouwerian logic," In *Fuzzy Automata and Decision Processes*, M.M. Gupta, G.N. Saridis, and B.R. Gaines (Eds.), North-Holland, Amsterdam, The Netherland, 1977, pp. 221-234.
184. D. Dubois and H. Prade, "Upper and lower images of a fuzzy set induced by a fuzzy relation – A fresh look at fuzzy inference and diagnosis," In Tech. Report

(L.S.I., Univ. P. Sabatier, Toulouse, France), n° 265, 1987, 36-66.
185. Y. Peng and J.A. Reggia, "Diagnostic problem-solving with causal chaining," *Int. J. of Intelligent Systems*, 2, 265–302 (1987).
186. M. Dorolle, *Le Raisonnement par Analogie*, Biblio. Philo. Contemp., P.U.F., Paris, France, 1949.
187. M. Hesse, *Models and Analogies in Science*, Sheed & Ward, London and New York, 1963. Also Notre Dame University Press, 1966.
188. P.H. Winston, "Learning and reasoning by analogy," *Communications of the ACM*, 2 3 , 689–703 (1980).
189. J.G. Carbonell, "A computational model of analogical problem solving," *Proc. 7th. Inter. Joint Conf. on Artificial Intelligence (IJCAI 81)*, Vancouver, BC, 1981, pp. 147–152.
190. J.G. Ganascia, "AGAPE et CHARADE: deux techniques d'apprentissage symboliques appliquées à la construction de bases de connaissance," Thèse d'état, Université de Paris-Sud, Orsay, 1987.
191. L. Bourrelly and E. Chouraqui, "A formal approach to analogical reasoning," In *Approximate Reasoning in Expert Systems*, M.M. Gupta, A. Kandel, W. Bandler, and J.B. Kiszka (Eds.), North-Holland, Amsterdam, The Netherlands, 1985, pp. 87–104.
192. J.D. Ullman, *Principles of Database Systems*, Computer Science Press, 1983.
193. T.R. Davies and S.J. Russell, "A logical approach to reasoning by analogy," *Proc. of the 10th Inter. Joint Conf. on Artificial Intelligence (IJCAI 87)*, Milano, Italy, August 23-28, 1987, pp. 264–270.
194. S.J. Russell, *The Use of Knowledge in Analogy and Induction*, Pitman, London, UK, 1989.
195. D. Coulon and J.M. David, "Inférences de nature analogique pour retrouver des informations dans une base de données textuelles," *Actes Conf. Cognitiva*, Paris, France, 4-7 juin 1985, Publ. by CESTA (Paris), pp. 885–891.
196. H. Farreny and H. Prade, "About flexible matching and its use in analogical reasoning," *Proc. Europ. Conf. on Artificial Intelligence*, Orsay, France, July 11-14, 1982, pp. 43–47.
197. C. Stanfill and D. Waltz, "Toward memory-based reasoning," *Communications of the ACM*, 2 9 , 1213–1228 (1986).
198. A. Collins and R. Michalski, "The logic of plausible reasoning: a core theory," *Cognitive Science*, (1988).
199. I. Arrazola, A. Plainfossé, H. Prade, and C. Testemale, "Extrapolation of fuzzy values from incomplete databases," *Information Sciences*, 1 4 (6), 487-492 (1989).
200. J. Doyle, "A truth maintenance system," *Artificial Intelligence*, 1 2 , 231–272 (1979).
201. E. Charniak, D. McDermott, and C. Riesbek, "Data dependencies," In *Artificial Intelligence Programming*, Lawrence Erlbaum Associate Eds, 1979, pp. 193–225.
202. D. McAllester, "A three-valued truth maintenance system," In Tech. report TR-473, M.I.T., AI Lab, 1978.
203. D. McDermott, "Contexts and data dependencies: a synthesis," *IEEE Trans. on Pattern Analysis and Machine Intelligence*, 5, 237–246 (1983).
204. R.M. Stallman and G.J. Sussman, "Forward reasoning and dependency-directed backtracking in a system for computer-aided circuit analysis," *Artificial Intelligence*, 9, 135–196 (1977).
205. J. Goodwin, "A theory and system for non-monotonic reasoning," Ph.D. Thesis, Univ. of Linkoeping, Sweden, 1987.
206. G. Brewka, "Tweety – still flying: some remarks on abnormal birds, applicable rules and a default prover," *Proc. of the 5th National Conf. on Artificial Intelligence (AAAI-86)*, Philadelphia, PA, 1986, pp. 8–12.
207. D. Poole, "A logical framework for default reasoning," *Artificial Intelligence*,

3 6, 27–47 (1988).
208. P. Morris, "Curing anomalous extensions," *Proc. of the 10th Inter. Joint Conf. on Artificial Intelligence (IJCAI 87)*, Los Angeles, CA, 1987, pp. 437–442.
209. P. Morris, "The anomalous extension problem in default reasoning," *Artificial Intelligence*, 3 5, 383–399 (1988).
210. S. Hanks and D. McDermott, "Default reasoning, non-monotonic logics, and the frame problem," *Proc. of the 5th National Conf. on Artificial Intelligence (AAAI-86)*, Philadelphia, PA, 1986, pp. 328–333.
211. A.L. Brown, Jr. and Y. Shoham, "New results on semantical nonmonotonic reasoning," In *Non-Monotonic Reasoning*, M. Reinfranck, J. De Kleer, M.L. Ginsberg, and E. Sandewal (Eds.), Proc. of the 2nd Inter. Workshop, Grassau, FRG, June 13-15, 1988, Lecture Notes in Computer Science n° 346, Springer-Verlag, Berlin, pp. 19–26.
212. K. Inoué, "On the semantics of hypothetical reasoning and truth maintenance," In Tech. Report TR-356, ICOT, Japan, 1988.
213. A.L. Brown, Jr., "Logics of justified belief," *Proc. 9th Europ. Conf. on Artificial Intelligence*, Munich, Germany, 1988, pp. 507–512.
214. M. Reinfrank, O. Dressler, and G. Brewka, "On the relation between truth maintenance and autoepistemic logic," *Proc. Inter. Joint Conf. on Artificial Intelligence (IJCAI-89)*, Detroit, 1989, 1206-1212.
215. Y. Fujiwara and S. Honiden, "Relating the TMS to autoepistemic logic," *Proc. of Inter. Joint Conf. on Artificial Intelligence (IJCAI-89)*, Detroit, 1989, 1199-1205.
216. J. De Kleer, "Choices without backtracking," *Proc. of the Amer. Assoc. for Artificial Intelligence Conf. (AAAI-84)*, Austin, 1984, pp. 79–85.
217. J. De Kleer, "An assumption-based truth maintenance system," *Artificial Intelligence*, 2 8 (1), 127–162 (1986).
218. J. De Kleer, "Extending the ATMS," *Artificial Intelligence*, 2 8 (1), 163–196 (1986).
219. J. De Kleer and B.C. Williams, "Back to backtracking: controlling the ATMS," *Proc. of the 5th National Conf. on Artificial Intelligence (AAAI-86)*, Philadelphia, PA, 1986, pp. 910–917.
220. J.J. Finger and M.R. Genesereth, "RESIDUE: a deductive approach to design synthesis," T-R STAN-CS-85-1035, Stanford University, Stanford, CA, 1985.
221. M. Cayrol and P. Tayrac, "Exploitation de la méthode du consensus dans les ATMS: la résolution CAT-correcte," *Proc. of the 8th Workshop on Expert Systems and Their Applications*, Avignon, 1988, Vol. 3, pp. 85–99. Published by EC2, Nanterre, France). See also "ARC: un ATMS basé sur la résolution CAT-correcte," *Revue d'Intelligence Artificielle* (Hermès, Paris), 3(3), 19–39 (1989).
222. O. Dressler, "Extending the basic ATMS," *Proc. 9th Europ. Conf. on Artificial Intelligence*, Munich, Germany, 1988, pp. 535–540.
223. H. Freitag and M. Reinfrank, "A non-monotonic deduction system based on (A)TMS," *Proc. 9th Europ. Conf. on Artificial Intelligence*, Munich, Germany, 1988, pp. 601–606.
224. R. Reiter and J. De Kleer, "Foundations of assumption-based truth maintenance system: preliminary report," *Proc. of Amer. Assoc. for Artificial Intelligence Conf. (AAAI-87)*, Seattle, WA, 1987, pp. 183–188.
225. M.O. Cordier, "Unification contextuelle et raisonnement hypothétique," *Actes 6ème Congrès AFCET-INRIA Reconnaissances des Formes et Artificial Intelligence*," Antibes, France, 1987, pp. 787–795.
226. M.O. Cordier, "SHERLOCK: hypothetical reasoning in an expert system shell," *Proc. of the 9th Europ. Conf. on Artificial Intelligence*, Munich, Germany, 1988, pp. 486–491.
227. K. Inoué, "Problem solving with hypothetical reasoning," In Tech. Report TR-379, ICOT, Japan, May 1988.
228. J. Martins and S. Shapiro, "Reasoning in multiple belief spaces," *Proc. of the*

8th Inter. Joint Conf. on Artificial Intelligence (IJCAI-83), Karlsruhe, Germany, 1983, pp. 370–373.
229. J. Martins and S. Shapiro, "A model for belief revision," *Artificial Intelligence*, **3 5**, 25–79 (1988).
230. P.T. Cox and T. Pietrzycowski, "Causes for events: their computation and applications," *Proc. of the 8th Inter. Conf. on Automated Deduction*, Oxford, U.K., 1986, pp. 608–621.
231. Y. Shoham, "Chronological ignorance: experiments in non-monotonic temporal reasoning," *Artificial Intelligence*, **3 6**, 279–331 (1988).
232. D. McDermott, "Artificial intelligence, logic and the frame problem," In *The Frame Problem in Artificial Intelligence* (Proc. of the 1987 Workshop), F.M. Brown (Ed.), Morgan Kaufmann Publ. Inc., Los Altos, CA, 1987, pp. 105–118.
233. M.L. Ginsberg and D.E. Smith, "Reasoning about action I: a possible worlds approach," *Artificial Intelligence*, **3 5**, 165–195 (1988).
234. J. McCarthy and P. Hayes, "Some philosophical problems from the standpoint of artificial intelligence," In *Machine Intelligence 4*, B.Meltzer and D.Michie (Eds.), Edinburgh University Press, Edinburgh, Scotland, 1969, pp. 463–502.
235. S. Hanks and D. McDermott, "Non-monotonic logic and temporal projection," *Artificial Intelligence*, **3 3**, 379–412 (1987).
236. P. Hayes, "A logic of actions," *Machine Intelligence*, **6**, 495–520. B. Meltzer, D. Michie, eds., Edinburgh Univ. Press, Scotland, 1971.
237. P. Hayes, "The frame problem and related problems in artificial intelligence," In *Artificial and Human Thinking*, A. Elithorn and D. Jones (Eds.), Josey-Bass, San Francisco, CA, 1973.
238. E. Sandewall, "An approach to the frame problem and its implementation," In *Machine Intelligence 7*, B. Meltzer and D. Michie (Eds.), Edinburgh Univ. Press, Edinburgh, Scotland, 1972.
239. F.M. Brown (Ed.), *The Frame Problem in Artificial Intelligence (Proc. of the 1987 Workshop)*, Morgan Kaufmann, Los Altos, CA, 1987.
240. F.M. Brown and S.S. Park, "Action, reflective possibility, and the frame problem," In *The Frame Problem in Artificial Intelligence* (Proc. of the 1987 Workshop), F.M. Brown (Ed.), Morgan Kaufmann, Los Altos, CA, 1987, pp. 159–174.
241. C.B. Schwind, "Action theory and the frame problem," In *The Frame Problem in Artificial Intelligence* (Proc. of the 1987 Workshop), F.M.Brown (Ed.), Morgan Kaufmann Publ., 1987, pp. 121–134.
242. M.L. Ginsberg and D.E. Smith, "Reasoning about action II: the qualification problem," *Artificial Intelligence*, **3 5**, 311–342 (1988).
243. M.P. Georgeff, "Many agents are better than one," In *The Frame Problem in Artificial Intelligence* (Proc. of the 1987 Workshop), F.M. Brown (Ed.), Morgan Kaufmann Publ. Inc., Los Altos, CA, 1987.
244. V. Lifschitz, "Formal theories of action," *Proc. of the 10th Inter. Joint Conf. on Artificial Intelligence (IJCAI 87)*, Milano, Italy, 1987, pp. 966–972.
245. C.B. Schwind, "A tense logic based theory of actions," Report GRTC/208, GRTC-CNRS, Marseille, France, 1988.
246. S.A. Kripke, "Semantical analysis of modal logic I, normal propositional calculi," *Zeitschr. f. Math. Logik u. Grundl. d. Math.*, **9**, 67–96 (1963).
247. S.A. Kripke, "Semantical considerations on modal logic," *Acta Philosophica Fennica*, **1 6**, 83–94 (1963).
248. E. Lafon and C.B. Schwind, "A theorem prover for action performance," *Proc. of Europ. Conf. on Artificial Intelligence (ECAI 88)*, München, Germany, 1988, pp. 541–546.
249. C.B. Schwind, "Un démonstrateur de théorèmes pour des logiques modales et temporelles en PROLOG," *Actes 5ème Congrés Reconnaissance des Formes et Intelligence Artificielle*, Grenoble, France, 1985, pp. 897–913. English version: "A PROLOG theorem prover for temporal and modal logic", In Research

Report LISH/386, Marseille, France, Jan. 1984.
250. E.W. Beth, "Semantic entailment and formal derivability," *Medelingen van de Koninklijke Nederlandse Akademie van Uetenschappen*, Amsterdam, **18**, 309–342 (1955).
251. R.M. Smullyan, *First Order Logic*, Springer-Verlag, New York, 1968.
252. V. Lifschitz and A. Rabinov, "Miracles in formal theories of action," *Artificial Intelligence*, **38**, 225–237 (1989).
253. C. Alchourron, P. Gärdenfors, and D. Makinson, "On the logic of theory change: partial meet contraction and revision functions," *The Journal of Symbolic Logic*, **50**, 510–530 (1985).
254. P. Gärdenfors and D. Makinson, "Revision of knowledge system using epistemic entrenchment," *Proc. of the 2nd Conf. on Theoretical Aspect of Reasoning about Knowledge*, M.Y. Vardi (Ed.), Morgan Kaufmann, Los Altos, CA, 1988, pp. 83–97.
255. D. Dubois and H. Prade, "Epistemic entrenchment and possibilistic logic," In Tech. Report IRIT/90-2/R (Univ. P. Sabatier, Toulouse, France), 1990.
256. P. Gärdenfors, *Knowledge in Flux: Modeling the Dynamics of Epistemic States*, MIT Press, Cambridge, MA, 1988.
257. K. Segerberg, "On the logic of small changes in theories," Auckland Philo papers, Auckland Univ., New Zealand, 1986.
258. M. Moreau, "Epistemic semantics for counterfactuals," To appear in *Journal of Philosophical Logic*, 1990.
259. D.G. Bobrow and P.J. Hayes (Eds.), "Special Volume on Qualitative Reasoning about Physical Systems," *Artificial Intelligence*, **24**, 1–491 (1984).
260. D. Kayser, "Le raisonnement à profondeur variable," *Actes des 2èmes Journées Nationales du PRC-GRECO Intelligence Artificielle*, Toulouse, France, 14-15 mars 1988, pp. 109-136.
261. A.R. Anderson and N.D. Belnap, Jr., *Entailment – The Logic of Relevance and Necessity*, Princeton University Press, Princeton, NJ, 1975.
262. P.B. Thistlewaite, M.D. McRobbie, and R.R. Meyer, *Automated Theorem Poving in Non-Classical Logics*, Pitman, 1988.
263. N. Da Costa, "On the theory of inconsistent formal systems," *Notre Dame Journal of Formal Logics*, **14** (4), 497–510 (1974).
264. W. Carnielli and M. Lima Marques, "Reasoning under inconsistent knowledge," Report Université de Campinas, Brazil, 1988.
265. G. Bodiou, *Théorie Dialectique des Probabilités Englobant leurs Calculs Classique et Quantique*, Gauthier-Villars & Cie, Paris, 1964.
266. J. Sallantin, "Représentation d'observations dans le contexte de la théorie de l'information," Thèse d'Etat, Université Pierre et Marie Curie, Paris, 1979.
267. D. Dubois and H. Prade, "An introduction to possibilistic and fuzzy logics (with discussions and a reply)," In *Non-Standard Logics for Automated Reasoning*, P. Smets, E.H. Mamdani, D. Dubois, and H. Prade (Eds.), Academic Press, New York and London, 1988, pp. 287–326
268. E. Neufeld and D. Poole, "Probabilistic semantics and defaults," *Proc. 4th AAAI Workshop on Uncertainty in Artificial Intelligence*, Minneapolis, MN, 1988, pp. 275–282.
269. C. Froidevaux and C. Grossetête, "Graded default theories for uncertainty," *Proc. of the Europ. Conf. on Artificial Intelligence (ECAI-90)*, Stockholm, Sweden, August 1990.
270. B. D'Ambrosio, "A hybrid approach to reasoning under uncertainty," *Int. J. of Approximate Reasoning*, **2**, 29–45 (1988).
271. K.B. Laskey and P.E. Lehner, "Belief maintenance; an integrated approach to uncertainty management," *Proc. of the 7th Nat. Conf. of Amer. for Artificial Intelligence*, Saint Paul, MN, Aug. 21-26, 1988, pp. 210-214.
272. G.M. Provan, "An analysis of ATMS-based techniques for computing Dempster-Shafer belief functions," *Proc. of the 9th Joint Conf. on Artificial Intelligence*

(IJCAI-89), Detroit, Aug. 20-25, 1989, pp. 1115-1120.
273. D. Dubois, J. Lang, and H. Prade, "Handling uncertain knowledge in an ATMS using possibilistic logic," To appear in *Proc. of the 5th Inter. Symp. on Methodologies for Intelligent Systems*, Knowville, Tennessee, Oct. 25-27, 1990, North-Holland.
274. D. Makinson and P. Gärdenfors, "Relations between the logic of theory change and nonmonotonic logic," *Report of RP2 1st Workshop on Defeasible Reasoning and Uncertainty Management Systems (DRUMS)*, Albi, France, April 26-28, 1990 (available from IRIT, Univ. P. Sabatier, Toulouse, France).
275. J. Bell, "The logic of nonmonotonicity," *Artificial Intelligence*, **4 1**, 365–374 (1989/90).

INDEX

Abductive reasoning, 416, 421
Abnormality (predicates), 363–366
Analogical reasoning, 418–424
ATMS, 434–438
Autoepistemic logic, 356–359, 369

Bayes theorem, 412–413
Bayesian network, 412–416
Belief function, 392–393, 406, 456

Causality, 412, 416
Certainty (degree of) 390–391, 393, 396, 399–401, 405
  vs. truth (degree of), 386–388, 396
Certainty factor, 332–334
Circumscription, 362–369
  with priority, 369
Closed world assumption, 339, 362
Conceivable, 351, 356–358
Conditional logics, 377–385
Conjecture, 387–388, 409
Context, 436–437
Contraction, 450–452
Contraposition, 329, 333–334, 341, 346-347, 353–354, 358, 368, 376, 381, 408

Data dependencies, 432
Decision procedure, 355, 358
Default, 342
Default (without prerequisite), 346–347, 353–354, 358
Default logic, 342–350, 358, 369, 374–375
Default reasoning (and approximate reasoning), 399–400
Default theory, 342, 345, 349–350, 358, 379, 381
Defeasible reasoning, 381
Dempster's rule, 393
Diagnosis problem, 412, 416–417

Environment, 434–437
Epistemic entrenchment, 451

Equality predicate, 335, 366, 368, 370, 375
Exceptions (rules with), 326–327, 331–332, 334–337, 342–343, 346–350, 354–355, 359–361, 366, 368, 374–375, 388, 390–391, 393–394, 398, 400, 404, 423–424, 428–430
Expansion, 356–359
Extension, 342–346

Fixed point, 343, 352–356, 369, 372
Frame problem, 439–443
Functional dependency, 420
Fuzzy logic, 394–401
Fuzzy pattern matching, 386
Fuzzy predicate, 386, 396, 398–399, 404

Honest theory, 359
Hypothetical reasoning, 424, 434, 438

Implication (weak), 341
Interpretations (fuzzy set of), 387–388
Intuitionistic logic, 355

JTMS, 432–433
Justification, 424–429, 431–433

Label, 434–438
Likelihood logic, 361–362
Logic of "All I know", 359–361
Logic of justified belief, 433
Logic of minimal knowledge, 359
Logic of relevance, 438

Modal logics:
  K45, 356–357, 359
  M, 355, 358, 362
  S4, 355–358
  S5, 355–356, 358–359, 361
Model:
  (minimal), 367, 371–372
  (preferential), 367
Monotonicity, 329

Necessity measure, 398, 406
Negation (as failure), 339
No-good, 434, 437–438
Nonmonotonicity, 327, 331, 335, 340, 342–343, 345, 349, 351, 355, 359–360, 362, 365, 368–369, 371–376, 379, 381
Normal default, 342–348, 350, 358

Ordered default theory, 349

Plausibility function, 392–393, 406
Possibilistic logic, 385–392
Possibility, 362
Possibility measure, 362, 385
Preference (in default), 345, 348–349
Preferential models, 367
Prime implicant, 438
Probability:
  (probabilistic logic), 392
  (conditional), 405, 412–415
Qualification problem, 439
Quantifier:
  (fuzzy), 402, 404
  (numerical), 327, 329–330, 401–411
  (relative vs. absolute), 405

Ramification problem, 439
Ramsey principle, 377, 452

Reasoning by case, 354, 411, 436, 453
Relational model (for diagnosis), 416–418
Restricted monotonicity, 340
Revision, 327–328, 330, 449–452
Rough implications, 382–384
Rule-based systems, 331–334

Semi–monotonicity, 348
Semi–normal default, 347–349
Similarity, 418–424
Sorites paradox, 394
Specific(ity), 335, 347–348, 353, 387-388, 390–391, 393, 407, 410
Stratification, 339, 433
Sub–implication, 367–368
Supposition-based logic, 369–376

Temporal logic, 440–447
Theories of action, 438–449
TMS, 424–433
Transitivity (weak), 340
Truth (degree of), 394–396, 398
  vs. certainty(degree of), 386–388, 396
Truth maintenance, 424–438

Uncertainty (logics of), 384–394

Call for Papers
FOURTH INTERNATIONAL CONFERENCE
Industrial and Engineering Applications
of
Artificial Intelligence and Expert Systems
(IEA/AIE-91)
Waiohai Hotel, Kauai, Hawaii
June 2–5, 1991

SUBMISSION DEADLINE OCTOBER 1, 1990

Sponsored by ACM/SIGART and The University of Tennessee Space Institute, in cooperation with AAAI, IEEE Computer Society, International Association of Knowledge Engineers, Canadian Society for Computional Studies of Artificial Intelligence, International Neural Network Society, and ECCAI. Submit four copies of an extended abstract written in English, 6–8 pages by October 1, 1990 to Dr. Jim Bezdek, Program Chair IEA/AIE-91, Division of Computer Science, University of West Florida, Pensacola, FL 32514, USA. Phone (904) 474-2784, Fax: (904) 474-2096.
E-mail: JBEZDEK@UWF.BITNET

How to design an effective database system

DATABASE DESIGN FOR INFORMATION RETRIEVAL
A CONCEPTUAL APPROACH

RAYA FIDEL

It's a well-established fact that a database system that works makes work easy and more efficient. Organizations worldwide rely on databases to organize data for a variety of functions. But to make a database work is not so easy—especially when you don't have a pre-established process, workflow, or framework upon which to base it.

When all you know is that a database is needed, but you don't know the details of its contents or how the data will flow, *Database Design for Information Retrieval* is the one book that shows you where to start. In straightforward terms, you'll find out how to initiate analysis—the first key step in good database design. You'll learn a variety of ways to conduct data requirements analysis and documentation, and you'll learn how to represent their outcomes in a "data dictionary" that establishes the purpose of the database based solely on the needs of those who will use it.

Written for the expert and novice alike, *Database Design for Information Retrieval* is the last word on the first step in database design for organizations that must create a system when nothing currently exists. $29.95

At bookstores or order direct from the publisher. Call 212-850-6148 or write M. Schustack.

WILEY

JOHN WILEY & SONS
Business/Law/General Books Division
605 Third Avenue, New York, NY 10158-0012
In Canada: 22 Worcester Road, Rexdale, Ontario M9W 1L1

JOHN WILEY & SONS, Attn: M. Schustack
605 Third Avenue, New York, NY 10158-0012
Please send me _____ copy(ies) of DATABASE DESIGN FOR INFORMATION RETRIEVAL (1-82786-X) @ $29.95 per copy plus applicable sales tax.
☐ Payment enclosed, Wiley pays postage/handling
☐ Bill me ☐ Bill my firm/institution
Bill my ☐ VISA ☐ MasterCard ☐ American Express
Signature_____
Acct. #_____ Exp._____
Name_____
Address_____
City/State/Zip_____

Price higher in Canada and subject to change.